The Handbook of Continuing Professional Development for the Health IT Professional

The Handbook of Continuing Professional Development for the Health IT Professional

Edited by
JoAnn W. Klinedinst
MEd, CPHIMS, PMP, DES, FHIMSS

CRC Press
Taylor & Francis Group
Boca Raton London New York

CRC Press is an imprint of the
Taylor & Francis Group, an **informa** business

CRC Press
Taylor & Francis Group
6000 Broken Sound Parkway NW, Suite 300
Boca Raton, FL 33487-2742

© 2017 by HIMSS
CRC Press is an imprint of Taylor & Francis Group, an Informa business

No claim to original U.S. Government works

Printed on acid-free paper

International Standard Book Number-13: 978-1-1387-2090-9 (Hardback)

Library of Congress Cataloging-in-Publication Data

Names: Klinedinst, JoAnn, editor.
Title: The handbook of continuing professional development for the health IT professional / [edited by] JoAnn W. Klinedinst.
Description: Boca Raton : Taylor & Francis, 2017. | Includes bibliographical references.
Identifiers: LCCN 2016050154| ISBN 9781138033238 (paperback : alk. paper) | ISBN 9781138720909 (hardback : alk. paper) | ISBN 9781315313290 (eBook)
Subjects: | MESH: Medical Informatics | Professional Competence | Education, Continuing
Classification: LCC R855.3 | NLM W 26.5 | DDC 610.285--dc23
LC record available at https://lccn.loc.gov/2016050154

Visit the Taylor & Francis Web site at
http://www.taylorandfrancis.com

and the CRC Press Web site at
http://www.crcpress.com

Printed and bound in the United States of America by
Edwards Brothers Malloy on sustainably sourced paper

My journey in health information technology would not have been possible without the leadership, support, mentorship, and guidance of H. Lynne Miller, RN, MSN, RN-BC. At Doylestown Hospital, Doylestown, PA, Lynne was a highly respected nurse leader who moved from administration to information technology and led the implementation of the organizational-wide hospital information system.

Working together, Lynne taught me many lessons about healthcare informatics even before it was named a discipline. She taught me about the value of efficient and effective hard work. She taught me about teamwork. She taught me clinical protocol. Moreover, she taught me that OS not only stands for "operating system" but "left eye" too.

As someone who embodies all that continuing professional development and lifelong learning encompass, I dedicate this book to H. Lynne Miller, RN, MSN, RN-BC. Thank you for the many lessons you shared with me and for our friendship that remains today.

JoAnn W. Klinedinst, MEd, CPHIMS, PMP, DES, FHIMSS
Vice President, Professional Development
HIMSS North America

Contents

SECTION I   POSITIONING THE HEALTH IT PROFESSIONAL FOR LIFELONG CPD

SECTION II   ESTABLISHING AND NURTURING YOUR CAREER

Foreword

To professionals in health information technology (health IT) and those who are considering a career in the field, it's common knowledge that not only is healthcare changing, but it is changing at an incredibly fast pace. The change is driven by a number of factors, including reimbursement policies, new medical devices and technologies, the continuing demand for improved quality and access, and the demands of a very diverse population. The change is also driven by health IT that is capable of generating data (i.e., big data) to drive quality improvement, cost savings, increased efficiency and population health improvement. In other words, health IT, used to its full potential, is a vital resource to drive the transformation of healthcare.

While healthcare is changing, health IT is also evolving at an equally fast pace as the field moves beyond the hectic pace of implementation of the past decade to deeper integration with devices and to big data and analytics. For the professional in health IT, this evolution of healthcare and of health IT can portend job security and an increasing array of challenging and rewarding career opportunities. Health IT enables providers to improve the care of large numbers of patients, to make the work of doctors, nurses and other clinicians more productive and satisfying, and to get care to more people more quickly than previously possible. The health IT professional is a key contributor to these outcomes.

This *Handbook of Continuing Professional Development for the Health IT Professional* offers a personal roadmap for the individual who has the drive and motivation to dedicate a career to improving health through IT. This book addresses all the essential elements that are important to career success in the field and provides examples that make those elements "come alive" in a very practical way.

Central among these elements is knowing and appreciating the importance of continuing professional development (CPD). Completing formal education to earn a Bachelor's, Master's, or other advanced degree is important. It provides the groundwork for a career that will span decades into the future. It provides the essential competencies for getting that first professional job and/or for advancing in a career that has already been launched. However, one of the most important personal perspectives that should accompany those competencies at graduation is a love of lifelong learning: learning that will continue to advance growth at each stage of development from career start to continued advancement to ever more responsibility, challenge, and reward. Lifelong learning requires that you use every opportunity for CPD. You'll identify your professional potential, create your personal brand, and develop your career roadmap as the foundation for continuing development. The roadmap will challenge you to constantly learn and to find your own "sweet spot" of work-life balance as you follow the roadmap.

Once you have designed your path forward, your plan to move down that path will require that you find the way to nurture your career day by day. As the chapters of this book explain, you'll find that professional associations provide invaluable learning opportunities at conferences, seminars, and other educational events. Many will provide certifications and professional designations that represent your advancing specialized knowledge. They'll also provide invaluable networking opportunities where you'll grow your circle of colleagues and build professional friendships that will reap benefits as you continue your journey.

You'll volunteer for professional and community organizations. Here the opportunity to give back is rewarding, and here you'll also find an ever-expanding network of professionals and community leaders in a wide array of fields, in and out of healthcare, that will expand your insights and your professional and personal relationships.

In this book, the authors describe the importance and the role of learning from others along our career paths. This may take the form of working with a mentor, of a 360-degree assessment, of professional coaching, and of other strategies that offer a mirror of ourselves from the perspective of leaders and colleagues—sometimes with words and insights that are hard to hear. For these strategies to work, we need to be prepared, with a lot of self-honesty, to accept objective praise and criticism and to internalize the learning that comes from that feedback. Learning is not always easy, but it's often the hard lessons from which we learn the most.

Finally, if you aspire to leadership in your health IT career, you'll find both formal opportunities for leadership (i.e., position authority) as well as informal opportunities that call on your own personal style and charisma in every project and every interaction in which you are involved. The ability to lead can be learned; it is not a birthright and your continued professional development should have a focus on leadership development. Leadership requires a certain foundation on which to build your skills, as you'll learn from these authors. First, you must have a moral compass, derived from your values and professional ethics, to guide your actions and to gain trust. Additionally, interpersonal skills are particularly important, as are your abilities to communicate. Thirdly, you must value and advance inclusiveness, whether related to age, gender, race, ability, or other characteristics that differentiate the people around you.

This book discusses all of these continuous professional development opportunities, and more, with clarity and practicality. After you craft a career plan with a clear vision of your future, it is your sense of humor and humility that will get you through the rough "patches" that all learning entails. As you progress, you'll enjoy the rewards and appreciate the contributions that you'll find you are making to your community, your organization, and the people around you.

All the best to you!

Margaret Schulte
DBA, FACHE, CPHIMS

Acknowledgments

With a career spanning over 25 years, dozens of friends and colleagues have impacted my professional journey from health information technology to adult educator in a very positive way. Some, however, have had such a profound effect on me both personally and professionally that I wish to sincerely thank those people individually.

It was at Doylestown Hospital in Doylestown, Pennsylvania, where I started my health information technology journey. I wish to thank Brad Block, who provided me with so many opportunities in the MIS Department and beyond; Nancy Pericone, who worked with me tirelessly to automate critical administrative information in the Nursing Department; Emily West, who recognized the value of interfacing a standalone medical transcription application with the hospital information system; and Sheri Putnam, with whom I travelled the unchartered waters of grants administration many years before HI-TECH and Meaningful Use were ever law. Within the MIS Department at Doylestown Hospital, I wish to thank colleagues Lynne Miller and Geri Bender, who welcomed me to the team for my technical abilities; Kay Germeroth, who came to IT from the HIS Department and who has excelled as the health IT professional that she is today; and Beth Schindele, who was critical in helping with the adoption of shared ambulatory IT services. Special thanks to third-party vendor representatives Joel Berman for the many innovative ideas his company offered to our environment, and Dave Dewing, Christopher Sullivan, and Mary Britt Bishop for their support, guidance, and friendship throughout the various HIS sales cycles.

As a HIMSS volunteer, I worked with dozens and dozens of members over the years. I attended conferences (HIMSS17 will be my 21st consecutively attended conference); served on various committees like the Annual Conference Education Committee and the Advocacy and Public Policy Committee; I participated in task forces; I advanced to Fellow status, and I earned the CPHIMS. None of these opportunities would ever have been possible without the vision, leadership, and pursuit of excellence of HIMSS President and CEO Steve Lieber and Executive Vice President Norris Orms. Special thanks to those HIMSS staff who welcomed me into my various volunteer roles to further the mission of HIMSS: Karen Malone, as I served as a conference proposal paper reviewer when they were still reviewed on paper (1997); Margaret Schulte, as I served as her volunteer chair for the Annual Conference Education Committee (2002); Dave Roberts and Tom Keefe, staff liaisons for the Advocacy and Public Policy Committee, of which I was a member (2005); and Erica Pantuso for her work with me as I advanced to Fellow (1999) while also earning a HIMSS Leadership award (2004). In addition, there were various co-volunteers who influenced my career over a span of many years. From the Delaware Valley Chapter of HIMSS (DVHIMSS), I wish to thank Tom Boyd, Joe Miller, Tim Schoener, Randy Thomas, Charlene Underwood, and Pamela Wirth. From chapters scattered across the U.S., I wish to thank Patricia Dombrowski, John Hansmann, Cindy McKinney, Holly Miller, Carol Steltenkamp, John Templin, and Mike Zaroukian.

I wish also to thank my HIMSS North American colleagues Tom Leary, Karen Malone, Erica Pantuso, Joyce Sensmeier, and Pat Wise who support me each and every day. Also, I wish to thank my staff at the HIMSS Professional Development Department. Each strive every single day to meet and exceed the continuing professional development activities of our members: Gail Rice, Kerry Amato, Mara Daiker, Caroline Connelly, Deb Clough, Caitlin Peters, LaShawn Williams, Karla Shao, Maggie Van Vossen, and Jan Lugibihl.

I owe a debt of gratitude to Pennsylvania State University, University Park, PA, faculty who helped me appreciate the value of the principles of adult education: Kay Shuttuck, D.Ed., who demonstrated patience and kindness towards me as I returned to academia after many years; Melody M. Thompson, D.Ed., whose advanced knowledge, passion, and respect for the principles of adult education is truly admirable; and Davin Carr-Chellman, Ph.D., who served as my faculty advisor for my Masters' thesis that exposed the need for this type of handbook. Special thanks to my undergraduate professor Oguz N. Babüroglu of West Chester University, West Chester, PA, who demanded and received excellence of all of his students.

From a personal perspective, I wish to thank my husband Tom for his support over these many years for my professional responsibilities in the hospital setting that encompassed long hours, off-hours support and downtime, volunteer initiatives, and the many responsibilities of being a HIMSS employee, and the pursuit of a graduate degree. And to our children, Andrew and Amy, who I wish to thank for being awesome, kind, sensitive, and incredible young adults.

Lastly, I must acknowledge the extraordinary leadership of Carla Smith, HIMSS Executive Vice President, for her support, mentorship, and guidance of me throughout my career at HIMSS, and beyond. As Carla provides strategic oversight for HIMSS North America, I experienced first-hand, as a volunteer and now as a HIMSS employee, how Carla works tirelessly to ensure mechanisms are in place for HIMSS to positively transform health and healthcare through the use of information technology. It is through her vision, drive, and determination that volunteers and employees like myself have the opportunity to develop professionally. As my professional, personal, and academic champion, I am forever indebted to her strength, drive, and determination. And for this, thank you Carla.

Editor

JoAnn W. Klinedinst, MEd, CPHIMS, PMP, DES, FHIMSS is Vice President of Professional Development for the Healthcare Information and Management Systems Society (HIMSS). She is responsible for all aspects of education, professional development, and engagement for health IT professionals for 65,000 members (2016).

In her current position, Ms. Klinedinst oversees the HIMSS professional development portfolio, which includes many aspects of annual conference education, mission-critical virtual education, professional certification, continuing education unit management, career services, advancement, a focus on inter-generational professionals, and approved education partner administration. Prior to her appointment as a vice president, Ms. Klinedinst served as an HIMSS subject matter expert for content areas which included the enterprise information systems, management engineering and process improvement, and personal health records. Her extensive background as an engaged HIMSS volunteer and active member since 1991 has provided her with a unique lens by which to facilitate professional development for health IT professionals.

Prior to her position with HIMSS, Ms. Klinedinst held various management positions for over 16 years in the applications development and support discipline at Doylestown Hospital, Doylestown, Pennsylvania. During this time, she was responsible for the entire software development implementation life cycle across the hospital information system core and supplemental applications. Her core competency focus, along with her team, was on software implementation, training, upgrades, maintenance, and support of many applications.

Throughout her career, Ms. Klinedinst has recognized the importance of being an engaged volunteer. She began volunteering as an Annual Conference Education proposal reviewer in 1997 and continued until she assumed responsibility for the function in 2008. For HIMSS National, she served as chair of the Annual Conference Education Committee, was a member of the Public Policy Committee, and served on numerous task forces. She presented her own experiences at multiple HIMSS Annual Conferences spanning over 12 years. At the HIMSS State level, she actively engaged with the Delaware Valley HIMSS chapter as a member of the Communications Committee and Public Policy Committee. In addition, she held a Board-appointed position for the Project Management Institute's Healthcare Special Interest Group.

Ms. Klinedinst holds a Bachelor of Science degree in Business Management from West Chester University, West Chester, PA; a Master's in Adult Education (MEd) from The Pennsylvania State University, University Park, PA; and a Master's Certificate in IS/IT Project Management from Villanova University, Villanova, PA. She holds credentials for the Certified Professional in Healthcare Information Systems (CPHIMS), the Project Management Institute's Project Management Professional (PMP), and Leading Edge Institute's Digital Event Strategist (DES). She is a Fellow with HIMSS. She is actively pursuing the Fellow designation with the American College of Healthcare Executives (FACHE).

Currently, Ms. Klinedinst is a Member of the Board of Commission on the Accreditation for Management Healthcare Administration (CAHME) and previously served as a Commissioner on the CAHME Accreditation Council. She also serves on the Advisory Council for the Division of Health Information Management at Temple University, Philadelphia, Pennsylvania. Ms. Klinedinst serves as member of the Health Systems Management External Count of Loyola University Chicago. Ms. Klinedinst is a member of the American College of Healthcare Executives, the Professional Convention Management Association, and the Project Management Institute.

Ms. Klinedinst resides in Pennsylvania with her family.

Contributors

Jason Bickford joined Banner Health in 2005 where he has worked as an HIMS System Coordinator at Banner Estrella before being promoted to an IT Systems Consultant responsible for deploying Cerner's Content360 enterprise content management solutions. In 2010, he was promoted to the role of Department Applications Director, reporting to the Revenue Cycle team. In this system role, he leads a dynamic support department that provides operational and technical support planning for all HIMS Operations and Coding teams totaling 670 employees. The department services include application and vendor support management, projects portfolio management, IT service ticket management, technical support education, and serving as the IT business support liaison.

Richard E. Biehl teaches quality and systems engineering in the College of Engineering at the University of Central Florida. He's a Black Belt who has mentored many hundreds of Green Belt teams, mostly at Honeywell from 1995 to 2007. Now he specializes in using informatics to improve healthcare systems. Starting in 2016, Rick is serving as the Program Director for UCF's new online Master's Degree in Healthcare Systems Engineering. In January, he published a book on Data Warehousing for Healthcare Informatics through CRC Press.

Dr. Anthony Blash received his Bachelor's in Computer Science from Kean University, his Bachelor's in Pharmacy from Long Island University and his Doctor of Pharmacy degree from Creighton University. Dr. Blash also completed his Pharmacy Informatics residency at Creighton, and is currently responsible for the Healthcare Informatics concentration of the Pharm.D. Curriculum at the Belmont University College of Pharmacy in Nashville, TN. As a result of meeting the Healthcare Information and Management Systems Society's (HIMSS) rigorous standards for quality healthcare education, The College of Pharmacy at Belmont University was named the society's inaugural HIMSS Approved Education Partner (AEP).

Dr. Tiffany Champagne-Langabeer is an assistant professor at the UTHealth School of Biomedical Informatics where she teaches health informatics, telehealth, and technology management. Prior to working at UT Health, she served as the founding vice president of Healthconnect, the ONC funded health information exchange for southeast Texas. Dr. Champagne-Langabeer is also a registered dietitian with a passion for preventive healthcare. She received her PhD in Healthcare Management from UTHSC. Dr. Champagne-Langabeer is a member of HIMSS, AMIA, ACHE, and the Academy of Nutrition and Dietetics. She co-authored several articles in peer-reviewed journals, including *JHIM*.

Michelle Cotton has been responsible for overseeing Meaningful Use compliance for the past two years as a Clinical Informatics AVP at HCA. Before that, Michelle spent 12 years in Internal Audit and was heavily involved in auditing EHR implementation projects, including Meaningful Use compliance as defined within federal HITECH legislation. Additionally, Michelle has experience auditing legislation, including Sarbanes-Oxley and Stark/Anti-Kickback regulations, as well as auditing financial and compliance efforts across the company. Michelle is a graduate of Western Kentucky University where she earned her Bachelors of Science in Accounting and Masters of Business Administration. She has earned CPHIMS, CPA, CIA, CFE, and CCA certifications.

Selena Davis has 25 years of combined experience in the Canadian healthcare and health informatics industries and in research and academia. She is Principal of an independent Health Informatics consulting firm and her current professional work includes Adjunct Professor in Department of Family Practice, Faculty of Medicine at UBC, Health Informatics Project Director for the Kootenay Boundary Division of Family Practice; and Engagement Lead for BC Patient Safety and Quality Council. Selena holds both PMP and CPHIMS-CA certifications and is currently pursuing her PhD in Health Informatics at University of Victoria.

John Eckmann is an accomplished health information technology professional with vision and proven successes navigating complex initiatives from feasibility to reality. His experiences as an health IT professional include numerous care settings: clinical, acute, post-acute, etc. As an executive who leverages best practices to achieve results, he is recognized as a leader who contributes value. Additionally, he is aware of the industry's trending reports indicating careers in information security and privacy are much needed and one of the top ten fastest growing professions. He has recently completed a postgraduate certificate in Information Assurance, Security and Privacy at the University of North Carolina at Greensboro. Since 2006, he is a CPHIMS. He served on the HIMSS Enterprise Information Systems Steering Committee in 2006.

Vic Eilenfield served as the Nation's Interim Deputy National Coordinator for Health Information Technology at the Department of Health and Human Services. He is now President and CEO of a health information technology firm focusing principally on health information exchange at national and regional levels, including those between the Departments of Defense (DoD) and Veterans Affairs (VA). During his military career, he managed the military EHR program as well as data warehousing and analytical resources programs. Consulting in the private sector, he informs corporations' responses to national rule-making processes in the area of health information technology.

Christopher B. Harris has 21 years' experience in healthcare. He spent more than 8 years as an accomplished Information Services leader within academic medical center organizations with broad understanding of the IS role, including governance, planning, project management/delivery, aligning change sponsorship for success, and developing staff. He has demonstrated success over 13 years in top-tier consulting organizations and has a proven track record of large technology-enabled change in complex academic multiple entity healthcare institutions.

John P. Hoyt, FACHE, FHIMSS is Executive Vice President Emeritus, HIMSS Analytics at the Healthcare Information and Management Systems Society, the largest U.S. not-for-profit healthcare caused-based organization focused on providing global leadership for the optimal use of information technology. While a full-time Executive Vice President, Mr. Hoyt was responsible for providing executive leadership and direction to HIMSS Analytics worldwide, where he also provided direction for all Stage 6 and Stage 7 validations and derivative research. Now as EVP Emeritus, Mr. Hoyt continues to conduct Stage 6 and Stage 7 validations, conduct consulting engagements globally and is the principle architect and interpreter of the revised acute care EMRAM standards which were announced at HIMSS 2016 in Las Vegas for use in 2017.

Throughout his healthcare career, Hoyt has been instrumental in defining business and IT strategy as well as selecting, implementing, and integrating mission-critical healthcare information systems across the enterprise. Before joining HIMSS, Hoyt served as a hospital Chief Operating Officer and twice as a Chief Information Officer with various healthcare organizations, accumulating in over 22 years of hospital executive committee leadership experience. Mr. Hoyt served in consultancy practices, including IBM Healthlink Services and First Data Health Systems Group.

Hoyt holds a BSBA in Economics from Xavier University in Cincinnati, Ohio, and an MHA from St. Louis University in Missouri. He is an HIMSS Fellow and a Fellow of the American College of Healthcare Executives (ACHE).

Dr. Christine A. Hudak is Professor and Director of the Health Informatics program at Kent State University, School of Library & Information Science. She is also a Contributing Interdisciplinary Faculty Member in the School of Digital Sciences. She has more than 30 years of experience in Health Care Informatics, including teaching, instructional development, systems analysis, systems implementation and data analysis. Her professional affiliations include the AMIA, ANIA ASHIM, HIMSS, and the National Institutes of Health Informatics in Canada. She is a member of the Health Informatics Society of Ireland and is a United Kingdom Certified Health Information Professional. She received her BSN. from Case Western University. Her MEd in postsecondary education and her PhD in Urban Education Administration were both earned from Cleveland State University (CSU), focusing on adult learning, curriculum development, instructional design, educational administration and computer uses in education. Her dissertation title was: "Organizational Factors in the Implementation of End User Computing Systems in Ohio Hospitals."

Valayia Jones-Smith is a Healthcare Management consultant and a Professional Coach. Valayia is a dynamic, highly experienced healthcare management consultant with more than 20 years of healthcare experience. Her coaching focuses on the future vision of her clients and how they can achieve those visions as quickly and efficiently as possible. Valayia is board certified in Healthcare Management from the American College of Healthcare Executives, a 360 Reach Master Personal Branding Strategist, and a Five O'Clock Club Certified Career Coach. Valayia also holds several other professional certifications in both healthcare and professional coaching.

David Lafferty is a senior technology executive with a unique mix of business acumen and technical expertise. He possesses a strong background of diverse industry experience, spanning the consulting, Fortune 100 distribution, healthcare, and manufacturing industries. Currently the Chief Information Officer for Tidewell Hospice, he is responsible for information technology as well as building and property management. David previously served as the Corporate Director of Information Technology with Plexus Corp., a global EMS provider, where he was responsible for worldwide IT infrastructure, support, and operations. Prior to this role, David led IT for a

$150 million division of McKesson Medical-Surgical in Hartford, CT. He has also held various senior level technology roles with Tech Data Corporation; Reptron; Metamor Worldwide, an information technology consulting firm; and CNA Insurance. David has co-authored a number of SQL Server training guides and was a contributing editor for leading technology trade publications including Network Magazine and Windows Magazine. He obtained his Bachelor of Science degree from DeVry University in Chicago, and has further studied various executive courses at MIT/Sloan School of Business and Florida State University. David holds a CPHIMS and is a certified health care CIO (CH-CIO). He is currently seeking his MBA from Webster University.

Dr. Jean Ann Larson has 30 years of experience as a healthcare executive partnering with leaders, executive teams and organizations to help them become more effective while bringing results-oriented strategic change into their organizations. In April 2016 she was appointed Leadership Development Officer for the University of Alabama, Birmingham Health System and the School of Medicine. During her career she's served as an assistant hospital director, a Chief Learning Officer, VP of Patient Safety and Quality and as a leadership and strategic change consultant. During her career she has worked with numerous leadership teams to develop strategy, engage their teams and become more effective leaders. She has a BS in Industrial Engineering, an MBA and a doctorate in organizational change from Pepperdine University. She is a past board member and industry award winner in both the Healthcare Information and Management Systems Society (HIMSS) and the Society for Health Systems of the Institute for Industrial Engineering. She is a Fellow in the American College of Healthcare Executives and a Life Fellow in HIMSS. She was recently named a Fellow in the Institute for Industrial and Systems Engineers. She is a keynote speaker, author of four books and she has taught in the executive education programs of both Southern Methodist University's Cox School of Business and the University of Texas—Dallas' Naveen Jindal School of Management. Her most recent book, *Organizational and Process Reengineering Approaches for Health Care Transformation*, was named the 2015 Book of the Year by the Healthcare Information and Management Systems Society.

Dr. Kay S. Lytle is the CNIO with Duke University Health System and a Clinical Associate for Duke University School of Nursing. She is a CPHIMS and recognized as a FHIMSS by HIMSS. She is also certified as an Informatics Nurse and as a Nurse Executive Advanced (NEA-BC) by the American Nurses Credentialing Center (ANCC). Dr. Lytle has spent the last 20 years working with a wide variety of clinical information systems. Her primary focus has been on implementation and maintenance. Her research interests include evaluating process and clinical outcomes associated with electronic health records.

John a. Mandujano, CPHIMS, PMP was Top Freshman Debater of Boston College, New England Novice Debate Champion, an alternate to the U.S. International Discussion and Debate Team and 3rd place speaker in the Leonard Persuasive Speaking Contest. As a Distinguished Toastmaster, he spoke at two Toastmasters International Conventions as part of the Accredited Speaker Program. John was an employee of Adventist Health Systems from 2007 to 2013. As a technical advisor, he has consulted at Fidelity Investments, Gillette, Northeastern University, Empire Blue Cross Blue Shield, Blue Cross Blue Shield of Massachusetts, Blue Cross Blue Shield of Michigan and PharMerica.

Dr. Laura Marks graduated from the University of Nebraska Medical Center with a Doctor in Pharmacy in 1993. Since that time Laura has installed over 12 different Pharmacy Information Systems and was a leader in CPOE development and implementation in 2010. Laura, in cooperation with her CIO, created a Clinical Informatics team under the auspices of the IT Department at Faith Regional Health Services in 2014. Faith has attested for MU2 for two consecutive years, created a Clinician and Patient portal, and advanced the usability of the EMR during her tenure.

Pamela V. Matthews is an accomplished Information Technology leader with over 25 years of experience focused on health information technology, strategic planning, IT operations and management, and clinical informatics. She has worked in management consulting, served as a CIO of a nationwide healthcare provider and worked for several healthcare provider systems leading clinical IT initiatives and operations including a major academic medical university. She has served on several boards and advisory councils as well as participated on federal grant endeavors and state specific initiatives. Most recently, she was Vice President of Education and Business Development at College of Healthcare Information Management Executives (CHIME). Prior to CHIME, Ms Matthews worked over eight years at HIMSS in various capacities and launched the HIE and Financial Systems content area. Ms. Matthews is a Registered Nurse with a bachelor in Industrial Engineering and a Master's in Business Administration. She is an Adjunct Professor at Northern Kentucky University, College of Informatics in graduate education where she developed and teaches the program's first course in health information exchange. Ms. Matthews makes numerous presentations and has published articles on health information technology, strategic planning, clinical informatics and practice automation, quality outcomes and healthcare information exchange.

Kristin Myers is an Executive IT Leader with extensive experience in IT Management, Change Management and Program Management. She has a proven record of significant accomplishments leading strategic planning, selection processes, process improvement and health care technology initiatives for multi-year Epic EMR and Revenue Cycle implementations, Accountable Care and Population Health, Meaningful Use, Interoperability and Health care reform programs such as DSRIP. Reputation for developing a strategic plan, collaborating with clinical and operational stakeholders, building a cohesive, dedicated team, and implementing systems that are on time, on budget, and on target in generating business value and operational efficiencies.

Deborah Newman is an experienced professional with over 20 years of progressive leadership experience in complex healthcare organizational operations with an emphasis on fostering a well-balanced operational vision. She is currently the Director of Quality & Performance Improvement/Risk Management/Accreditation Management at Virginia Commonwealth University. Her professional achievements include robust strategic skills in both urban and rural settings—including risk management, high reliability and patient safety, quality improvement, accreditation, process improvement, management engineering, accreditation, and auditing—which focus on attention to continual change and the evolving landscape of healthcare. She provided system management to Xerox ACS Midas for over 12 years and was a Senior Systems Analyst.

Colonel Kevin P. Seeley is the CTO at Headquarters USAF, Office of the Surgeon General. As CTO he is responsible for the lifecycle of clinical and business systems at 75 healthcare locations worldwide. He directs Enterprise Network, Information Support, Global Service Center, Infrastructure Modernization, Information Assurance, and Systems Implementation, Integration, and Standardization Operations. His most recent positions include: CIO, Air Force Medical Operations Agency; COO, Defense Health Agency Health Information Technology Infrastructure

Support Branch; Commander, 7th Medical Support Squadron; Acting Commander and Administrator, 7th Medical Group; and Chief Enterprise Architect, Air Force Medical Support Agency.

Bonnie Siegel is an Independent Career Consultant in the health IT and higher education IT industries. She most recently was a Consultant at Witt Kieffer in Oak Brook, Illinois, a preeminent healthcare and higher education executive search firm. She specialized in recruiting CIOs, CTOs, Clinical IT leaders, and other health IT senior leadership positions. Bonnie formerly held executive search leadership roles at Sanford Rose Associates, Cejka Search, and Hersher Associates. She began her healthcare IT career at Dorenfest & Associates, where she was a consultant and led health IT market research studies. Bonnie presents at national health IT conferences and writes a CIO career management blog for www.healthsystemcio.com. She was an adjunct professor at the University of Illinois at Chicago for their Masters of Health Informatics program, is a fellow member of Healthcare Information and Management Systems Society (HIMSS) and a member of the American Nursing Informatics Association (ANIA). Bonnie has a Bachelor's degree in Biology Education from the University of Illinois, Champaign-Urbana, Illinois. Bonnie Siegel may be reached at https://www.linkedin.com/in/bonniesiegel.

Dr. Detlev H. (Herb) Smaltz is a business-savvy, innovative technology executive with 25 years of global experience in healthcare technology leadership positions. He has held CIO positions at a 20-bed community hospital, a 300-bed academic medical center, an 1100-bed/5-hospital academic medical center, 5-state managed care region and 7-country region (Europe). Dr. Smaltz was the first-ever CKO for $6.2 billion, 39,000 FTE global healthcare system. He is the Founder & CEO of an analytics tech start-up company. Dr. Smaltz was twice awarded CIO Magazine's CIO-100 Innovation Award. He is a recognized leader in the healthcare industry; Fellow in HIMSS; member of the HIMSS Board of Directors, 2002–2005 & Vice-Chair, 2004–2005; Fellow in ACHE Dr. Smaltz has provider, managed care, academic and entrepreneurial experience and is frequently published and a frequent conference/symposia speaker.

Joseph J. Wagner, as the Vice President of TELUS Health, has been responsible for the U.S. professional services team for the past 9 years. Prior to that he was the VP & CIO of Broward Health in Fort Lauderdale Florida. He served as HIMSS Chapter President for South Florida and New York and is currently the Treasurer of Central Florida HIMSS. He is also currently the HIMSS Chair for the Integration and HIE committee. Prior to this, he served on several other HIE committees that were responsible for white papers or other deliverables. He has presented to Columbia University MSH candidates (multiple times) on what it is like to work as a Provider, Consultant or with a healthcare applications firm, assisting them with their decisions on where in healthcare they fit best.

Dennis Winsten has over 30 years in the application of computer systems to healthcare as an entrepreneur with his own healthcare systems consulting corporation. He has published extensively in books and professional journals and has spoken at numerous national and regional professional meetings. Affiliations include: Fellow, HIMSS; Fellow, Clinical Laboratory Management Association and Board of Directors, 2011–2013 and 1990–1993; Association for Pathology Informatics; Clinical and Laboratory Standards Institute-Committee on Automation and Informatics. He has served as Clinical Systems Editor for Healthcare Informatics and Clinical

Laboratory Management Review and is on the editorial board for Advance for Laboratory Administrators.

Dr. John R. Zaleski is Chief Informatics Officer for Bernoulli Enterprise, a leader in real-time data integration and enterprise patient safety surveillance. He has been awarded 7 U.S. Patents; has written 3 seminal books on medical device integration & analytics; is a contributing author to the *Dictionary of Computer Science, Engineering and Technology* by CRC Press; and has authored over 50 published journal articles, conference symposia presentations, and continuing medical education training sessions. Dr. Zaleski has 30 years of professional experience; has led IRB-approved clinical trials and the development of three clinical product lines, including achieving Class II FDA approval on each, and is a certified analytics professional. He is President of the Philadelphia Chapter of INFORMS; is a Senior Member of IEEE; a member of AMIA, and a member of HIMSS.

Dr. Joyce A., Zerkich has been a Project Manager for over 20 years (PMP certified) and a CPHIMS for over 6 years. She has Master's degrees in Information Technology/Business and MBA and a Master's certificate in Project Management. She helped author *Implementing Business Intelligence in Your Healthcare Organization.*

Introduction

Although I serve as editor of *The Handbook of Continuing Professional Development of Health IT Professionals*, this resource would not be possible without the generosity of health IT professionals who volunteered their time and talent to produce content that spans 26 chapters. Their insights, experiences, and examples serve as excellent resources for anyone interested in developing, maintaining, or enriching a continuing professional development (CPD) plan.

The source of inspiration for this Handbook was the result of work on my Masters' thesis at Pennsylvania State University. Through my research, which was informed by my experience, I knew that there was a tremendous need to create a resource so that health IT professionals could learn from others on how to continually develop professionally. While I myself engaged in CPD throughout the course of my career, my vision was to create a resource to articulate what I believed was important to health IT professionals globally.

Why do so? Because the environment of a health IT professional is one which is fast-paced, dynamic, ever-changing, and global. And because of this, professionals should recognize that "change and uncertainty require lifelong learning," as suggested by Edwards and Usher (2000) in Dzubinski et al. (2012, p. 103). And, as a health IT professional engaged in helping to positively affect patients and the care that is delivered, "Professional development is a part of [one's] professional responsibility and accountability and [is] essential to organisational [sic] and professional success" (Cleary et al., 2011, p. 3562).

Continuing to develop professionally is critical for not only health IT professionals but also others who strive to maintain personal competency in one's chosen profession. I trust that this Handbook will be valuable to you in your pursuit of your professional (and personal) goals.

JoAnn W. Klinedinst, MEd, CPHIMS, PMP, DES, FHIMSS
HIMSS North America

References

Cleary, M., Horsfall, J., O'Hara-Aarons, M., Jackson, D., & Hunt, G. E. (2011). The views of mental health nurses on continuing professional development. *Journal of Clinical Nursing, 20*(23–24), 3561–3566.

Edwards, R., & Usher, R. (2006). A troubled space of possibilities: Lifelong learning and the postmodern. In P. Sutherland & J. Crowther (Eds.), *Lifelong Learning: Concepts and Contexts*. New York, NY: Routledge.

A Personal Testimony

Times are changing the workforce dynamics everywhere, and health IT is no exception. We're playing by a completely different set of rules these days. Getting ahead and staying ahead in a highly competitive industry like ours requires not only high performance, but also collaborative relationships, effective workplace habits, and a go-getter mindset. Leading in this territory to thrive, not merely survive, is no easy feat. In today's world and in the foreseeable future, health IT professionals will need to engage in high-quality professional development if they are to keep pace with industry shifts and, at the same time, align their career aspirations with a deeper commitment to helping deliver the best patient care and outcomes. While the exact path that each of us might take in this daunting endeavor may differ, this handbook certainly helps make our direction much clearer.

> We are like dwarfs sitting on the shoulders of giants. We see more, and things that are more distant, than they did, not because our sight is superior or because we are taller than they, but because they raise us up, and by their great stature add to ours.
>
> **John of Salisbury**
> *12th-century theologian*

This handbook packs wisdom from many experts who inspire us to aim higher, see farther, and dream larger. In 26 chapters edited and organized into five major sections, each building upon the next, more than two dozen industry leaders from across academia, provider, payer, product, and consulting settings weigh in to prescribe a practical approach to lifelong learning for health IT professionals and offer up a great toolbox of many "things"—*tools, tactics, teachings, and themes*—that we must embrace and apply to push professional development and success forward with confidence. The editor lays down a solid framework for us to build upon, emphasizing the importance for health IT professionals to reflect on their purpose and mission to direct their learning, and highlights throughout the handbook very specific examples of ways to help the self-directed learner.

By applying the concepts and tactics shared in this handbook as tools for continuing development, I have been able to seek and pursue many rewarding career experiences and benefit both professionally and personally from finding sense of purpose, satisfaction of accomplishment, and commitment to the community in what I do. I continue to receive far more than I give to our community, and I'm inspired to stay true to my career ambition of enhancing clinical, operational, and patient-facing processes with technology-enabled design and innovation to make care delivery robust, efficient, and sensitive to those who are most vulnerable. For all of these reasons and more,

I have come to realize that there really is no substitute for lifelong learning. Indeed, knowledge alone can take people to places where money and power cannot!

All who are impatient and imaginative about making healthcare better, sooner through technology will find this handbook to be thought-provoking, comprehensive, informative, and invaluable. This practical guide to all aspects of professional development ought to be in the possession of every health IT professional aspiring to be a high-performing leader and with every progressive leader seeking to attract, engage, and inspire health IT talent.

Santosh S. Mohan, MMCi, CPHIMS, FHIMSS

POSITIONING THE HEALTH IT PROFESSIONAL FOR LIFELONG CPD

Chapter 1

Identifying Your Professional Potential

By Bonnie Siegel
FHIMSS

Contents

Abstract

Health IT professionals must have a solid grasp of one's skills and abilities. By reviewing the various tools that can help evaluate one's strengths, weaknesses, opportunities, or threats, health IT professionals can then create a tactical roadmap to achieve career goals based on the results of the various tools used.

Keywords:

Carer planning
Career narrative
Resume
Network
Negotiating

The Demand

It is a great time to be a health information technology (HIT) professional. The good news is that there is an increased demand for qualified talent. The reasons are many:

- Marketplace competitiveness
- IT security needs
- Enterprise data analytics and optimization of the electronic health record
- Patient safety and clinical quality
- Baby boomers retiring
- Value-based healthcare and quality-driven metrics
- Expansion of IT services with mergers, acquisitions, connections to community physicians and new facilities
- Project management needs in all areas

Whether you are looking internally at your current employer for your next career move or making the big move to another organization, you need to identify your own skills, attributes, strengths and weaknesses and match them to the right job, culture and organization. Hiring managers are looking for talented IT professionals. Do you have the skills, attributes, experiences, and background to match this demand? This chapter will help you identify your career potential and suggest tools and ideas to create a successful roadmap or plan for your health IT career.

Where Are the Health IT Jobs?

The options for health IT jobs are vast. Here are some of the organizations that you should consider:

- Hospitals/health systems
- Academic medical centers
- Physician organizations/medical groups
- Consulting firms
- Software vendors
- Biotechnology/research companies
- Pharmaceutical companies
- Associations

- Government/military
- Academia/education
- Start-ups

If you currently work in a health organization and want to move into an IT career, consider becoming a "super-user" of your electronic health record system, volunteering to be on an implementation project, or applying for an IT opening. This is a common pathway for many successful IT careers. A super-user is described as a non-technical person who has mastered the use of the installed computer system and has the ability to communicate to others how to best utilize the system. Super-users can be nurses or other clinicians, financial, administrative, or departmental staff. Their ability to learn a computer system and train others makes them valuable liaisons between the IT department and their own areas. If you are drawn to data, love working with people, and can communicate effectively with others, a super-user position can be a great stepping stone to a health IT career. If you do not have an opportunity at your current employer or you are new to health IT, follow the steps in this chapter to make an IT career roadmap.

What Are the Health IT Positions?

Health organizations seek all levels of IT talent from entry level to VP level and C-Suite. Hiring managers and recruiters want to fill new or replacement positions with the most qualified individuals that meet their specific criteria. The "ideal" health IT background for the management level includes:

- Five-plus years of health IT management experience
- Bachelor's degree from an accredited college or university, masters preferred
- Successful track record implementing clinical, financial, and administrative systems
- Excellent communication, people and project management skills, and customer service savvy

Here is a list of frequently used health IT titles at many different levels:

Sample Health Information Technology Positions

Senior Vice President, Chief Information Officer
Vice President, Chief Information Officer
Vice President of Technology
Vice President, Clinical Systems
Vice President, Information Technology
Vice President, Enterprise Analytics
Vice President, Project Management
Chief Applications Officer
Chief Advanced Analytics
Chief Clinical Information/Informatics Officer
Chief Health Information Officer
Chief Information Officer
Chief Information Security Officer
Chief Medical Information/Informatics Officer
Chief Technology Officer
Deputy Chief Information Officer
Associate Vice President, Clinical Applications
Associate Vice President, Program Director

Regional Information Technology Director
Senior Director of Information Technology
Enterprise Technology Architect
Director, Clinical Informatics
Director, Clinical Information System
Director, Analytics
Director, Electronic Health Record
Director, Applications
Director, Telecommunications
Director, Web Development
Director, Technology Operations
Director, Technology and Information Services
Director, Information Security
Manager, Ambulatory Electronic Health Record
Manager, Information Technology
Network Manager
Project Leader or Manager
Application or Systems Analyst
Application or Project Coordinator

Evaluate Yourself

Whether you are beginning a health IT career or preparing to advance your career, you need to assess your skills and abilities. Do you have the proper education and training? Can you communicate detailed processes effectively? Do you listen more than you talk? Are you open minded, able to see several ways to accomplish the same tasks? Do you have an experienced mentor to guide you? Have you taken the time to learn the healthcare business and learn the clinical side? Have you cultivated your interpersonal and customer service skills? The following activity is an excellent way to evaluate your skills, qualifications, and abilities and pull together material to help develop your resume. The material you need to gather to be organized will include: older versions of your resumes, accurate names of previous organizations and their demographics, correct titles and dates of positions, number of staff and descriptions of key accomplishments for each position, all degree and certification information, and names of professional affiliations and memberships. Review your past projects and write down key facts to include in your resume. Hiring managers and recruiters will ask you for details on your work and life history and this activity will help you prepare.

Health Information Technology (HIT) Career Planning Activity

1. List all previous positions with:
   a. Employer names and descriptions
   b. Dates
   c. Responsibilities, number of staff
   d. Titles reported to
   e. Accomplishments
   f. Reasons for leaving
   g. What you liked and disliked about each job

2. List all other pertinent experience
   a. Education, degrees, certifications, licenses
   b. Professional organizations
   c. Public speaking
   d. Volunteer activities
   e. Sports
   f. Government
   g. Interests and hobbies
3. Which positions have you enjoyed the most? Why?
4. Which projects did you find the most enjoyable? Why?
5. Which projects would you never be willing to do again? Why?
6. What type of environment is most comfortable for you (entrepreneurial, for-profit, not-for profit, large, small, etc.)? What work environment do you like the best?
7. How would you rate your people management skills?
   a. Excellent
   b. Good
   c. Average
   d. Fair
   e. Poor
8. How would you rate your project management skills?
   a. Excellent
   b. Good
   c. Average
   d. Fair
   e. Poor
9. Do you enjoy managing projects? Why or why not?
10. What kind of projects do you enjoy?
11. What vendor systems and products do you know well?
12. Identify your greatest challenges. How have you handled these situations? What have you learned?
13. Have you presented to senior executives and did you feel comfortable?
14. What are your long-term career goals?
15. Can you relocate? Yes_____ No_____ If yes, what is your geographic preference?
16. Based on your ratings and evaluation, what skills do you need to acquire or improve in the short term?
17. Develop a plan to acquire those important skills through:
    a. Education and training
    b. Experience
    c. Working with a mentor
    d. Professional associations

The Resume

Your resume is your most important career document. It represents your career narrative in reverse chronological order, not a curriculum vitae format. The reader of your resume, whether a hiring manager or recruiter, will expect it to be readable and look good. Your resume and career narrative will be assessed and consumed across many platforms, databases, mobile apps, and devices and your look and tone have to be excellent. Career advisors have many approaches to formatting resumes, but for the health IT industry, stick with a conservative style.

Tips for Crafting Your Resume

- Prepare your resume like an executive summary of your work history and why you are qualified.
- Utilize easily readable fonts like Calibri, Tahoma or Cambria in size 11 or 12.
- Write out your entire work history not just the last ten years, do not restrict yourself to one or two pages.
- Place contact information on top: Name, address, city, state, email and cell phone.
- Write a career summary paragraph with specific key words and phrases that make your health IT experiences stand out.
- Include key demographic facts about your employers; they add credibility to your background and aid the reader in his or her understanding of your experiences.
- Craft your professional experiences in reverse chronological order with brief descriptions of your employers before your job titles.
- Include all job titles under each employer separately with separate accomplishments.
- Bullet point key accomplishments in a list for each job title and begin each bullet with an action verb (Developed, Managed, Implemented, Planned, Led, etc.).
- List your key projects, describing your management experience and time and money saved.
- Name vendors and products you have worked with, since they can be unique in health IT.
- End your resume with education, including degrees and dates, memberships, awards, publications, presentations.
- Spell and grammar check your resume.
- Ask others to critique your resume.

Avoid These Resume Writing Problems

1. Boring: Listing of just responsibilities with no mention of accomplishments; generic phrases not related to health IT or current trends.
2. Brief: Less than two pages is unwise if you have been a professional for more than two years.
3. Wordy: Multiple sentences in bullets; long, wordy paragraphs; no white space to rest reader's eye; looks too crowded and busy.
4. Gaps: Do not leave off the first ten years of employment; or have holes in your history. If unemployed, add independent consultant as current role; explain any gaps of employment during your work history.
5. Slick/Salesy: Overuse of bolding, underlining, shading, multiple columns, multiple fonts and sizes; never use pictures or decorative graphics.
6. Acronyms: Avoid acronyms or unusual abbreviations not known to health IT or the general public.
7. Humble: Lack of key accomplishments that set you apart in health IT; lack of employer descriptions.
8. Egotistical: Use of the first person, use of exaggerated titles and egocentric language or opinions.
9. Personal: Do not include anything personal, salary or references (Figure 1.1).

To help you visualize a well-crafted health IT resume, here is an example:

Your Name

12 Your Street	XXX-555.1212
Your City. Your State XX111	sampleresume@XXXX.com

SUMMARY

A proven business director who specializes in driving excellence via continuous process improvement within healthcare organizations capitalizing on proven skills in clinical informatics, data analysis and health information management Over eleven years' experience in fast-paced, entrepreneurial and intellectually stimulating environments; an effective leader who works well with others or alone and relentlessly drives toward optimizing efficiency and maximizing effectiveness. Key areas of expertise:

PROFESSIONAL EXPERIENCE

LARGEST HEALTH SYSTEM, City, State   2008–present
The largest health system in the Big City region with $5.8 billion of annual revenue; comprised of eight hospitals and 25,000 employees that provide quality healthcare services annually to more than 150,000 inpatients and over 500,000 outpatients.

Assistant Vice President of Clinical Applications   2011–present
Responsible for the enterprise clinical systems and reporting to the Vice President, Chief Information Officer Lead a team of 75 IT professionals and contractors.

- Develop the clinical systems strategic roadmap for the health system and the eight hospitals
- Serve in the Office of the CIO and attend executive and Board meeting as needed
- Recruit and build a high-performing clinical applications team and work within the established budget
- Partner with all key stake holders including senior executive leaders, physicians and clinical department heads for all clinical implementation projects and ongoing systems maintenance
- Developed a strategic "roadmap" which was published to the repository enabling successful bulk testing of more than 10,000 (product) items contained on formulary across seven hospitals

Director of Clinical Information Systems   2009–2011
Recruited to the IT department after a successful clinical and electronic health record information system implementation from the Leading Clinical Systems vendor. Reported to the Assistant Vice President of Clinical Applications.

- Built the department to 30 by recruiting other clinical IT leaders to help design and maintain the new system
- Established customer service and strategic plans to help build credibility with department heads and physicians
- Provided timely implementations and optimizations of systems for all clinical areas

Project Manager – Pharmacy Information Systems   2008–2009
Recruited to the new computer system project team to lead the enterprise-wide deployment of the Big System pharmacy solution and corresponding data conversion "cut over" responsibilities. Challenged with implementing in a fast-paced environment with limited resources, stringent timelines and budgetary constraints; reported to the Assistant Vice President of Clinical Applications.

- Established credibility by partnering with pharmacists, consultants and senior executive leadership during the first week of tenure to quickly evaluate and understand current/future state processes, design decisions and stakeholder influence to regain project accountability
- Developed a strategic "roadmap" which was published to the repository enabling successful bulk testing of more than 10,000 (product) items contained on formulary across seven hospitals
- Integrated Pharmacy order entry and barcode medication scanning, EMAR validation, mobile device viewing, and CDM charge code validation to ensure integrity with the bill dropping process

LEADING RETIREMENT COMMUNITY , Mid-size City, State   2005–2008
A holding company which has developed and manages many full service retirement communities nationwide offering its 22,000 residents ownership in maintenance-free living accommodations. Recently recognized by FORTUNE Magazine as one of the top "100 Companies to Work For" in 2008 and 2009.

Figure 1.1   Sample resume.

Director of Business Process Improvement   2006–2008
Identified by the Vice President of Operations as a high potential Director to join an elite start-up team of internal Six Sigma consultants. Challenged with executing projects, establishing a Six Sigma disciplined process improvement program within the corporate Operations department, developing a metrics reporting system with Key Performance Indicators, influencing change management at the senior leadership level and recruiting and training belt resources to execute projects.

- Elevated resident satisfaction scores from 73% to 85 % in one year by targeting dining process variability, eliminating bottlenecks through cycle time reductions, standardizing processes and implementing control plans necessary for sustainability.
- Established a project pipeline which defined approximately $1.75 million of potential cost-saving opportunities.
- Added more robust quality assurance capabilities throughout the organization by introducing the Balanced Scorecard approach to the quarterly review process and geared agendas to consistently embrace the concept of continuous improvement.
- Established "critical mass" and momentum within three weeks of initial project engagement by leading a cross functional mix of Operations team members through the design and implementation phases necessary in creating an infrastructure of excellence.

Director of Project Management – Operations   2005–2006
Recruited to take over and turn around a failed asset management software implementation, halt escalating costs associated with the original deployment, identify root cause and establish a best practice model. Reported to the Vice President of Operations.

- Formulated a reimplementation plan renewing a sense of urgency within 35 days of initial start by conducting a gap analysis and identifying and presenting shortfalls to senior leadership to influence change.
- Launched the Rapid Design process reengineering methodology responsible for eliminating over 200 unnecessary processes and standardizing work flow across 23 retirement communities.

LEADING CLINICAL SYSTEMS CORPORATION, Big City, State   2000–2005
A global healthcare information technology corporation with $1.3 billion of annual revenue that offers its 6,000 health organization clients information solutions to optimize and improve their healthcare processes.

Senior Solutions Delivery Consultant   (2003–2005)
Promoted to manage complex project implementations "highly visible" to executive management at two large healthcare delivery systems. Challenged with strengthening client/vendor relationships, identifying client strategic imperatives and influencing decisions associated with their capital request/purchasing process. Projects involved automating healthcare processes via transforming highly paper-intensive business to electronic data management.

- Re-established credibility with strategic accounts by identifying project deviations, renegotiating contracts, facilitating contact change orders and maintaining overall project overhead and profit margins.
- Increased project team's productivity numbers by 38% by reallocating resources, shuffling roles and responsibilities, reducing travel, and reengineering the remote support process.

Application Specialist   2000–2003
Spearheaded efforts in a consultative role to implement entire suite of software solutions to include into acute care facilities throughout North America. Led notable client engagements and project successes.

- Played a key role in client leadership's successful initiative to reduce costs in excess of $1.5 million associated with the off-site storage of paper medical records by orchestrating the application of technical data storage strategies and the digitizing of "paper based" health information.
- Empowered client teams to improve data quality specifically reducing the number of scheduling and registration errors per day to a level below 1% by creating systemized workflow and instructing on data quality best practices.

HEALTHCARE CONSULTING PRACTICE, Big City, State   1999–2000
A global services firm that offers healthcare solutions via consulting, technology and out-sourcing services that drive improvements to their clients' business performance.

Figure 1.1   (continued) Sample resume.

Application Consultant – Sales and Marketing 1999–2000

Promoted to build strategic relationships with new and existing clients, increase customer base and maximize existing account sales. Challenged with creating marketing and sales forecasting plans, developing an updated pricing model, and reducing RFP response time.

- Instrumental in generating approximately $65,000 in new revenue within 6 months of promotion by broadening the business line from selling software to also providing professional consulting services.

Application Consultant – Implementations (1999)

Hired to implement clinical and patient accounting information systems throughout the long-term care industry in North America. Executed software implementations including requirements gathering, process design, development of data conversion, communication procedures and user acceptance testing.

- Eliminated project backlog by 50% from 12 to 6 in a 6 month duration by averaging one project completion per month contributing to the company's ability to beat "Wall Street's" 4th quarter earnings projection for fiscal year 1999.

REGIONAL MEDICAL CENTER, *Big City, State* 1997–1999

A 700+ bed Joint Commission accredited academic medical center nationally recognized for its geriatric center, neonatal intensive care unit and burn center.

Health Information Systems Administrator

Hired into a newly created role to act as the liaison between the Medical Records and Information Technology departments.

- Raised worker productivity levels on all reportable metrics by automating Health Information Management processes to optimize workflow and reassigning departmental roles and responsibilities.
- Played a key role in the hospital's ability to recoup approximately $750,000 in accounts receivable by analyzing and presenting data illustrations which influenced senior leadership's decision to execute on their collection strategy.

EDUCATION AND PROFESSIONAL CERTIFICATIONS

College of State, City, State
- Bachelor of Science - Health Information Management - May 1997

American Health Information Management Association, Chicago, IL
- Registered Health Information Administrator (RHIA) - January 1998

Breakthrough Management Group, City, State
- BMG Certified Six Sigma Black Belt – Process Improvement Methodology January 2008
- Lean For Transactional Processes – Lean SCORE Methodology - February 2008

PROFESSIONAL AFFILIATIONS

- American Health Information Management Association (AHIMA)
- Healthcare Information and Management Systems Society (HIMSS)
- International Society of Six Sigma Professionals (ISSP)

Figure 1.1 (continued) Sample resume.

Cover Letter

Your cover letter can be written directly in an email addressed to a specific person or attached as a separate document. It should be one to two paragraphs and include all of your contact information. Verify the name, title, and address of the person receiving the cover letter. State your reasons for your interest in the position and why you are uniquely qualified. Ask for confidentiality.

Resume/cover letter writing is an ongoing task and you may have several versions when applying for different positions. To help you prepare different versions, read the job description carefully and include keywords that show you fit the required criteria. Your resume and your cover letter can help you open the door to an interview.

Contacts and Networking

To land a job in health IT or to advance your current health IT role, you need to expand and grow your network. Your colleagues, associates, friends, family and recruiters are a wealth of connections and knowledge to help you. Reach out to them with calls or emails and send them your resume. You can invite them to lunch and remind them of your experiences. Follow up with them and send thank-you notes.

References

Choose your references wisely and stay in touch with them. Make sure they will be your champions. Never put their names and contact information on your resume, but have a separate list available upon request. You will need to have three to five business references such as previous managers, peers or subordinates. They will need to know your leadership skills and be able to give an example of what you have done. Be sure to prepare them ahead of time and let them know that they may receive a call from a prospective employer.

Social Media

Utilize LinkedIn to your best advantage; it is your professional branding tool. It is a great way to market yourself in a very competitive world. Refresh your online presence frequently. Here are some key factors in conveying the "best" professional profile:

- Professional photo: Use one in business attire, ideally taken by a professional photographer.
- Connections: Build up your connections to 500+; reach out to many health IT leaders in the industry.
- Career summary: Write one or two paragraphs describing your career; include keywords important to health IT.
- Experience: List all of your key positions, employers and years of experience; not a duplicate of your resume or as lengthy.
- Groups: Be active on LinkedIn and join health IT groups; follow their discussions.
- Publications, presentations, projects: Add your unique events and increase your exposure.
- Recommendations, skills: Note any recommendations and acknowledgment of skills.

A well-written LinkedIn profile is an excellent part of your career narrative and can be a stepping stone to a new position. Use other social media with caution; Twitter, Facebook, and personal blogs can appear to be harmless, but personal photos, strong opinions and comments are easily retrieved by hiring managers and recruiters while doing candidate background and media checks. Research your online presence on a regular basis by doing a Google search. Be upfront with potential employers on any less-than-flattering public reports like bankruptcy, DUIs, or other items that they may find.

Interviewing/Negotiating

There are several different methods used to interview health IT candidates. Internal candidates as well as external candidates may follow the same process. You may be involved in one or more of these methods:

- Phone interviews (can take an hour or longer)
- In-person interviews (one-on-one, group or panel, meal interview)
- Video conference interview (desktop, laptop, or video conference center)

Each of these methods will have different approaches. With a phone interview, speak clearly and slowly with confidence and enthusiasm. With an in-person interview, wear formal business attire, arrive early, use a firm handshake, have eye contact, sit up straight, listen more and talk less. A video interview is similar to an in-person interview but requires that you provide good lighting and neutral surroundings behind you to avoid distracting elements. Be realistic, candid, and truthful with your answers. This is your chance to show your interpersonal skills and style.

Major Gaffes to Avoid at In-Person Interviews

1. Getting lost and arriving late.
2. Being discourteous to administrative staff and receptionists.
3. Carrying a briefcase in one hand and a glass of water in the other, so as not to be able to shake hands when you meet someone.
4. Dressing too casually—such as an open polo shirt underneath a jacket or no tie for a man, or a casual dress or slacks outfit for a woman—for a formal selection committee meeting.
5. Wearing excessive amounts of cologne or perfume.
6. Using slang or profanity during the interview.
7. Looking down or not making eye contact with anyone.
8. Over-selling one's abilities, being pompous, and talking too much.
9. Bringing unsolicited presentations or handouts.
10. Not listening, not taking notes, and not answering questions directly.

Be prepared to answer situational questions like *STAR* behavioral-based questions:

- **S**ituation or **T**ask you faced
- **A**ction you took: What was done and how it was done
- **R**esult of your actions

To be skillful at interviewing, you need to practice and be prepared. That is why it is important to know everything about yourself and the hiring organizations. Spend extra time doing research on the organization and the executives. Know your accomplishments and achievements and be able to articulate why you believe you are qualified for the position (Figure 1.2).

Let's review the best way to answer these questions. Recall your experiences and write them down with as much specific detail as you can remember. Vary your stories and be concise. Reread the job description; because the employer will want to match their needs, not your desired job. Practice and rehearse your answers and be honest.

After the interview, follow up with thank-you emails or even a handwritten note. It is an honor to be interviewed. View it as a life achievement and the next step on your career ladder. Stay in close contact during the active phase of interviewing. Whether chosen to move forward or not selected, ask for feedback.

CURRENT SITUATION/JOB HISTORY
- Tell me about your current situation.
- Describe your current environment/position.
- What title do you report to?
- What aspects of your current position do you like most?
- What aspects of your current position do you like least?
- How many staff do you manage, directly or indirectly? What is the largest number of staff that you have managed? When?
- Describe your computer systems experience in healthcare, applications, and electronic medical record systems, etc.
- Describe your management style. How do people perceive you as a manager, leader?
- Do you attend meetings or present to senior executives? Please explain.
- Describe your strengths and any weaknesses.

WHY CONSIDERING A CHANGE
- Why are you looking for a new opportunity now?
- What don't you like about your current job? What else? What else?
- Is your organization aware that you are looking for something else?

DESIRED POSITION, LOCATION, TOWN SIZE
- What is your ideal next job?
- What would be most important to you? Why is this important to you?

OTHER OPPORTUNITIES
- Have you had the chance to look at other opportunities?
- Have you received any other serious interests?
- Have you scheduled any interviews yet? Have you attended them?
- What did you like/dislike about what you have already seen?

TIMEFRAME FOR DECISION
- What timeframe do you need to part with your current situation?
- Are there any obligations you have that may affect your decision to make a move at this time (house, children in school)?

FAMILY SITUATION AND PRIORITIES (these are optional but may come up)
- Is there another person we need to consider?
- Will someone else be relocating with you?
- What else should I know about you that I haven't already asked?

OUTSIDE INTERESTS/NEEDS/HOBBIES
- What are your hobbies/outside interests?
- What do you enjoy doing most?

CURRENT INCOME AND MINIMUM TO RELOCATE
- What is your current salary and bonus?
- Is there anything else in the way of benefits and compensation that is important to you?

Figure 1.2 Sample interview questions.

Negotiating

Congratulations, you are a finalist for a health IT position and may receive an offer. What do you need to do? You want to come out a winner in the negotiation process and leave no bad feelings behind. Be ready to discuss your needs and know which ones are deal breakers if not met. Here is an outline of suggested items you need to have clarified during negotiations of an offer.

1. Title
2. Base salary/performance yearly bonus percentage, sign on bonus

3. Reporting relationship(s)
4. Benefits
5. Basic health: major medical, dental, vision, life insurance, disability
6. Retirement: 401k, 403B, SERP, deferred compensation, other benefit packages
7. Perks: mobile and handheld devices, PC/laptop, vehicle allowance or travel expense, allowance, data-lines, memberships, paid tuition for self or family members
8. Health and drug screen
9. Psychometric screening
10. Paid time off/vacation: Current number of weeks, paid holidays, sick days
11. Office support/location
12. Relocation: Temporary housing, moving of household goods, realtor visits, rent stipend
13. Unusual or rare relocation items: Sale of house, down payments, housing stipend, boats, horse, etc.
14. Upcoming events already scheduled
15. Start-date/availability date

Here are some examples of negotiation scenarios to be aware of:

Surprise Verbal Offers

Be prepared in case a hiring manager extends an offer to you verbally. This is not the best scenario but it can happen, so review the list of suggested items even before the first interview and do your best with the negotiations. If you are working with a recruiter, they can handle the negotiations if they are aware of your needs.

Counteroffers

Your current organization may find out that you are actively looking for another opportunity. This is a hazardous situation. They may decide to let you go or, in an effort to keep you, offer you a counteroffer. It can include a promotion, a title change, more money, and/or increased benefits. This is tempting but remember, a counteroffer benefits the organization, not you. Step away wisely from these types of offers. You will be considered disloyal for thinking of leaving, and accepting a counteroffer almost always leads to regret.

Serious Multiple Offers

You are lucky if you ever experience multiple job offers at once. These are rare occurrences, but they do happen. Be prepared to do your due diligence on all the pros and cons of each organization and their offers.

Deal Breakers

Be realistic about your demands and needs, and include items that are important to your family. Relocation issues are at the top of the deal-breaker list. Try to solve them before a job offer. Research the new area completely—housing, schools, taxes, quality of life, etc.

In conclusion, it is best if your recruiter can handle negotiations for you. Share your complete salary, benefit and housing needs, as well as other demands with the recruiter. Be careful not to accept counteroffers from your current employer. Know what your "true" deal breakers are, and be realistic in your demands.

Conclusion

To best identify your health IT professional potential, you need to develop a health IT Career Action Plan. This chapter includes action steps to help guide you. Review the health IT opportunities and be realistic about your abilities. Target and research health IT organizations and learn the industry vendors and products. Complete the Health Information Technology (HIT) Career Planning Activity to help you learn about your skills and abilities. Consider moving forward with an advanced degree and certifications. Develop your skills to manage managers and seek out ways to lead IT projects or become a "super" user. Prepare an outstanding resume and cover letter and use keywords unique to the health IT industry. Identify internal/external mentors and build your connections on LinkedIn. Take care of your references and treat them like gold. Don't forget to have a work-life balance. Practice your interviewing skills and be prepared. Good luck with your career in health IT.

Additional Resources

Siegel, B. (2012, February to 2016, June). Collection of career management blog articles. Retrieved from http://healthsystemcio.com/?s=Bonnie+Siegel.

Siegel, B. (2012, February). What Makes a Successful Healthcare IT Professional? Presentation at the HIMSS12 Conference, Las Vegas, Nevada.

Siegel, B. (2015, October). Career Development: So You Want to Be in the C-Suite? Presentation at HIMSS Midwest Fall Technology Conference, Detroit, Michigan.

Chapter 2

Creating a Personal Brand

By Valayia Jones-Smith
FACHE, CPHIMS, PCMH CCE, PMI-PBA CCP

Contents

Abstract

Establishing one's identity based on skills, abilities, values, ethics, and other attributes is important for health IT professionals. To do so, identify ways to create a "self-package" that markets one's professional and personal best.

Keywords:

Personal brand
Professional brand
Visibility
Credibility
Clarity
Consistency

Introduction

When you hear the word branding, what are the first thoughts that come to mind? For most, the word branding is associated with a business or products. Very few of us would think of ourselves as a brand. However, each one of us is the most unique brand that exists: there is no other brand just like you.

Personal branding is fast becoming the primary method to be influential, indispensable, and incredibly happy at work.

Following is a three-step process that will help you uncover and express your brand in a way that will help you reach your goals.

First we will start with defining "what is a brand?" as it applies to personal branding. William Arruda's definition of a brand is "YOUR unique promise of value" (http://williamarruda.com). Picture your brand as being at the intersection of three connecting circles and at each of the three circles are the words "Promise," "Unique," and "Value": what is unique to you, what is the promise you commit to delivering, and what has value to the people who are making decisions about you.

When you think of some of the world's strongest brands such as Apple, Google, or McDonald's, not only are you able to immediately recognize these brands by their logos, but also each brand illicits words, feelings, and associations that each of us has tied to the brands. What makes these strong brands is that the words, feelings and association that are tied to the brands is consistent for each brand. When you think of the Apple brand, what are some of the words that come to mind? One of those words may be innovative. Why, because most everything Apple does is innovative. Apple distributes innovative products that consumers don't even realize they want or need. Apple's innovation extends past their products: you can see it in their packaging and in their stores, which have "Genius Bars" instead of check-out lines. Why is this important? Well there are two reasons. One is branding is based on authenticity. Branding is not about creating a fake image for the outside world or convincing people about something that isn't true. It is based on what is true, genuine, and real. Ann Morrow Lindbergh stated, "The most exhausting thing you can be is insincere" (http://www.brainyquote.com/quotes/authors/a/anne_morrow_lindbergh.html). The second reason Apple is a strong brand is that they are known for some "thing" and not a hundred "things." Take a moment to think of what words would be used when your name is said.

The goal is to think about what your brand is and how you can use your brand to deliver value for yourself, for your career, for your team, and for your organization. You may be asking yourself, "Why do I need to think of myself as a brand?" Simply because the world of work has changed forever! There was a time when an organization managed its employees' careers since things were static. Today, it isn't uncommon for most to have worked at least ten jobs by the age of 40. Based on a study by the U. S. Bureau of Labor Statistics, those born in the years of 1957–1964 held, on average, 11.7 jobs from ages 18 to 48, with 27% holding 15 or more jobs (http://www.bls.gov/nls/nlsfaqs.htm#anch41). Companies are aware of this and expect the best from you while you are there. To succeed in this new world of work, you need to be your best self and integrate what makes you exceptional for everything you do to prove your value to your organization.

The DITCH Framework

Based on the research of Arruda and Dib, there are three actions that are critical to successful branding: DITCH, DARE, DO.

DITCH

A "Ditch" is something you need to eliminate. It could be a success strategy that got you where you are today but won't take you further, or, it could be a mindset or habit that will get in the way of your success. You need to be willing to ditch "it" and you need to be actively understanding what these things are you need to remove, so that you can get them out of the way and be successful.

DARE

A "Dare" is a risk you need to take. By doing so, you need to step outside your comfort zone. You need to be able to take calculated risks to get noticed and move your career forward.

DO

A "Do" is an action you take every single day to build and nurture your personal brand. You can't expect your brand to be built for you. You need to be deliberately delivering on your brand daily.

Reach 1-2-3 Success ™ !

Reach 1-2-3 Success™! is a personal branding process. It is comprised of three steps:

1. Extract. Unearth/uncover your brand by digging deep into who you are to figure out what your brand is about.
2. Express. Communicate your brand to your target audience.
3. Exude. Align your brand environment with everything that surrounds you. This is the easiest part as you are now crystal clear about your brand and have a communication plan for your brand to make it visible to others.

Notice that each word of the Reach 1-2-3 Success™! phases begin with the letters "EX". The reason is because your brand, although based in authenticity, is held in the hearts and minds of those around you—"EX" = external. Actually, it is what others think that counts.

Before examining each phase of the branding process, let me take a moment to discuss the benefits and what is in it for you to unearth and live your brand.

You:

■ Do a lot of introspection so you can increase your self-awareness.
■ Increase your visibility and presence.
■ Stand out from others who do what you do and share your job title.
■ Put yourself in control of your career.
■ Increase your wealth, since strong brands are paid more than commodities.
■ (Most importantly) Increase your achievement and professional fulfillment because you are aligning who you are with what you do and how you do it.

These are the benefits to you. But why would an organization want its people to build their brands? Some organizations are concerned about personal branding. They worry about having thousands of individual brands in the industry. Organizations need to deliver a consistent experience to their stakeholders. It is true that organizations need their employees to deliver on the brand promise consistently. And there is an important distinction between consistency and conformity: conformity may come across as fake or inauthentic but it isn't transparent. Consistency is the key.

One great example of consistency is the Nordstrom brand. In the Nordstrom employee manual it states, "deliver the finest customer service." Nordstrom does not dictate how an employee should "deliver the finest customer service." This allows each employee to deliver on the brand promise in a way that is authentic to them. The employees will be engaged and motivated and will deliver their best in support of the company's objectives. At this point, you should have a better understanding of the benefits of personal branding for both yourself and your organization.

Extract

By further examining the "Extract" phase of the 1-2-3 Success! Model, we identify three separate components. The first component starts with the "promise" of the brand definition, which is "your unique promise of value." Promise relates to your authenticity. In uncovering your brand, take a look at yourself introspectively as well as getting feedback from those around you. What types of things do you need to know? Do you know your vision, purpose, values, and passions? These are referred to as your VPs for your personal brand.

Your vision is what you see as possible/desirable for the world; something you could not accomplish yourself.

Your purpose is your role in turning your vision into reality.

Your values are your operating principles; you carry them with you every day. They impact how you behave, how you feel.

Your passions are those things that get you out of bed early on a Saturday morning to do. When you can connect your passions with your work, you are unstoppable!

Another important element of your brand is goals. Goals give your brand direction. They help you identify what things you want to do, what things you don't want to do and how you can eliminate things because they are not connected to those goals. You need to think about where you want to go and how will your brand get you there. When it comes to goals, you will want to document your goals and read them every day. Why? Because you are resetting a part of your brain called the RAS (Reticular Activating System). It's the part of your brain that decides what makes it into your conscious mind and what doesn't. Every day, a person is bombarded with over 700 billion stimuli, and only a tiny, tiny fraction make it into their conscious mind. You want to make sure what makes its way into your conscious mind is that which is self-serving. This is why reading your goals every morning is important. The act of reading them resets your RAS and says this is important to me and be on the lookout for anything that will help me reach these goals. What you see that day will be different from what you will see if you do not read your goals. All of us have experienced our RAS in action. Perhaps you have decided what color, make, and model you are going to buy for your next vehicle. Maybe a red BMW? As soon as you make that decision, you suddenly start to notice all the red BMW's on the road. That is your RAS at work. Your "DO" here is to document your goals and read them regularly.

Up until now we have been discussing your brand from the inside out: who are you, your vision, your purpose, your values, your passion, your goals. You also need to get feedback from the outside in. The question is what do people think about you? What words would they use to describe you? Are they the same words you would use to describe yourself? Would they all use the same words to describe you or would they all be different depending on who you talk to? To help understand your brand and your reputation from the outside in, it is helpful to use a tool called the 360Reach personal branding assessment, assessable at www.360Reach.me. This tool gives you a good understanding of your brand attributes, which are the adjectives people use to describe you. The DARE is to seek and be open to feedback. All strong brands seek feedback and take action as a result of what they learn.

The last thing we need to remember when uncovering your brand is you need to eliminate the word "FINE!" Nobody gets excited in life about things that are fine. When you hear the word "fine," you also think of average, adequate, OK, and acceptable. Do you want people describing your work that way? Probably not! Yet we accept one's mindset that the way to succeed is to fix our weaknesses. When you fix your weaknesses, you become "fine" at a lot of things. That is the opposite of branding. What strong brands do is take the things they are great at and become exceptional at them. They maximize it and they maximize the visibility of it.

Regarding your weaknesses, think about the following. For any weakness identified you should ask yourself this one question: "Will this weakness get in the way of my success?" If the answer is yes, then you absolutely need to work on it. If the answer is no, what you need to do is ignore it, and then you need to focus next on your strengths. Identify which ones will be most helpful to you and which is going to enable you deliver on superlatives. The goal is to have people using words such as best, outstanding, or exceptional when they think of you.

The DITCH is to stop fixing weaknesses and start working on strengths. The question you need to be thinking about is what do you want to be known for? How do you instill everything you have learned about yourself in the Extract phase and use it as a way to define the brand called you?

The second area of "unique promise of value" is the "unique" piece. Branding is about differentiation. What do you have in common with your peers, but most importantly what sets you apart from others? What is your brand differentiation? An example to think about is MasterCard, Visa, and American Express. What is the difference between a Visa or a MasterCard versus an American Express card? What makes someone choose to pay an annual membership fee of $450 to carry an American Express versus carrying a card with no fee like MasterCard or Visa, when they all have the same function of letting you make purchases? When you dig deeper into the practice of maintaining a membership with a credit card, is there something available from American Express that isn't available from the others? When you think about what you do and your ability to do that job, you are in a sense functioning as the MasterCard or Visa. If you think of yourself as your job title, you are interchangeable with anyone else who shares that job title. But when you start thinking about that unique experience that you deliver such as those things that you deliver, in addition to the competence of being able to do your job, that's when you are thinking about yourself as a brand. When you think about your brand, you need to think about what you have to offer and who your audience may be. Then, make sure you are always relevant and compelling to them. That's the lesson for a strong brand. The DARE here is to know that differentiation and flaunt your quirks. Take those things that make you YOU and make them visible. And, as William Aruda says, "What makes you unique, makes you successful."

The third element of "unique promise of value" has to do with the "value." The value is not determined by you but rather by your target audience, by the people making decisions about you, and those that influence them. That includes people both internal and external to your organization. You need to know who this group is so you may build your brand and increase your visibility in front of them. Personal branding is not about being famous; rather, it is about being selectively famous.

After you learn about yourself introspectively and through external feedback, you will distill these learnings into what is called your personal brand statement (PBS). This statement is for you. It is NOT your elevator pitch that you share with people you meet. It is an internal statement that you use to remind yourself to be on-brand every day in everything that you do. You need to place your PBS somewhere so that you will see it every day.

Once you are clear about your brand, including what is authentic to you, what is differentiating you from your peers, and what is relevant and compelling to your target audience, you are ready for the Express phase of the personal branding process.

EXPRESS

In the Express phase, the focus is on the "ilities":

- Visibility. Making sure your target audience sees you
- Credibility. Demonstrating your unique promise of value in everything you do

Visibility and credibility is a combination of show and tell. In this phase you will use your communications wheel, which shows which communications vehicle(s) you are going to use. At the center of the wheel is your message—your thought leadership—what you want people to know. You apply that message to all communications. When choosing the tools/methods to use for your communication wheel, be sure it is something you enjoy doing and that it reaches your target audience. Some of the tools/methods to consider using to develop your communication wheel are social media, public speaking, or volunteering. If you don't enjoy public speaking, then it is not a tool that should appear on your communication wheel.

There is certain branded content that we all need, like your 3D brand bio, your headshot, and your thought-leadership content. Your 3D brand bio is much more than a list of accomplishments: it expresses who you are, what makes you great, and why people should care. The 3D brand bio makes your target audience want to get to know you. It has your personality, your values, your passions, and the things that you want other people to know about you. And your headshot is a way for people to be able to connect a face with some information and content.

Thought-leadership content is what you want to be known for by others. It might have to do with your area of expertise for example, like patient engagement or population health. Or it could have to do with your thoughts on leadership or building relationships. This can come in the form of interviews, blog posts/comments, articles, presentations, or videos.

In the Express phase of the process we deliver on the 3 C's of branding:

- Clarity. Being clear about who you are and who you are not
- Consistency. Always being that
- Constancy. Always being visible to the people who need to know you

If you don't show up in Google do you exist? Have you have ever googled yourself? Have you ever googled someone else? If so, then following logic if you are googling others, then they are googling you. Many will make decisions about you based on what Google reveals. DO google yourself regularly. Your Google results can change as quickly as the weather in Texas.—so google yourself regularly.

There is a phenomenon that is making Google more important in your personal branding. That phenomenon is called Digital First. Digital First describes how we more often form first impressions online before we connect with people in the real world. The term was described in Mitch Joel's book *Ctrl Alt Del: Reboot Your Business. Reboot Your Life. Your Future Depends on It* (Business Plus, 2013). Two concepts are really important to the Digital First phenomenon. The first is primacy. Primacy relates to the fact that we believe the first thing we learn and we remember it. This is important because if someone is learning about you first on the Web, then what they learn becomes permanent. That becomes who you are. When primacy is combined with another concept called anchoring, this is why you need to focus on building your brand in bits and bytes. Anchoring means that once you have formed an opinion of something, even if you receive new data that contradicts that opinion, you make the new data fit with the initial belief. This is why it is imperative that you make sure the virtual world "you" is consistent with the real world "you."

Without even realizing it, when someone googles you they are looking at five measures of online ID. They are evaluating you based on value, relevance, validation, purity, and diversity. To increase volume and relevance, use social networking sites, your own web site, web portals, or thought-leadership sites. Thought-leadership sites are those sites specific to your area of expertise where you can post content or comments and include blogs, publications, etc. Key social networking sites to focus on include LinkedIn, Google+, Twitter, and Facebook.

When people google your name, they have become very skilled at using the appropriate filter words to achieve the desired search results. Part of your personal branding process is determining what filter words are associated with you and being sure that everything you post on the web contains those words. This contributes to purity. One possible way to determine the filter words associated with your name is by looking at your top skills and endorsements on LinkedIn.

Diversity speaks to having different types of content. You do not want to convey your brand just in text on the web. You want to make sure you are using videos, images, images of yourself, and real-time content so people can get a truer, richer experience. Having a professional headshot is absolutely critical and is a worthwhile investment while building your brand. The DARE—get a professional headshot and use it.

Video is the new frontier when it comes to personal branding. Thanks to high-speed Internet, video, or video-sharing sites like YouTube, it is easy to create, view, and share video content. Go to www.personalbranding.tv and learn how to build your brand in both the real and virtual world. DARE to produce your first video.

The last of the five measures, validation is becoming more and more important. Validation is less about what you say, but more about what other people say about you. Do other people back up what you say about yourself with recommendations and testimonials? People make decisions about each other based on the feedback of others. Get comfortable sharing what others think about you and make a plan to get testimonials, endorsements, references, and recommendations.

EXUDE

In the third phase of Exude, you align your brand environment. That means you make sure everything that surrounds you sends the same on-brand message. Your brand environment consists of:

- Your personal appearance
- Your office environment
- Your personal brand ID system
- Most importantly, your professional network

Your appearance and office environment (and every decision you make in fact) says something about your brand. You want to ensure that you are reinforcing your brand message instead of detracting from it. The technique used to determine what is on—or off—brand is called "living in the inquiry". Ask yourself, "Is this on-brand for me?" and if the answer is no, make a plan to make it on-brand. The DARE is to brand your office. Even in organizations with very strict rules there are things you can do to make sure your brand is reflected in the items in your office. When you are communicating on behalf of your organization you are going to use their branding system. When you are communicating on behalf of yourself use your own personal brand ID system.

Your personal brand identity system is a critical component of your brand. It is made up of a signature color, a standard font, images, textures, a personal logo, and tagline. One of the most important elements of your brand identity system is your brand color. What color best represents your brand and how can you use it consistently to create recognition? Access the video at bit.ly/ brandcolor to help you determine which color best represents your brand. Use your brand color consistently to reflect your brand. When you communicate on behalf of your organization, use its brand color!

The most important part of your brand environment is your professional network or brand community. These are the people that can help extend your brand. You can look at it as a series of concentric rings. The ring closest to you has the people who know you best; the stronger your brand, the clearer the message to the people in the outer rings. The DITCH—drop the go-it-alone attitude. You need a network of resources to be successful.

Remember that your personal brand is your unique promise of value. It is authentic to you, differentiating from your peers and relevant and compelling to your target audience. It is the key to your professional success and fulfillment. Use the 1-2-3 Success process to unearth your brand, express it to your target audience and align everything that surrounds you so you exude a consistent, on-brand message.

Conclusion

Your Personal brand is:

■ Authentic
■ Differentiated
■ Compelling

Reach 1-2-3- Success™

■ Extract
■ Express
■ Exude

Remember to Ditch, Dare and DO!

We all need to think of ourselves as brands if we want to be successful. What you think you are portraying is usually not the same as how people are perceiving you. People's perception will win out every time. If you are thinking like a brand, that will translate into acting like a brand. A brand is a unique promise of value. Your brand is your unique promise of value. It is unique because it sets you apart from your peers. It's a promise because it is authentic to you and you commit to delivering it every day with everything you do. It has value to your target audience, the people who need to know you so you can be successful.

DO you leave your mark on everything you do? Every email you write, every meeting you attend, every teleconference you lead? And if not, how can you?

DARE be yourself be your best self. Personal branding is about giving yourself the mandate to be your best self—ALWAYS!

Reference

Arruda, W. and Dib, D. *Ditch, Dare, Do: 3D Personal Branding for Executives.* Hachette Book Group, NY, 2013.

Chapter 3

Diversifying Your Skillset

By Vic Eilenfield

MS, MHA, FACHE, CPHIMS

Contents

Abstract

While the health IT industry may be one's primary skills choice, review the importance and rationale of developing complementary skills to enhance one's professional and personal value to the organization or beyond.

Keywords:

Total Quality Management
Career Diversifications
Storyboard
Workplace Diversification
Professional Certification

Introduction

Remember when you were talking to your parents or other personal or academic mentors about applying for college? They often said, "You need a well-rounded application; It can't just be academics or sports. You need academics *and* sports *and* a record of community or civic involvement." That doesn't really change too much when you move into the workplace environment. We need to be diversified in the workplace as well.

Diversification in the Health IT Workplace

Let us begin to explore diversification that would be helpful in the health information technology (HIT) workspace by looking at the complexity of our health systems. The healthcare system is a surprisingly complex ecosystem filled with many subspecialty niches that do not have good parallels in other industries. In a physician practice alone there are over 150 specialties and subspecialties [1]. Add to this the specialization of the nursing profession, ancillary service providers (laboratory, pharmacy, etc.), and hospital administrative, information systems, and logistical operations and we see a vastly complex ecosystem that has few parallels. We've all heard the one about automated teller machines (ATMs), right? It goes something like this: "If bankers can figure out how to do secure transactions between thousands of competing banks around the world, then why can't the health IT community figure out how to share my health information?" It seems simple doesn't it? People who make such statements are completely unaware of the tremendous complexity of our healthcare system and the systems that support it.

As an example, in the niche of the health IT coding space there is great nuance in determining diagnostic codes far transcending the simple concept of "is this a withdrawal or a deposit?" The specificity of these concepts has greatly increased in recent years, such that a provider may not simply record that a patient has asthma; they must record whether the asthma is mild/intermittent, mild/persistent, moderate/persistent, severe/persistent, or other/unspecified and select from three subcategories to more finely qualify the diagnosis, resulting in 18 potential diagnostic codes for the presumably simple diagnosis of asthma. And these 18 codes are only a tiny fragment of the 69,000 codes in the 10th revision of the International Classification of Diseases (ICD-10) now required for use in the United States to support billing and multiple other clinical documentation-related activities. This is not your average ATM withdrawal! This example only begins to open the Pandora's box of health IT.

So what does this have to do with skill diversification in health IT? The number of diverse niches in which you could play a vital role in improving performance of your healthcare organization is huge. This example of the complexity of the workspace and the opportunities to fill multiple roles in one scenario just scratches the surface. Who helps the IT developers with determining how to expose clinical code pick lists for providers to appropriately code their clinical encounters? Who ensures clinical practice supports not only effective coding but optimizes accounts receivable? Who trains the providers to optimize their documentation while not adversely impacting the efficiency of their clinical activities? Who ensures clinical quality measures derived from the codes are reviewed and reported to the Centers for Medicare and Medicaid Services (CMS)? These questions begin to reveal the plethora of sub-specialties or experiential bases of health IT staff trying to optimize these complicated business practices in healthcare settings. Does your level of diversity help you fill one or more valued roles in this space?

Total Quality Management (TQM) and Healthcare

Most students of health IT, and others with business backgrounds have a reasonable understanding of quality management processes. Many of these quality assessment models dating back to Total Quality Management (TQM) and Healthcare evolved from Deming and Juran and strongly suggest that problem-solving in high-performing organizations be supported by robust, multidisciplinary teams [2]. The value of such a tenet cannot be understated. In complex systems, it is quite implausible that upper management will routinely be able to discern what the root cause of a problem is or define the best solution to that problem. Approaches similar to and evolving from TQM very frequently emphasize the power of using cross-functional teams in improving system processes to enhance performance and outcomes.

An analogy frequently used in the quality management or quality improvement space is that of the infection control challenge in clinical environments. When a hospital encounters an increase in hospital-acquired infections, can this problem be solved only by nurses? No! The entire patient care environment must be examined by everyone who enters it from provider hand-washing practices, to sterile supply, house-keeping services, ventilation system maintenance, nursing care and beyond. Are you serving as clinic staff with experience in hospital infrastructure (heating, ventilation and air conditioning systems) or perhaps a health IT person with a good background in quality management practices? The broader your diversity in such situations, the greater your value as a team member in these settings! Do you just bring one skill to the table or do you have a breadth of skills from which to assess challenges and improve organizational or system performance?

Skills Diversity and Professional Certification

Another way to view the diversity of skills necessary to make healthcare enterprises function effectively and efficiently is to look at the tremendous range of job roles and professional certifications in this space. Another chapter discusses certification programs in more detail, but as an example of diversity here are just a few adapted from a substantially more robust listing from Toms IT Pro [3]:

Database Job Roles

- Database Administrator (DBA)
- Database Developer
- Database Designer/Database Architect
- Data Analyst/Data Scientist
- Data Mining/Business Intelligence (BI) Specialist
- Data Warehousing Specialist

Health IT Certifications

- CAHIMS: Certified Associate in Healthcare Information Management and Systems
- CPHIMS: Certified Professional for Healthcare Information and Management Systems
- RHIA: Registered Health Information Administrator
- HCISPP: HealthCare Information Security and Privacy Practitioner

■ CompTIA Healthcare IT Technician
■ CPHIT: Certified Professional in Health Information Technology

Information Security Certifications

■ CISSP: Certified Information Systems Security Professional
■ CISM: Certified Information Security Manager
■ CompTIA Security +
■ CEH: Certified Ethical Hacker
■ GSEC: SANS GIAC Security Essentials

Project Management Certifications

■ PMP: Project Management Professional
■ CAPM: Certified Associate in Project Management
■ CSM: Certified ScrumMaster
■ CompTIA Project+
■ CPM: Certified Project Manager Certification

This list of 20 roles and certifications barely scratches the surface of the specialties in a hospital setting and this is just a slice of the IT space! Taking a more clinical focus, you may find your contribution in such clinical and administrative areas including:

■ Clinical provider: physician, nurse, physicians' assistant, nurse practitioner, laboratory or radiology technician, pharmacist or pharmacy technician, etc.
■ Clinical administration: Hospital or clinic administrator, finance officer or specialist, hospital facilities engineer or specialist, human resources, etc.

Developing your skills through on-the-job experience and acquiring additional training or certifications helps build a strong resume and contribution to the healthcare team. As an example of both experiential and academic maturation over a career, I will use myself to illustrate how skillsets can build on each other and make you a more valuable asset to your organization (Figure 3.1).

Looking back, I know that my opportunities were uncharacteristic and remarkably fortuitous, but it does provide an illustration of how one skillset builds upon another to offer an ever-increasing range of opportunities to diversify and contribute as a valued member of your organization.

Assessing Your Skills Diversification

If you have been in the health IT field for a few years, take a look at your diversity of knowledge, skills, abilities, and certifications. Consider building a storyboard or narrative as in the case study above. Even using a graphical storyboarding technique may be helpful. How do you picture yourself in the "story" of the healthcare environment? I've built a simple storyboard for illustration (Figure 3.2).

Case Study: Starting with a couple degrees in psychology, my first Army healthcare assignment was as a Company Commander of a brick and mortar hospital where I tended to the training and professional development of our healthcare team as well as their rewards and discipline [**human resource** skill set]. After a couple years, I was accepted to patient administration school and, upon completion of training, became the administrator of the medical records division of a small hospital [**medical records** skillset and first exposure to **health IT**]. Going back to school for my Master of Healthcare Administration years later, I completed a residency in health policy in the Pentagon [**health governance and policy** skillset]. I was selected to teach post-graduate education in patient administration and managed care to Army healthcare officers when health IT systems were evolving rapidly [**teaching/training skillset**]. This exposure and my professional network kept me in constant contact with IT staff causing my subsequent placement to be as Chief Health Informatics Officer in the Office of the Army Surgeon General [Major cross-over into **health informatics** – a strong link between IT and the clinical processes of care]. Working at this corporate level and with my background in health IT, I was recruited to serve as program manager for an enterprise data warehouse program supporting the Military Health System [**project management & data warehousing** skillsets]. Success with this program led to formal acquisition training and program management of the military electronic health record (EHR) program [**EHR & acquisition** skillsets]. And so on...

Figure 3.1   Example of experiential and academic maturation over one's career: Vic Eilenfield's Personal Journey.

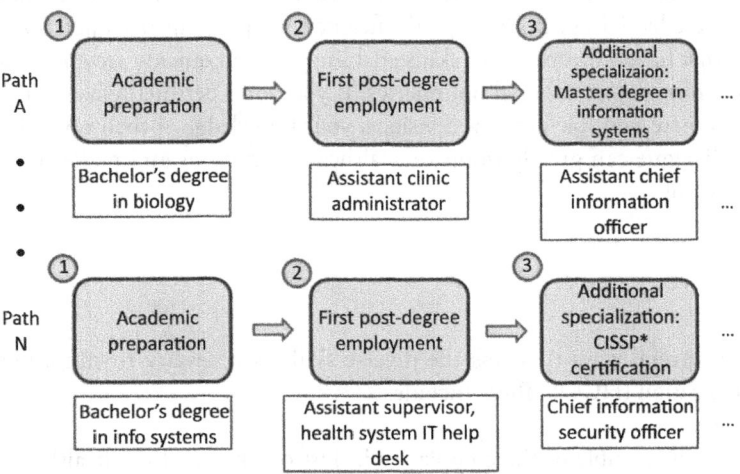

*CISSP – Certified Information Systems Security Professional

Figure 3.2   Storyboard technique (many alternative paths).

Does your resume reflect your experiential knowledge? Have you ever felt that you had much of the knowledge, but not the certification to better support your input on key decisions? If so, please review the chapter on professional certifications and consider going that extra step to become certified if it is an area in which you would like to see your career expand.

If you haven't been in the health IT field for long, consider mapping out skillsets, job roles and possibly certifications that can help you diversify your skills and make you a more valued member of the healthcare team over time. In this process, you would write down a number of job titles or skills that are associated with your position and that of others with whom you work, thus providing a multi-layered view of alternatives in job growth upon which you could proceed. While a subsequent chapter develops the concept of career mapping more fully, an exceptional tool that shows both vertical and horizontal diversification is that produced by the American

Health Information Management Association (AHIMA). Visit the link at http://hicareers.com/ CareerMap/ to see how interactive it is as an illustration of diversification possibilities for your career in the health IT space!

Work Diversification in the Health IT Setting: An Example

Another way of examining how diversification makes you a key player for your healthcare team is to look at a typical hospital environment and the usual problem-solving challenge. In this illustration from www.healthitoutcomes.com (Figure 3.3), you quickly see that many, if not most, challenges addressed in the healthcare environment impact a very broad range of hospital—or clinic—functions. While the scope and diversity of the outpatient setting is often more restricted than that of the hospital, the analogy is easy to follow.

While this representation has a lot of moving parts, it is a very simplified view of the hospital IT ecosystem. If you find yourself with a problem or process challenge in the billing department, what other team members would you bring to the table? Are you that team member who can easily talk across these soft boundaries in your healthcare organization? How does the billing system impact the EHR data sources and vice-versa? Can you discern the challenges a billing issue would have on provider credentialing? Both hospital efficiency and problem-free operation rely greatly on team members that have a diverse set of skills enabling them to quickly see and resolve challenges occurring across intra-organizational boundaries. If you don't personally have the requisite skills to operate across these multiple hospital divisions, your knowledge of their operations and who to bring into the dialogue can greatly improve healthcare operations and make you a more valued member of the team!

Conclusion

We've looked at several ways to assess the diverse skillsets necessary to run a high-performing healthcare organization (HCO). These include:

- ■ Examining an example of the complexity in just one niche of the healthcare environment (diagnostic coding).
- ■ Looking at common quality management practices that leverage multi-disciplinary teams for process improvement.
- ■ Reviewing a surprising breadth of job roles and certifications in the health IT space.
- ■ Viewing a case study in career health IT evolution.
- ■ Assessing a career map showing horizontal and vertical movement opportunities in health IT.
- ■ Reviewing a health IT ecosystem view of a hospital.

Ensuring high-quality products and processes is often dependent on having a diverse group of subject matter experts review and provide input on their part of the process. But who identifies all the various experts that might own a piece of the current process or the future improved process? Personally possessing a more diverse skillset enables you to identify the many contributing players to a process and perhaps play more than one role in the process resolution, making you a much more valued member of the healthcare team!

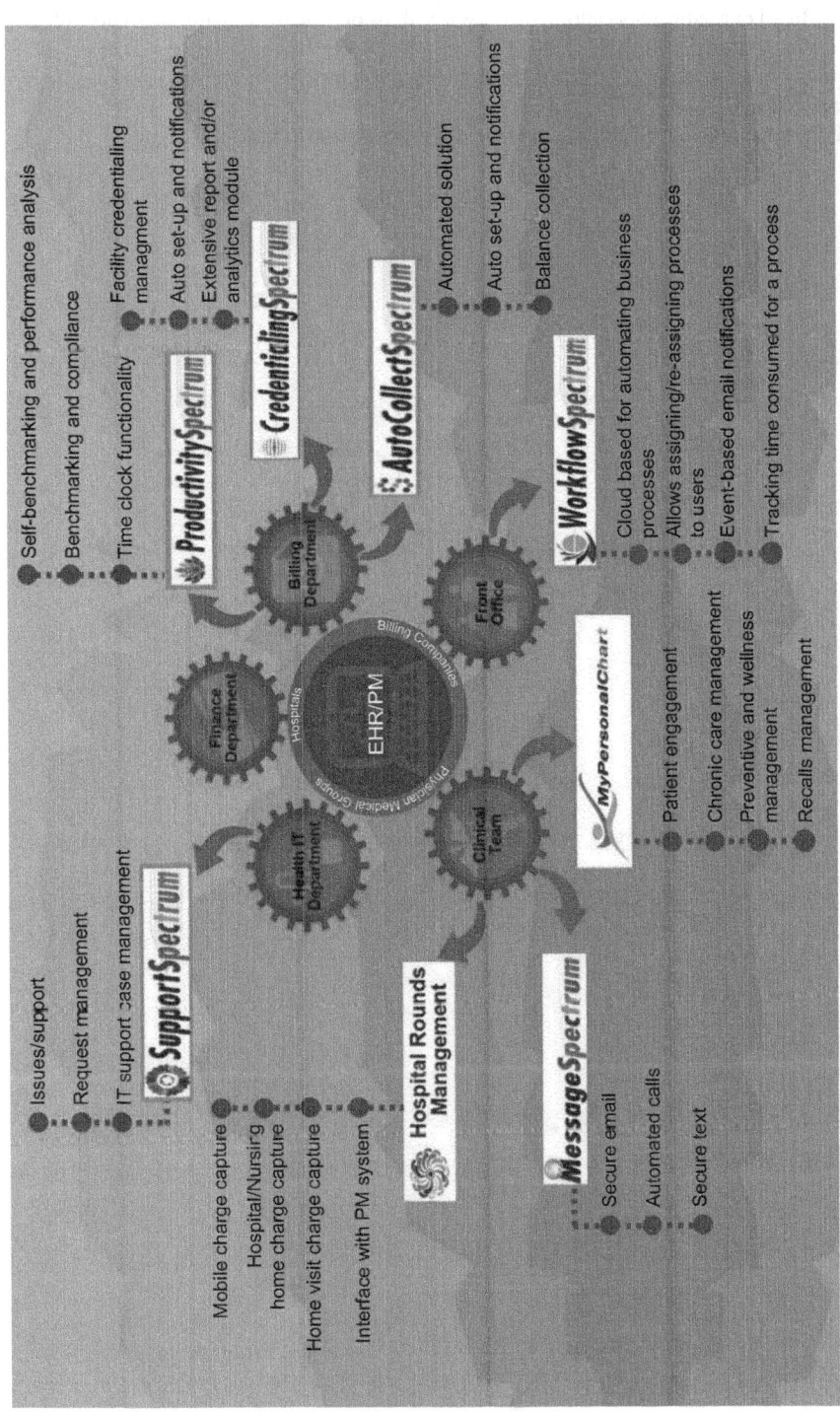

Figure 3.3 Diversification of problems occurring in a health IT setting. (Reprinted with permission from the Health IT Blog Network: http://www.healthcarescene.com.)

References

1. American Board of Medical Specialties, http://www.abms.org/member-boards/specialty-subspecialty-certificates/.
2. Total Quality Management (TQM), Inc.com, http://www.inc.com/encyclopedia/total-quality-management-tqm.html.
3. Toms IT Pro, http://www.tomsitpro.com/articles/best-it-certifications,1-1352.html.

Chapter 4

Developing a Career Roadmap

By Dr. Detlev H. (Herb) Smaltz

PhD, FHIMSS, FACHE

Contents

Abstract

Leveraging the value of a roadmap, health IT professionals need a plan of approach to navigate the career aspects of health IT. Identify the components of developing and implementing a career map designed to chart one's future.

Keywords:

Health Informatics
Career Roadmap
Introspection
Self-Assessment
Professional Networking
Mentor

Introduction

It seems like such a simple edict—plan ahead. Most of us that toil daily in the field of healthcare informatics certainly apply that edict to the myriad of initiatives that we lead or participate in over the years. Yet some of us tend to neglect that same edict when it comes to our own professional career development. One of my favorite childhood books was Lewis Carroll's *Alice's Adventures in Wonderland*. Recall the exchange between the Cheshire cat and Alice:

> *One day, Alice came to a fork in the road and saw a Cheshire cat in a tree. "Would you tell me, please, which way I ought to go from here?" she asked. "That depends a good deal on where you want to get to." was his response. "I don't much care where." Alice answered. "Then it doesn't matter which way you go" said the cat.*

Brilliant in its simplicity, yet it has such a deep and profound message.

I was recently going through my high school yearbook, which I haven't looked at in about five years. I wasn't going through it nostalgically to relive my high school years, which were uneventful to say the least, but rather to retrieve a doodling that I put together on a piece of butcher block paper some 33 years ago. I had just enlisted in the United States Air Force earlier that year to both fulfill a patriotic desire to serve (I grew up a military brat so that runs deep in me) as well as a means to an end—specifically to complete my baccalaureate education. I was just completing my technical training as a biomedical equipment repair technician (BMET) and was about to be transferred to my first assignment to MacDill Air Force Base in Tampa, Florida. I apologize for the handwriting (mine was never very good)—this is my original handwritten career roadmap (Figure 4.1).

What I continue to this day to find amazing is that, 33 years later, I'm actually on one of those career paths that I laid out in my own personal roadmap those many years ago. At the time, I didn't think much of it—I'm analytical by nature. So laying out a decision tree with all of the possible career paths that I could envision from the starting point I was currently at was just a simple way for me to visualize my career options. Yet that simple act of writing down, not just the end state goals, but the intermediate steps I might have to take in order to move to the next step on that roadmap, was empowering. If I wanted to move forward on the roadmap, I needed to take the next step, which in my case was enrolling in night school and completing my baccalaureate degree. Thereafter, it's a matter of taking the next incremental step on your roadmap.

The roadmap in Figure 4.1 above was completed by my inexperienced self, without benefit of a mentor at the time, and without benefit of help from any professional societies, like HIMSS (at the time I was not involved in IT so I wasn't a member yet). If I could redo it today, the figure below outlines the elements of an effective career roadmap (Figure 4.2).

Career Roadmap: The Foundation—Self-Understanding

Prior to embarking on laying out a career roadmap, introspection is an important foundational step. And in being introspective it's very important to be honest with yourself. It's not uncommon for some to fall into the trap of pursuing career paths that others have chosen for them, whether through the influence of parents, friends, or other well intentioned people in their life.

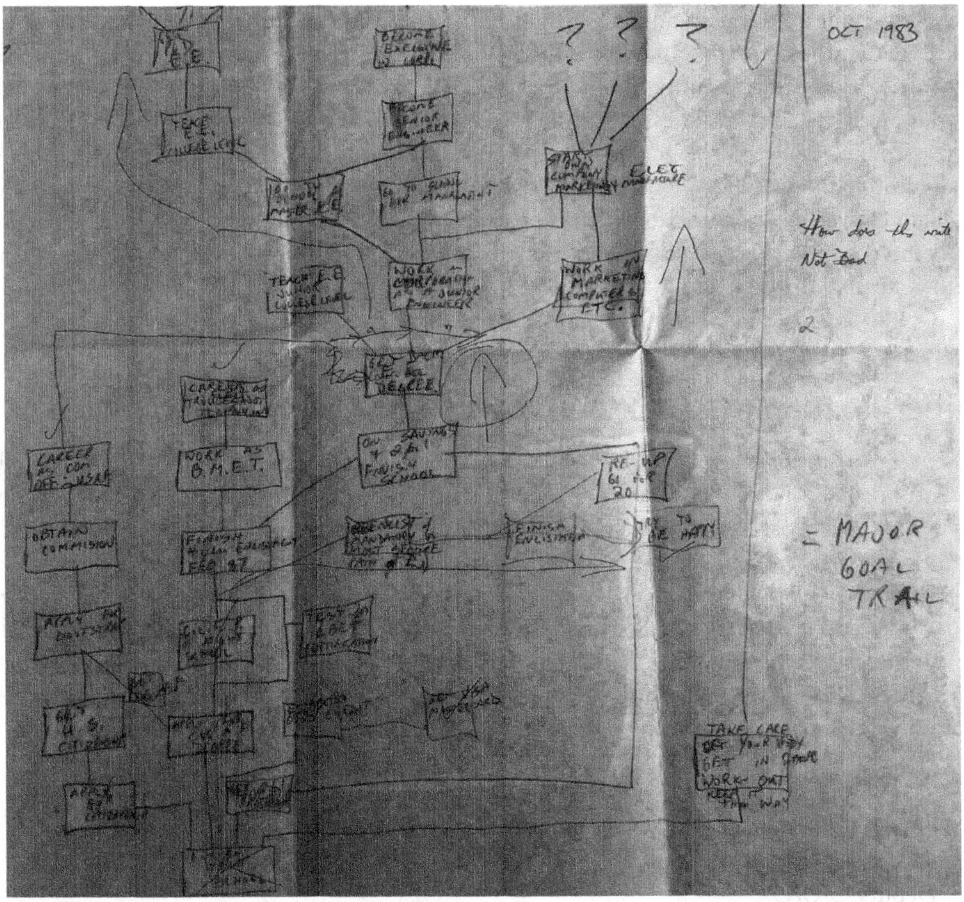

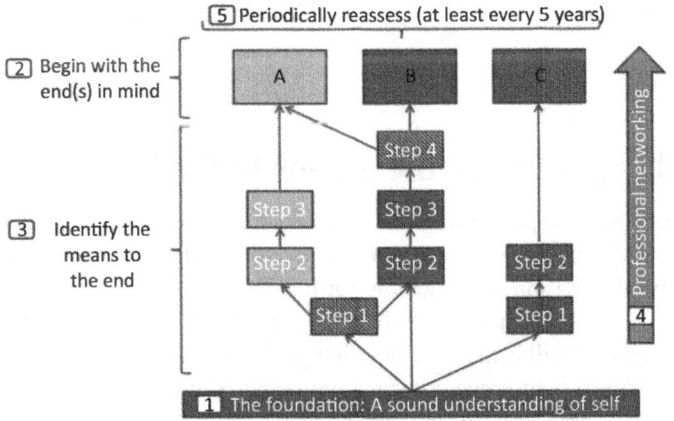

Figure 4.1   My own career roadmap—circa 1983.

Figure 4.2   Components of a career roadmap.

It's a good thing to discuss and gain insight with others you know and trust about what they believe, but in the end, you, and you alone, will ultimately have to live your career path every day. So it's important to think about what you like to do, what you don't like to do, what are your strengths and weaknesses. While a web search will provide a wealth of career-related self-assessment resources, the goal is to help you be truly introspective and gain a better understanding of your true self. A good example is the self-assessment survey provided by Claremont Graduate University [1], a link to which is provided in the 'Web Resources' section at the end of this chapter. Armed with an honest self-assessment, you are ready to move onto the next step in creating a career roadmap.

Career Roadmap: Begin with the End in Mind

Stephen Covey in his seminal work *The Seven Habits of Highly Effective People* [2] suggests that successful people tend to focus on the end goal that they are trying to achieve in all of their dealings in life. This is particularly true when embarking on drafting your own career roadmap. My own belief is that it's not as important to reconcile yourself to a single, "achieve it or bust" end goal. That, particularly in today's economy, is setting yourself up for frustration. Rather, conceive of a number of potential end goals that align with your self-assessment as outlined in Figure 4.2. For instance, for someone with a background as a pharmacy technician that has just graduated with a baccalaureate degree in healthcare informatics, after an honest self-assessment that suggests an affinity for managing people and leading teams, the following might be plausible roadmap goals:

A. Director, Pharmacy Information Systems
B. Director, Clinical Information Systems
C. Deputy CIO/CIO

The important thing is to leave plausible alternatives and not lock yourself into a single "be-all" end goal, recognizing that there are lots of forces potentially at work (e.g., the economy, a growing family, changes in your own desires, etc.) that will have an impact on how your career roadmap actually evolves. In essence, you are planning ahead for end goals that are all plausible and acceptable to you at the point in time that you are creating your roadmap.

Career Roadmap: Identify the Means to the End

Next, think through what steps you might need to take to achieve each of your stated end goals. For instance, one of the examples above, our healthcare informatics graduate pharmacy technician, could conceivable envision the following for her "B" path above to the Director of Clinical Information Systems. As you can see, the pharmacy technician in our example envisioned a distinct path that she believes will help her achieve her goal and thus has concrete intermediate goals/steps that she can take to help prepare her to move toward her ultimate goals as opportunities within her own or other organizations present themselves.

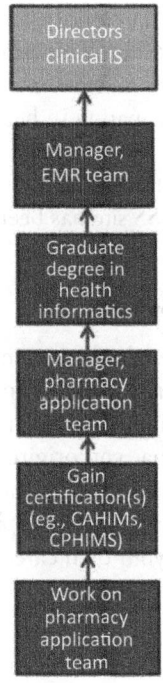

Career Roadmap: Professional Networking

Professional networking is an important component of a career roadmap for a number of reasons. First, by continuing to expand your network of professional friends and colleagues you are expanding the pool of people that might serve as references for new positions that you may want to compete for as you move through your career. Second, developing a strong and growing professional network, gives you greater visibility into how others are moving through their own careers to gain some validation for intermediate steps you believed you needed to take when you first built your career roadmap. Alternatively, the interaction with others in your professional network may suggest changes you may want to make to your career roadmap. Third, a professional network can be a great source of mentors that can help you continue to refine your career roadmap over time. Later in this book, Joseph J. Wagner (Section III: Learning from Others; Chapter 11: The Mentoring Process) is going to cover the mentoring process and Dr. Joyce A. Zerkich (Section III: Learning from Others; Chapter 15: Professional Coaching) will cover professional coaching, so I won't go into depth here. But I will say, seeking out and maintaining a long-time professional mentoring relationship with someone that you admire is a huge plus in helping you think through a career roadmap and also in evaluating career roadmap course changes from time to time. When I was a young healthcare administrator, I was leery about approaching senior leaders in my organization or professional society. I worried that they didn't want to be bothered with me; that they were too busy to care about me; etc. Nothing could be further from the truth. Almost all senior leaders love to give back—they love to mentor and relish the opportunity to work with young up-and-coming healthcare leaders, like you, to develop or evaluate your career roadmap, to serve as sounding boards when new opportunities present themselves, and to share lessons learned and give advice from their own experiences of navigating the same waters you are now trying to navigate. So take note—put your fears aside and simply ask. You'll be pleasantly surprised by the positive response.

If you haven't been able to get much traction in developing your professional network, I strongly urge you to consider greater participation in health IT professional societies like HIMSS. Not only do they offer career development services, but by participation in annual and state conferences and events, you naturally will begin to grow your network of colleagues that you benefit from for a lifetime. A web resource to the HIMSS site has been provided at the end of this chapter [3].

Career Roadmap: Periodic Reassessment

Finally, it's important to recognize that people change, industries change, economies change, such that it only makes sense to periodically take stock of your career roadmap and yourself to see if it still holds true or if changes are warranted. At the very least, pull your roadmap out every five years and assess not only the end goals that you originally listed but also the intermediate steps you thought you needed to take to achieve the goals and update your roadmap accordingly. Just like hospitals and health systems don't build a strategic plan one time and never update it, so, too, should you expect to periodically update your own career roadmap.

Conclusion

Know yourself. A good friend, Jaime Parent Associate CIO, Vice President, IT Operations, and Assistant Professor, College of Health Sciences, Rush University, once told me, "Do what you love and love what you do." Like Lewis Carroll's Cheshire cat, Jaime's words are brilliantly simple yet deeply profound. Seek out things you enjoy doing and love doing those, whatever level in the organization those may be. Don't let naysayers dissuade you from what you professionally gravitate toward. But above all, commit to creating your own career roadmap.

Key Takeaways

Commit to drafting a career roadmap with the following components:

1. Conduct and honest self-assessment to identify your strengths, weaknesses, likes and dislikes, etc.
2. Begin with the end in mind: Identify at least 2–3 plausible future career goals.
3. Identify the steps you believe you either need to take or that you believe will be useful in helping you move toward that desired end goal.
4. Develop and nurture your professional network throughout your career.
5. Reassess at least every five years to update your career roadmap.

Web Resources

Example of a Self-Assessment Tool: http://www.cgu.edu/PDFFiles/Career%20Development/ CDO016.HowToCreateACareerRoadmap.pdf.

HIMSS Career Development Site: http://www.himss.org/health-it-career-services.

References

1. How to Build a Career Roadmap, Claremont Graduate University, http://www.cgu.edu/PDFFiles/Career%20Development/CDO016.HowToCreateACareerRoadmap.pdf.
2. Covey, Stephen, *The Seven Habits of Highly Effective People*, Simon & Schuster, New York, NY, 1989.
3. Healthcare Information & Management Systems Society, Health Career IT Services, http://www.himss.org/health-it-career-services.

Chapter 5

Work-Life Balance: Does It Exist? Can You Achieve It?

By Dr. Jean Ann Larson

LFHIMSS, FACHE, FIISE

Contents

Abstract

Because the health IT environment is fast-paced and dynamic, a tendency exists to work long hours to implement, maintain, or update solutions. Determine the best approaches to protecting one's personal life from professional practice.

Keywords:

Work-life balance
Productivity
Values

Mission Statement
Roles
Relationships

Introduction

The ability to traverse the struggles and challenges of life is critical to our health and our lives. Workplace stress has long been cited as a major cause of rising healthcare costs and lower workplace productivity (Ganster and Schaubroeck 1991). We sense that if we could achieve work-life balance (WLB), it would help make workplace stress more manageable and we could live more satisfying, healthy and productive lives. The concept of WLB has existed for decades. As each generation gets busier and busier, often even before they enter the workforce, it seems that WLB becomes more of an elusive goal. This chapter will answer several questions such as: What is WLB and should we pursue it? What does WLB mean to different individuals at different stages of their lives? Who is responsible for helping us achieve it? What are strategies that we can employ to achieve it through the various stages of our lives.

WLB is defined as "being able to properly prioritize activities related to job, family, community, and self-development" (Wu 2016). Though the definition seems fairly straightforward, WLB happens differently for each individual. Our own understanding of WLB also changes throughout our lives as we take on different roles professionally and personally, and as those roles evolve over time. For example, for the role of parent, the demands, priorities, and rewards of that role change as you first become a parent, as your children grow up and then go out to live independent lives. At all these different times, what WLB means to us and how we achieve WLB with this particular role changes. Also, how this role and our other roles intersect and overlap will change. Thus, how we "achieve WLB" will be very different at different stages of our lives and present very unique challenges. I have found that just when I feel I am successfully creating WLB in my life, a role changes significantly or I take on a new role. The truth is that at any given moment, I am not achieving WLB. However, it is much like piloting a plane or a ship. At any given time, the plane is not headed directly toward its destination. In fact, 99% of the time it may be technically "off course." If this is true, how do planes or ships ever arrive at their destinations? Just as the pilot continuously makes very small changes to keep the plane on its intended flight path, we must make choices, big and small throughout the day, the week, the month and ultimately our life to make sure that we are achieving the things that are important to us and that we are maintaining key relationships with ourselves and others.

Creating WLB in your life, whatever that means to you at this point in your life, is critical to your health and productivity. But there is good news and bad news. First of all, though your organization or employer can help support—or at least not get in the way of WLB—it is ultimately up to you and the choices you make that will allow you to create it. Why? Because it looks different for everyone. What helps create balance in one person's life, may actually create stress for another. We all have different values and objectives, as well as different priorities that may change over time. Thus, you never achieve or arrive at WLB; you must constantly create it!

A particular challenge that IT professionals have is that they are under tough deadlines amidst constantly changing technologies and organizational priorities. If we allow ourselves to get caught up in the frenetic pull of multiple stakeholders with different priorities and different levels of appreciation and understanding of the complexities of our industry, we can end up in a downward spiral that makes us ineffective both personally and professionally, while making the concept of WLB seemingly out of reach and just another frustrating and impossible goal.

However, there are ways we can step off of this hamster wheel, identify what is important to us and what we want to achieve, and create balance in our lives. And as critical change agents for our organizations, we can show the way and role model WLB. As we modify our reactions and the choices that we make throughout the day, we can demonstrate to our peers, teams, and clients that there is a better way to deal with change in our organizations.

So what can we do? First recognize that *you alone* are responsible for creating WLB in your life, minute by minute. No one can or will ever create it for you. Plus if you wait, the right time will never come. But, you always have choices. The challenge is to be aware of when to make those choices and then to have to courage to make them and live by them! Even though you may be busy and stressed out, take the time to sit down to *thoughtfully and intentionally* identify what matters most to you. Specifically, you must discover, your governing values—those enduring, passionate, and distinctive core beliefs that do not change; your roles, which are key relationships and responsibilities; and ultimately your mission, which is your unique purpose in life. I realize that if you've never done this before, it can seem a very daunting task. It can also seem intimidating if we feel we may have removed ourselves far from who we are and who we want to be.

Developing Values

The important first step is to spend time developing and reflecting upon your values. To make it easier, walk yourself through a series of questions and journal your answers to them. Understand that they will evolve and become more clear as you refer back to them and as you begin to use them in your life to make choices and decisions around where you want to spend your time and energy. Ask yourself the following questions:

- What is really important to me?
- Why is it important?
- Throughout my life, what remains important to me?
- What would others say are my signature traits and strengths? (You may want to ask trusted colleagues and friends what they would say.)
- Where do my talents and passions lie?
- What gives me energy?
- What and who causes my eyes to light up?

Some sample values might include:

- To be balanced in hand, heart, mind and soul to bring out the best in myself and others.
- In all my dealings with others, I choose to assume that they are creative, capable, and complete.
- To be tolerant and compassionate toward all.
- To be grateful.
- To be continuously learning.
- To be curious and engage myself and those around me in lifelong learning and discovery—Values of curiosity, learning, sense of adventure, open-mindedness.
- To be fit and healthy.
- To be financially secure.
- To cherish family, friends, and loved ones.
- To be creative.
- To embrace all of life's changes.

Make sure that these values really are you and not those of someone you or someone else wants you to be. Later as you identify key roles and your goals and objectives, you'll get more specific around what these values mean to you. Record your values in a small notebook, journal, or on your phone or computer where you can refer back to them and reconnect with them annually, monthly, and weekly. To help you, see Appendix 5.1 for a values exercise that can help you with this process.

Developing Your Mission Statement

A mission statement is a powerful document that expresses your personal sense of purpose and meaning in life. It acts as a governing constitution by which you evaluate decisions and choose behaviors and the ways you engage with others personally and professionally. The process of writing a mission statement involves answering a series of questions:

■ What am I about?
■ What are my values? (Which you have already identified.)
■ What are the qualities of character I would like to emulate?
■ What is important to me?
■ What are my roles?
■ What things do I want to have that I feel are important?
■ What legacy do I want to leave?

Again, spend some time reflecting upon these questions and record your answers in your notebook or journal. For me, this step was challenging because I kept thinking that there should be a formula or process that would help me do this. Unfortunately, there is not. The good news is that this mission statement may be kept private and confidential. Also, I had to live with what I wrote down, grow into it and get comfortable with it. Even though I was teaching workshops on WLB, it took some time and courage for me to become vulnerable enough to share small parts of it. Since then, and through several professional and personal transitions, it has changed very little and it has helped me reinvent myself and accept new opportunities over most of my life. For more help and inspiration go to http://msb.franklincovey.com/inspired/mission_statement_examples for examples and some ideas to help you write your unique mission statement.

Your Key Roles and Relationships

Most of us live multi-faceted lives. In fact, we may relish the multiple roles that we take on. However, this can make WLB even harder to achieve. Incorporating your values and mission around your key roles and relationships can not only lead to a more satisfying life, they can serve as a compass to keep you in balance. Some roles you might wish to think about as you develop your values and your mission include:

■ Professional roles you assume at work. For example, are you a leader of a team? Are you the boss? What about a colleague to your peers? You are also an employee of your organization. This might be your formal title or description of what you do. For example, my current title is Leadership Development Officer. Key relationships I have include those with my two bosses as well as the leaders across the organization who I serve.

- You may be a spouse or partner.
- You may be a parent, a child, or both.
- You are a community member.
- You may have a relationship with a higher power, be a member or leader of a place of worship.
- You may be a member of a professional or recreational organization that is important to you.

I offer these examples and suggest you consider all of them and select the four to six most important ones in your life right now. Make sure that your values and mission are aligned around them and include them. This will ensure that you can create balance around all of your key relationships and roles. Often we find it hard to reconcile our work and personal lives because all of our goals are centered on just one or two roles, ignoring other parts of our lives that help define who we are.

In addition to identifying those key four to six roles that you play in your life, you should also intentionally identify the key relationships or people that these roles serve or relate to. For example, one of my roles is that of being a "mother." In that role, I have two key relationships that are important to me—the one with each of my two daughters. I am also a daughter and that key relationship is with my elderly mother. As I mentioned earlier, in my place of employment I am the leadership development officer and I have key roles with the CEO and the Chief of the Medical School to whom I report. As a relatively new employee, it is critical that I develop a healthy, trusting relationship with each of them. As an author, my relationship is to my readers and I must do my best to communicate to them and relate to their challenges.

There is also one key and sometimes neglected relationship that we all have in common. That is the relationship we have to ourselves. Similar to the safety message we hear on the airlines, before we help others with their oxygen masks during a time of emergency, we should first secure and put on our own. If we don't take care of ourselves, we cannot help others. Stephen R. Covey used the metaphor of "sharpening the saw." If the saw is dull, the wood cutter is unable to work at full capacity and cut down the number of trees he needs to cut down. Once he sharpens that saw, he can go back to working full speed ahead.

This metaphor is true of our lives. The key lesson here is that in order to be as effective in all of our roles, we must take time to take care of ourselves, refresh and recharge, and "sharpen our saw" in order to be at full capacity. To achieve WLB, it is vital that we manage not only our time, but our energy. In fact, some researchers now suggest that managing our energy is more important than managing our time (Loehr and Schwartz 2005). In order to manage both our energy and time, we need to care for ourselves on four dimensions: the physical, the emotional/social, the intellectual, and the spiritual.

On the physical side we need to care for our physical health and spend time and attention on exercising, eating healthy, hydration, and adequate rest and sleep. On the social and emotional side, we need to spend time connecting with our family, friends, and community. Intellectually, we should ask ourselves if we're challenging our minds. Are we learning new things? Are we reading? Are we finding new solutions and approaches to problems? Spiritually, are we connecting to a higher power or source however we choose to worship and acknowledge the divine? There is no one way to sharpen the saw for any one person—and the ways in which we sharpen the saw may change over time as our circumstances change.

Remember, you do not have to address every dimension every day. However, you should work on each of the four dimensions at least once a week—though some of you will prefer to do some of them on a daily basis. Here are some examples I've heard from friends and colleagues of how they sharpen the saw in each of the four dimensions. To sharpen the saw in the physical dimension we often select some sort of regular exercise and eating "healthy." Physical exercise for you may be anything from 30 minutes of daily walking or training for a race, marathon or triathlon. The key is to do what makes sense for you. Depending on your circumstances and what is most important for you to be doing to improve your physical health you may also select getting seven to nine hours of sleep each night, drinking 64 oz. of water per day, not skipping meals, or scheduling an important preventive checkup. Think about one or two physical activities that if you incorporated into your day-to-day life would help you improve or maintain good health.

For good emotional health, are you maintaining good relationships with family, friends and loved ones? Can you think of one thing you can do to nurture an important relationship in your life? It might be a date night with your spouse, a call to parents or grandparents in another city. Maybe you'll spend some focused one-on-one time with one of your children. As both of my children are living in different states than I am, I make sure to text them every morning to say "good morning" and let them know I am thinking of them. These are simple things but they help me stay connected daily to those who I love.

To keep your intellect sharp, are you reading, studying, taking classes, or learning? Do you have a reading list you're working your way through every day? Maybe you want to brush up on a foreign language or musical instrument. Maybe you have an interest or hobby you've always wanted to learn more about such as cooking, gardening, dance, yoga, or crafting. Find a good friend or family member to join you and you may be able to sharpen your saw intellectually, socially, and even physically.

What about your spiritual side? Similar to the other three aspects, how you engage and recharge spiritually is very personal and unique to each individual. For some, it is traditional worship in a church, synagogue, temple, mosque, or other faith-based community. Others connect to their spirituality through reading inspirational literature, meditation, journaling, reflective writing, or even walking in nature. Some experience spirituality within like-minded groups and others are engaged in a more solitary journey.

Now that you've previously identified your values, mission statement, and key roles and relationships, it is now time to write down your goals and objectives. Many people do this at least annually. Depending on how quickly your roles change, or if you are in a time of personal or professional transition, you may need to set or at least review your goals more frequently. For example, when I first started my business, I reviewed, assessed, and often reset my goals every 12 weeks. I had to do this because I was learning so much so quickly that some goals became obsolete or irrelevant within a few months. A resource I found helpful for developing and considering my goals and objectives at that time was a book entitled *The Twelve Week Year: Get More Done in 12 Weeks Than Others Do in 12 Months* (Moran and Lennington 2013). The authors' premise is that you ideally focus on only three goals or major objectives every 12 weeks. For each goal or objective, you list tactics that will help you achieve the highly specific and measurable goal. If at the end of the 12 weeks, you have not achieved that goal, you ask yourself the following questions:

1. Did you achieve the goal? If not, ask:
2. Did you successfully complete all the tactics for that goal?
3. If you made some progress but you still did not achieve the goal, you will need to investigate and employ new tactics that will allow you to achieve the goal. This approach is helpful if you have stretch goals where many of the tactics to achieve those goals might be determined by trial and error and in areas that are very new to you. A simple example of how this approach might work is to use losing 10 pounds as one of your key goals within the 12-week timeframe. If at the end of the 12 weeks, you have not lost the weight, you need to determine if you have a discipline problem or a problem with your tactics. If you've nailed all of your tactics but the weight still didn't come off, you'll have to investigate and try different tactics.

Weekly Planning: Put the Big Rocks in First

Every week review your goals and objectives and roles. For each goal, ask what one to two action items you can take *that week* to help move you toward achievement of that goal. Also for each key role in your life, ask what one to two things you can do to build upon and strengthen the relationship. Once you have your weekly list of action items for each of your goals, objectives and roles, schedule them into your day. Also include your "sharpen the saw" activities. Be realistic about your schedule. By scheduling these into your calendar as a commitment, you are putting the big rocks or most important activities in first. To keep me on track, I use the Franklin Covey weekly compass based upon Stephen R. Covey's book *The Seven Habits of Highly Effective People* (1989) and *First Things First* (Covey et al. 1994) in order to record the two to three important tasks for each of my roles and goals. It reminds me at a glance and every day of my important roles and goals as well as the ways in which I choose to "sharpen my saw" physically, intellectually, socially, and spiritually. Please see Appendix 5.2 for an example. In the example, the individual selected four key roles: that of boyfriend, team leader, friend, and volunteer. For each role, he recorded one or two important tasks he wanted to accomplish that week. He also filled out all four dimensions for sharpening the saw.

Daily Planning

Once you've identified your roles, set your goals and done your weekly planning, daily planning becomes very easy. However, there are a couple of tips that I've learned along the way. First, as much as possible, schedule those key activities or big rocks for a specific date and time on your calendar by making it an appointment or commitment you make to yourself to accomplish the task. Second, allow a certain percentage of "unscheduled" time on your calendar to take care of urgent activities and other things that you must handle immediately. When I didn't do this, I got frustrated when I couldn't get everything I had planned done. What I discovered was that I was overscheduling myself. As a healthcare professional and leader, it was unrealistic and undesirable to try to schedule and control every minute of my day. Depending upon your role and situation, you'll need to leave more or less unscheduled time on your calendar to handle the necessary urgent and important tasks that make up your day. Also, if you attend a lot of meetings as many of us do, make sure you allow ample travel time, preparation time, and time to follow up on action items. If you don't do this, you will make your day more hectic and rushed than it needs to be. Last but not least, be flexible. Some days you may feel that your priorities are changing almost hourly, so your schedule will need to flex accordingly. Most important, don't be too hard on yourself. By focusing on the one or two things you want to do around your key roles and goals, no matter how crazy the week gets, you'll be able to engage (most of the time) in those activities that speak to who you are and your deepest held beliefs.

Covey's Four Quadrants for Time Management

A model that will help you assess how you currently spend your days versus maybe how you'd like to spend them is Covey's four quadrant time management construct as illustrated in Figure 5.1. Think about the types of activities that keep you running all day and where you spend your time. Begin to think about the *importance* versus the *urgency* of your daily tasks.

	Urgent	Not urgent
Important	Quadrant #1 "Necessity" ——— Your key action: "Manage" ——— *Common activities* – Crises – Deadline-driven activities – Medical emergencies – Other "true" emergencies – Pressing problems. – Last-minute preparations	Quadrant #2 "Quality and personal leadership" ——— Your key action: "Focus" ——— *Common activities* – Preparation and planning – Values clarification – Empowerment – Relationship-building – True recreation
Not important	Quadrant #3 "Deception" ——— Your key action: "Use caution or avoid" ——— *Common activities* – Meeting other people's priorities and expectations – Frequent interruptions: – Most emails, some calls – Urgency masquerading as importance	Quadrant #4 "Waste" ——— Your key action: "Avoid" ——— *Common activities* – Escapist activities – Mindless tv-watching – Busywork – Just mail – Some emails – Some calls

Figure 5.1 Covey's four quadrants for time management. (Adapted from Stephen Covey's "First Things First," Covey Leadership, Inc. ©2003.)

Quadrant 1

It is very easy to get caught in the urgency trap. Some people I've worked with seemed at times to be addicted to urgency. As you can see from the graphic, quadrant 1 is comprised of activities that are both urgent AND important. Examples are deadlines, medical emergencies, and family emergencies. These are truly items that cannot be deferred and must be handled now. However, they can be *managed*. A very simple example is a project deadline. Assuming that you weren't just assigned the project, you usually have time to work on the project and complete it before it becomes a crisis. However, if you routinely leave everything to the last minute, you spend more time in quadrant 1 than is necessary.

Quadrant 3

Another way to get trapped in the urgency trap with even more negative implications is to spend time in quadrant 3. This quadrant is called the quadrant of deception because these are tasks that seem to be *urgent* but are not at all important. They demand our immediate attention but do not require it. Most of them can be deferred or even ignored in some cases. What are examples? Looking at your phone every time you get a ping for a social media update, ill-defined meetings, some emails, and frequent interruptions. You want to avoid this quadrant as much as possible.

Quadrant 4

Quadrant 4 activities which are defined as not urgent and unimportant need to be avoided as much as possible. This is the quadrant of waste. These activities include any kind of escapist type activities such as mindless TV watching, internet surfing, games, and busywork. So why would we go there? After too much urgency and stress we end in this quadrant to escape the pressure. Better to go into quadrant 2 for rest, recovery and rejuvenation. But be careful that these activities don't morph back into quadrant 4. We may also go here to procrastinate and avoid undesirable or seemingly overwhelming tasks. Understand why you are procrastinating. Are you lacking information, resources or are you overwhelmed or afraid of tackling the task? Some of my favorite remedies for my own procrastination include:

- Start the day with the task I've been procrastinating.
- Work on the task for just 10–15 minutes.
- At the end of each major step, start the next step so that it is easier to jump back in where I left off.
- Brainstorm what information I need, who I need to talk to or what resources I need to take the next step.

What are your ways to avoid procrastination? How can you employ them more frequently?

Quadrant 2

Quadrant 2 activities do not occur if we do not focus upon them and take time to do them. Why? Because they are not urgent and they do not pull on our attention the way urgent tasks do. It is critical to work-life and personal life leadership to focus our efforts in this quadrant. We must take time to prepare for the week and the important tasks and roles in our lives. It is the time that we spend clarifying our values, mission statements, goals and connecting with who we are. These are the tasks we spend in order to build relationships that matter to us. And quadrant 2 is where we take time for true recreation and sharpening of the saw.

Conclusion: So How Does This Help with Work-Life Balance?

Most people live half their lives "below the line" on the unimportant tasks and activities. This leads to frustration, a sense of being out of control, and lots of stress. The bottom line is that we must live above the horizontal line of Covey's time quadrant and focus upon and do the important things as much as possible. Otherwise, we'll find ourselves reacting to every urgent stimulus.

So what's the secret of WLB? First it doesn't just happen. You have to create it. Year by year, month by month, week by week, and day by day as your life changes and as you evolve and grow. Like the earlier mentioned airplane crossing the country, you're 99% off course or not in balance any given time. Just like the adjustments that the pilot makes that allows the plane to travel from point A to point B, for you, it is the constant adjustments and decisions that you make during your day that allows you to do what matter most and feel a sense of balance. When you feel that you are making the right choices and navigating your life's journey, stress decreases and you can have some sense of peace and accomplishment. The bad news is that sometimes making the right decisions can be difficult as we are distracted and pulled in many different directions. The good news is that when you frequently connect to who you are—your mission, vision and values—it makes it easier to make the hard decisions.

In the words of Mahatma Gandhi:

> Your beliefs become your thoughts,
> Your thoughts become your words,
> Your words become your actions,
> Your actions become your habits,
> Your habits become your values,
> Your values become your destiny.

References

Covey, S. R. 1989. *The Seven Habits of Highly Effective People.* New York: Simon & Schuster.

Covey, S. R., A. R. Merrill, and R. R. Merrill. 1994. *First Things First.* New York: Fireside.

Ganster, D. C., and J. Schaubroeck. 1991. Work stress and employee health. *Journal of Management* 17 (2): 235–271.

Loehr, J., and T. Schwartz. 2005. *The Power of Full Engagement: Managing Energy, Not Time, Is the Key to High Performance and Personal Renewal.* New York: Simon and Schuster.

Moran, B. P., and M. Lennington. 2013. *The 12 Week Year: Get More Done in 12 Weeks than Others Do in 12 Months.* Hoboken, NJ: Wiley.

Wu, S., Nhengzheng, X., Li, F., Xiao, W., Fu, X., JIang, P., Chen, J. et al. 2016. Work-recreation balance, health-promoting lifestyle and suboptimal health status in southern China: A cross-sectional study. *International Journal of Environmental Research and Public Health* 13 (339): 1–16.

Appendix 5.1: Values Exercise

Identifying and prioritizing one's values can be a challenge. It may take time, be uncomfortable and highlight areas where your current life is not congruent with what you value most.

First, look at the list of potential values as brainstormed by others and circle or highlight up to 50% that might be your values. **Second**, in the column on the right, add any values that you don't see.

Being kind	Serving the less well-off	Financial independence
Being involved in politics	Health and energy	
Doing something worthwhile	Loving relationships	
A strong marriage or partnership	Intellectual growth	
Integrity	Being a good listener	
Religious beliefs	Being a good leader	
Professional success	Personal excellence	
Credibility in my profession	A balanced life	
Peace of mind	Discipline	
Self-sufficiency	Ability to influence	
Law and order	Ability to make things happen	
Open mindedness	Compassion	
Individual freedom	Being a risk-taker	
Success and achievement	Preparing children for adulthood	
Family happiness and well-being	Being a good team player	
Social issues and causes	Being funny	
Love	Trust in God	
Creativity	Tolerance of others	
Music excellence	A wide range of friends	
Art and Beauty	Standing firm on principles	
Financial excellence	Being decisive	
Fairness and justice	Patriotism	

Third, pick out the top 10 values that are closest to your heart *(Highlight or underline each one).*
Fourth, rank in order of importance one that you feel is number one, then number two and so on.

Some times short words and phrases do not quite catch the overall impact of a value. Write what these values mean to you in your life using "To" statements.

My core values are: *1st Draft*

To
To
To
To
To
To
To
To
To
To
To
To

Appendix 5.2: Weekly Compass Example

[Your company]
Job exchange proposal

[Select date]

Overview

1. Job exchange background and description

2. Job exchange scope

3. Advantages and disadvantages

4. Deliverables

5. Affected parties

6. Affected business processes or systems

7. Implementation plan

8. High-level timeline/schedule

Approval and authority to proceed

We approve the job exchange proposal as described above and authorize the team to proceed.

Name	Title	Date

[Your company]
Job exchange summary and report

[Select date]

Overview

1. Job exchange background and description
2. Job exchange scope
3. Deliverables – summary of achievement
   - Activities
   - Time spent
   - Observations
4. Affected business processes or systems-observed effect
5. Timeline/schedule analysis
6. Positive observations
7. Opportunities for improvement
8. General comments

| Report author approval | Date | Report author approval | Date |

ESTABLISHING AND NURTURING YOUR CAREER

Chapter 6

The Role of the Professional Association

By Dr. Anthony Blash
Pharm.D., BCompSc, CPHIMS

JoAnn W. Klinedinst
MEd, CPHIMS, PMP, DES, FHIMSS

Contents

Abstract

With a goal of assembling members of like topics, professional associations offer many benefits. Identify the ways health information technology (health IT) professionals will gain valuable insights into the many facets of associations for health IT and beyond.

Keywords:

Career development
Membership
Volunteer
Leadership
Chapter
Professional Growth
Personal Growth

Introduction

Professional Associations (also called professional bodies, professional organizations, or professional societies) are generally defined as a group of individuals with a general field of interest or expertise that comes together to advocate, set standards, and speak for the respective profession in local, regional, national and international discussions with other legislative or professional bodies.[1,2] The association may also provide support, educate, certify, and facilitate meetings for member, individuals interested in the profession and the public. Table 6.1 lists a representative sample of health information technology (health IT) professional associations.

Professional Associations

As Table 6.1 shows, the cost of one-year active membership varies between organizations. Even if you're a cash-strapped new hire, joining a professional association will likely be one of the best investments you'll ever make. Most associations will offer different types of membership:

Active student: This member is a full- or part-time student on the pathway to a certification or degree that may or may not reflect the profession represented by the association. The student member's dues are usually the lowest of the membership categories.

General members: General members make up the body of the association. These are professionals in the workplace, working within the profession.

Corporate members: Corporate membership allows a company to enjoy benefits similar to an individual in terms of being in a position to network, advocate, set standards, and represent the respective profession in local, regional, national, and international discussions with other legislative or professional bodies. A company with a number of employees who would benefit from joining the association may choose to join as a group.

Affiliate members: An Affiliate Member is characterized as a person engaged in a commercial enterprise doing business with or providing goods or services to members.

Other: Additional membership types may be available, but these represent the most common.[2–4]

Table 6.1 Health Information Technology (health IT) Professional Associations

Acronym	Association Name	Focus	Individual Annual Membership Cost	Website
ACHE	American College of Healthcare Executives	Healthcare executives, US	$150.00–$325.00	http://www.ache.org/
AHIMA	American Health Information Management Association	Many aspects of healthcare, US	$175.00–$185.00	http://www.ahima.org/
AMIA	American Medical Informatics Association	Many aspects of healthcare, US and international	$45.00–$350.00	https://www.amia.org/
ANIA	American Nursing Informatics Association	Nursing, US	$79.00	https://www.ania.org/
API	Association for Pathology Informatics	Pathology, US	$0.00–$225.00	http://pathologyinformatics.org/
ASHP	American Society of Health-System Pharmacists	Pharmacy, US	$49.00–$305.00	http://www.ashp.org/
CHIME	College of Healthcare Information Management Executives	Healthcare Information Management Executives, US	$375.00	https://chimecentral.org/
HFMA	Healthcare Financial Management Association	Healthcare Financial Management Executives, US	$315.00	https://www.hfma.org/
HIMSS	Healthcare Information and Management Systems Society	Many aspects of healthcare, US and international	$30.00–$199.00	http://www.himss.org/

(Continued)

Table 6.1 (Continued) Health Information Technology (health IT) Professional Associations

IMIA	International Medical Informatics Association	Physicians, international	http://www.imia-medinfo.org/new2/
SIIM	Society for Imaging Informatics in Medicine	Biomedical imaging, US	http://siim.org/
AATP	American Association for Technology in Psychiatry	Psychiatry, US	http://www.techpsych.org
AMDIS	Association of Medical Directors of Information Systems	Medical directors, US	http://www.amdis.org
IAHSS	International Association of Healthcare Security and Safety	Healthcare security, international	http://www.iahss.org
NCHICA	North Carolina Healthcare Information and Communications Alliance	Healthcare Data Exchange, US	http://nchica.org/
WEDI	Workgroup for Electronic Data Interchange	Healthcare Information Exchange, US	http://www.wedi.org/
ACDM	Association for Clinical Data Management	Clinical Data Management, US	http://www.acdm.org.uk/
CSMI	The Cyprus Society of Medical Informatics	Physicians, Cyprus	http://www.csmi.org.cy/

Note: The price column values are: IMIA $0.00–$100.00; SIIM $0.00–$200.00; AATP $45.00–$75.00; AMDIS $185.00–$385.00; IAHSS $50.00–$150.00; NCHICA $25.00–$300.00; WEDI $0.00–$300.00; ACDM $60.00; CSMI $22.00

HISI	Health Informatics Society of Ireland	Healthcare, Ireland	$0.00–$55.00	https://www.hisi.ie/
SHINE	Scottish Health Information Network	Healthcare, Scotland	$0.00–$60.00	http://www.shinelib.org.uk/
ACHI	Australasian College of Health Informatics	Healthcare, international	$0.00–$60.00	http://www.achi.org.au/
ATHS	Australasian Telehealth Society	Telehealth, international	$25.00–$50.00	http://aths.org.au/
AVI	Association for Veterinary Informatics	Veterinary, US	$0.00–$35.00	https://avinformatics.wildapricot.org/
MIM	Belgian Society for Medical Informatics	Physicians, Belgium	$30.00–$60.00	http://www.bmia.be/en/home/
HIMAA	Health Information Management Association of Australia Limited	Health Information Management, Australia	$0.00–$385.00	http://www.himaa2.org.au/
HiNZ	Health Informatics New Zealand	Healthcare, New Zealand	$20.00–$189.00	http://www.hinz.org.nz/
IAMI	Indian Association for Medical Informatics	Healthcare, India	$100.00	http://www.iami.org.in/index.aspx

(Continued)

Table 6.1 (Continued) Health Information Technology (health IT) Professional Associations

ADA	Americaan Dental Association Center for Informatics and Standards	Dental, US	$0.00–$552.00	http://www.ada.org/en/member-center/member-benefits/practice-resources/dental-informatics
	AcademyHealth Health Information Technology (HIT) Interest Group	Health care delivery and management, US	$45.00–$200.00	http://www.academyhealth.org/index.cfm
ASIS	Association for Information Science and Technology Health Informatics (HLTH)	Various disciplines, US	$40.00–$140.00	http://www.asis.org/SIG/hlth.html
MLA	Medical Library Association, Medical Informatics Section	Medical librarians, health professionals, information sciences professionals, US	$50.00–$130.00	http://www.mlanet.org/p/cm/ld/fid=532
NASCIO	National Association of State Chief Information Officers	State Chief Information Officers, US	$0.00–$500.00	http://www.nascio.org/
IHTSDO	International Health Terminology Standards Development Organisation	Data standardization, international	Free	http://www.ihtsdo.org/

Why Join a Health Information Technology Professional Association?

Joining a professional association is a great way to meet people. Membership grants you access to health IT professionals at the state, regional, and national levels. It gives you a structured opportunity to meet other health IT professionals—those with equivalent experience, leaders in the field, and people just entering the profession. You will be exposed to new ways of thinking about the world of health IT, meet potential employers and make friends. Health IT professional association members may contribute professionally through engagement at meetings and conferences.

Membership may also provide other benefits, such as a subscription to the association's journal, swift communication on key issues that may affect the health IT professional, attendance at meetings for reduced rates, and the opportunity to experience and participate in Special Interest Groups (also known as SIGs) designed for your subspecialty.[1,5]

Member Benefits

Personal and Professional Growth

On a resume, membership in a health IT professional association shows an understanding of the importance of professional networking. Current and future employers value a person dedicated to staying current and connected to their profession. Employers also want to know that a person's skill extends beyond the classroom. Opportunities to obtain knowledge and experience are available through the many volunteer opportunities offered in professional associations.

The association can assist in skills development by offering classes and presentations in your field. There may be opportunities to earn and maintain professional certifications or other credentials. Being recognized in this way validates your skills and demonstrates a high level of competence in your chosen profession.

Opportunities to volunteer also bring value to the member. Members who volunteer experience benefits far beyond the actual act of volunteering. Associations need the time and talent of volunteers to help shape and support key projects affecting the profession. Volunteering on a service project or committee you are passionate about will motivate you, which in turn will motivate others. As a volunteer, you may have opportunities to organize people and resources while participating in professional service projects. You may also gain valuable field experience by volunteering.

Association members also have the opportunity to mentor and be mentored. Most associations offer mentoring programs. Within the professional association your area of expertise may be nurtured and shared with members of greater and/or lesser experience. If your passion has not yet been promoted by the association, you may be given ample space, support, and opportunity to turn your ideas into action.[4–7]

Role in Shaping the Profession

In the association's policy-making body, sometimes called the House of Delegates, recommendations concerning the profession and its members are made. Usually any member may submit proposals for consideration by the House of Delegates. Accepted proposals are then used to position health IT as an influencer in the area of legislative and political decision-making. Your association's actions assist in ensuring that health IT is actively supported in influencing and shaping health and healthcare policy.

Voice in Washington

Your professional association monitors legislative activity on issues that may affect the future of its members, such as the Health Information Technology for Economic and Clinical Health (HITECH) Act and Meaningful Use progress. Professional associations may also represent health IT interests before the U.S. Congress and Federal regulatory agencies. The association is your partner and advocate in efforts to identify and offer guidance on critical issues regarding technology in the U.S. healthcare system.

Leadership Opportunities

Participation in the governance of the professional association offers a service to the profession and to the members while providing a sense of satisfaction to the member serving in this capacity. Association members may serve as local, regional or national committee chairpersons, chapter officers or members of the House of Delegates. There will be ample opportunity to develop or exercise leadership skills that may also be used in community or professional capacities.[3,6,8–11]

Chapter Activities

In most professional associations, local association members are also recognized as members at the national level. Your local or regional chapter may offer many opportunities for involvement. Usually there are chapter meetings, conferences, community service projects, socials, fundraisers, elections and membership drives to name a few. Members may also have the opportunity to develop and present on topics of importance to the profession or the community.[3,4,10]

Association Activities

Continuing professional education and community outreach are important components of health IT association activities. Members will be able to learn while earning or maintaining professional licensure or other credentials. Many programs and activities are sponsored by professional associations to assist and support the credentialing efforts of their members. Nonmembers may also be able to participate in professional development activities sponsored by the association, but usually at a significantly higher enrollment cost.

Because of the number of individuals involved, associations are able to effect change faster and have a much greater impact than just one person. Some notable efforts are described below.

AMIA: EHR-2020 Task Force

Our nations' healthcare system is in the midst of an unprecedented transformation that is designed to improve the safety, efficiency, and quality of patient care. The HITECH Act instituted incentive programs for the meaningful use of certified electronic health records (EHR) technology. EHRs can help advance care in ways that paper records cannot. EHRs can improve patient and provider access to data, and also improve the quality of care that patients receive by helping healthcare providers identify potential safety issues and better follow up with patients on long-term care goals. However, turning paper health records into electronic health records is not enough. The electronic health record will provide the most benefit when the information is standardized, structured, and stored in uniform ways.[8,12–15]

Meaningful use of EHR technology has the potential to prevent medical errors, decrease unnecessary healthcare costs, reduce paperwork, and improve the quality of healthcare. This task force creates recommendations and advises the American Medical Informatics Association Board on Electronic Health Record (EHR) functionality, integration with workflow, and safety and efficiency of care.[6,16]

HIMSS: Interoperability and Health Information Exchange Committee

Because the health information exchange landscape continues to evolve, interoperability becomes a key driver toward achieving secure, lower cost and higher quality patient care. Interoperability is the foundation for a learning healthcare system where the best evidence is generated, shared and applied for collaborative patient care.

The Interoperability & Health Information Exchange Committee focuses on the advancement of interoperability and standards that help drive health information exchange.[13,16,17]

Career Development

Professional associations provide many opportunities for members to explore their career options. Career fairs are traditionally held during annual meetings and give members the opportunity to interview with companies from all over the country and possibly the world. Regional and local conference meetings may also feature career fairs which gives attendees the opportunity to interact with representatives from the health IT industry while staying closer to home.[5,18]

International Membership

Some Associations are global in scope or are members of international federations. This allows the member to collaborate with chapters or similar associations outside of the United States. The member then has the opportunity to participate in global initiatives, exchanges, or conferences.[8,13,19–23]

Special Interest Group Membership

The term health IT encompasses a large number of subgroups, and all health IT association members are not the same. Your individual areas of expertise and research are likely represented in a SIG by the professional association. A SIG is defined as a subgroup within a larger group where members share information or research in specialized fields. Joining a SIG within the association allows members to discuss and research items of importance related to the member's specific sub-specialty with professionals of similar interests.[13,21,23,24]

Annual Conferences/Meetings

Annual meetings are meetings of the general membership of an association. These meetings are held annually in various cities across the country and provide information on career options and legislative issues affecting health IT. The annual meeting also provides many opportunities for interactions with companies and products focused on health IT. These meetings may also serve as a location for health IT-related certification examinations and continuing education seminars. The presenters and presentations at the annual meeting represent the best the industry has to offer. Topics are contemporary and can set the tone for the national or global health IT conversation for the year. Local chapter representatives may elect regional officers at this time and propose topics for resolution. The annual meeting may also host elections for national association officers. Members have the opportunity to meet with colleagues from across the nation and around the world.[7–9,19] The annual meeting is also a platform for the bestowing of awards. The association may recognize a Book of the Year, exceptional leadership, innovative practices, scholarship recipients, or other professional developments. Table 6.1 lists select association annual meeting details for the next 3 years, where available.

Subscription to Association Publications

A few health IT associations sponsor their own journal, while others recognize an independently published work as the official journal of the association.

> The *Journal of the American Medical Informatics Association* (JAMIA), the American Medical Informatics Association's (AMIA) official peer-reviewed journal, has articles on health IT-related studies, legislature affecting the profession, analytics and big data, and original research. Information is presented in a clinical practice-oriented format.[25]
>
> *Methods of Information in Medicine,* is the official journal of the International Medical Informatics Association (IMIA) and of the European Federation for Medical Informatics. It is also the official international journal of the German Association for Medical Informatics, Biometry and Epidemiology. The journal covers articles in health information technology, statistical analyses of medical data, and epidemiology.[26]
>
> *The Online Journal of Nursing Informatics (OJNI)* is an official journal of the Healthcare Information and Management Systems Society (HIMSS) Foundation. Articles published in the peer-reviewed journal address the theoretical and practical aspects of nursing informatics as it relates to the field of nursing.[27]
>
> *Telemedicine and e-Health,* an official journal of the American Telemedicine Association, is a peer-reviewed journal covering telemedicine and management of EHRs. The journal has articles on telemedicine in home healthcare, remote patient monitoring, and disease management in rural health battlefield care, nursing home, assisted living facilities, maritime, and aviation settings. Association members will usually receive discounted subscriptions to their association's journal.[28,29]

Other Benefits Available to Members of Some Associations Include

- Professional liability insurance, which may be provided for free or reduced prices for association members.

- Life insurance, home insurance, and auto insurance.
- Financial services such as scholarships, association credit cards, loans, credit unions, or money market accounts with partner financial institutions.
- Discounts in the community on car rentals.[2]

Membership Case Study

Why do members get involved with association? What do they get from volunteering? Here, a member shares her story.

JoAnn W. Klinedinst, MEd, CPHIMS, PMP, DES, FHIMSS
Vice President, Professional Development
HIMSS North America

My involvement with professional associations has been pivotal in my development as a health IT professional. While working in the Management Information Systems (MIS) Department of a local hospital in Southeastern Pennsylvania, United States, I realized that healthcare was the place for me. At the time (early 1990s), a career in health IT was not viewed as positive since the industry lacked advanced technology and offered lower pay than the IT industry in general. However, I welcomed the family-like atmosphere among many of the departments in this small, community hospital setting.

After being hired in the MIS Department for my knowledge of PC-based applications for word processing, database, and spreadsheet applications, I started getting more involved in the technical aspects of implementing MEDITECH through report writing, dictionary building, and other activities. While my degree was in business management, I had little knowledge of the hospital setting. As a result, I began exploring various professional associations that could provide additional education and training to supplement my healthcare knowledge.

After a search of many different types of organizations, I joined HIMSS in 1991. I did so because of the thought leadership that was available through peer-reviewed themed journals which allowed me to expand my knowledge in the areas of telehealth, clinical systems applications, the computer-based patient record, and many others. Further, HIMSS held an annual conference that combined education, exhibition, and networking. For me, this was a great start on my journey to begin my understanding of health IT. (And that journey still exists today.)

Much to my surprise, my involvement in HIMSS was not only accessing thought-leadership journals but much more. I attended my first conference in 1995 (San Antonio, TX) and was immediately captivated. After a few years, I decided that I too had experiences to contribute and responded to my first call for proposal on a poster session entitled "Critical Success Factors of Application Upgrades." I was accepted and actually earned recognition for the best post session overall. And I was hooked.

In addition to speaking at a HIMSS annual conference three times over ten years at HIMSS, I also served as a paper reviewer for many years. Through this experience, I decided that I wanted to serve on the Annual Conference Education Committee so I also applied for an appointment by the HIMSS Board of Directors. There were no guarantees that I would get appointed but I wanted to try. Much to my surprise, I was selected for a two-year term (1999–2000) and served as chair in 2000. This was such an honor. To think that someone from a small community hospital could be recognized for her skillsets and abilities was just amazing to me. And this is true today as well: HIMSS welcomes the involvement of individuals from all different types of stakeholders. The only differentiating factors are a willingness to serve the health IT sector.

As my appointment came to an end on the Annual Conference Education Committee, I applied for an appointment to the Advocacy Committee. I too was accepted for a two-year term. By this point, I was very engaged in my local DVHIMSS (Delaware Valley) chapter, and served on the State Advocacy Committee. My responsibilities included setting up the appointments for attendees to meet with their legislative representatives: all 110 attendees. While advocacy was a different area for me, I learned quite a lot which helped me to become even more well-rounded as a health IT professional.

As I progressed in my volunteer efforts with HIMSS, I realized that I may not always want to work in health IT so I diversified my professional association involvement and joined the Project Management Institute (PMI). Because so much of what I did in health IT was project-focused, I decided that PMI was a good fit for me as well. I served in a variety of capacities for the PMI Healthcare SIG. While I wanted to diversify, I kept coming back to health IT. At the same time, I became involved in various Special Interest Groups (SIGs) with HIMSS: the Supply Chain Management SIG, Long-Term Care SIG, and the Project Management SIG. All provided an opportunity to engage but without the commitment of a HIMSS Board appointment.

One advantage to becoming involved with a professional society as an active volunteer is that one can earn points for advancement. HIMSS has advancement opportunities for Senior Member and Fellow. Many of these activities contributed to my overall advancement score and I became a Fellow in 2000.

And another advantage to becoming an engaged volunteer is earning points for certification. After I earned the FHIMSS, a new certification was being launched by HIMSS called the Certified Professional in Healthcare Information and Management Systems (CPHIMS). I decided to study and then sit for that exam. Again, my involvement in HIMSS definitely prepared me to understand the vast body of health IT knowledge. So, with 200 of my closest friends on a Sunday morning at HIMSS02 Atlanta, we were the first to be seated to take the exam. I passed and now was both a FHIMSS and a CPHIMS.

As an engaged volunteer, one has the opportunity to work with peers both nationally and internationally. And this recognition sometimes results in an industry or service award nomination, as it did for me. I was nominated and selected for the HIMSS Leadership Award based on my many years of involvement with HIMSS. While I never expected anything like this, professional associations do recognize their well-deserving members. And I happened to be one who was recognized. And a moment I still remember to this day.

While still involved with PMI and HIMSS jointly, I decided to earn the Project Management Professional (PMP) certification. I had the experience needed to apply and had also enrolled in Villanova University's Masters Certificate in IS/IT Project Management (which is still available today). Based on three modules, the third was devoted to preparing for the PMP exam. I completed the certificate and then sat for the exam. Although I failed the first time, I decided to try again. This exam was (and still is) highly rigorous but I felt I had the competencies to succeed. And I passed on my second try.

With my time approaching an end on the Advocacy Committee, I decided that I would apply to sit on the Ambulatory Information Systems Committee. Since I had moved from the acute setting to the ambulatory setting in my workplace, this made sense to me. At the same time, HIMSS was hiring subject matter experts like myself and others. I interviewed for and was selected as the Director of Enterprise Information Systems. Fortunately for me I was hired; however, my volunteer involvement with HIMSS came to an end as a paid employee.

While my experience may be atypical, one never knows where an engagement with a professional association may lead. To this day, I see vendors that I worked with at my community hospital who also exhibit at the HIMSS Annual Conference and Exhibition. While some may have retired, I still seem to find a person or two who I worked with some 20 years previously.

Conclusion

Our best advice to those interested in joining a professional association is to not only join but also get involved. There are many ways to become involved with professional associations and some require a minimal commitment while others require longer terms. Based on your level of commitment, your rewards may be immediate or perhaps long term. Regardless, your experience with professional association involvement may be as priceless as ours has been. While my (JoAnn's) role has changed from a practicing health IT professional to one who serves the professional development needs of the health IT professional, I too am searching for that next professional association that will help me learn and grow as an education professional. Please consider not only joining a professional association or two of your choice but also getting involved. Both you and your career will benefit immensely.

References

1. Hovekamp TM. Professional associations or unions? A comparative look. *Library Trends.* 1997;46(2):232–245.
2. Graner B. Membership in a professional organization. *The Prairie Rose.* 2010;79(4):10.
3. Ayres EJ, Hoggle LB. 2011 Nutrition informatics member survey. *Journal of the Academy of Nutrition and Dietetics.* 2012;112(3):360–367.
4. Adler-Milstein J, McAfee AP, Bates DW, Jha AK. The state of regional health information organizations: Current activities and financing. *Health Affairs.* 2008;27(1):w60–w69.
5. Anderson BL. Nursing informatics: Career opportunities inside and out. *Computers in Nursing.* 1992;10(4):165–170.
6. Greenes RA. Strategic planning activities of the American Medical Informatics Association. *Journal of the American Medical Informatics Association: JAMIA.* 1994;1(3):263–271.
7. Honey M, Newbold S. Initiatives to support the emergence of nursing informatics. *Studies in Health Technology and Informatics.* 2009;146:107–111.
8. Special issue: APAMI 94. Asia Pacific Association of Medical Informatics conference. Singapore, November 10, 1994. *International Journal of Bio-Medical Computing.* 1995;40(2):77–163.

9. Proceedings of the 1st TTUHSC Radiology Informatics Conference on Advanced Technologies for Radiology Operations. *Journal of Digital Imaging.* 1998;11(4 Suppl 2):1–47.
10. Ayres EJ, Hoggle LB. ADA nutrition informatics member survey: Results and future steps. *Journal of the American Dietetic Association.* 2008;108(11):1822–1826.
11. Greenwood K, Murphy J, Sensmeier J, Westra B. Nursing profession reengineered for leadership in landmark report: Special report for the alliance for nursing informatics member organizations. *CIN: Computers, Informatics, Nursing.* 2011;29(1):66–67.
12. Osheroff JA, Teich JM, Middleton B, Steen EB, Wright A, Detmer DE. A roadmap for national action on clinical decision support. *Journal of the American Medical Informatics Association.* 2007;14(2):141–145.
13. Peltonen L-M, Topaz M, Ronquillo C, et al. Nursing informatics research priorities for the future: Recommendations from an international survey. *Studies in Health Technology and Informatics.* 2016;225:222–226.
14. Embi PJ, Payne PR. Clinical research informatics: Challenges, opportunities and definition for an emerging domain. *Journal of the American Medical Informatics Association.* 2009;16(3):316–327.
15. Petrakaki D, Barber N, Waring J. The possibilities of technology in shaping healthcare professionals: (Re/De-) Professionalisation of pharmacists in England. *Social Science and Medicine.* 2012;75(2):429–437.
16. Payne TH, Corley S, Cullen TA, et al. Report of the AMIA EHR 2020 Task Force on the status and future direction of EHRs. *Journal of the American Medical Informatics Association.* 2015;22(5):1102–1110.
17. Committee H-IHIE. Improving Patient Care through an HIE. http://www.himss.org/library/health-information-exchange/improving-patient-care?ItemNumber=47235.
18. Staggers N, Lasome CEM. RN, CIO: An executive informatics career. *Computers, Informatics, Nursing: CIN.* 2005;23(4):201–206.
19. Berleur J, Nurminen MI, Impagliazzo J. *Social Informatics: An Information Society for All? In Remembrance of Rob Kling: Proceedings of the Seventh International Conference'Human Choice and Computers'(HCC7), IFIP TC 9, Maribor, Slovenia, September 21–23,* 2006. Vol 223: Springer; 2007.
20. Mantas J, Ammenwerth E, Demiris G, et al. Recommendations of the International Medical Informatics Association (IMIA) on education in biomedical and health informatics. First revision. *Methods of Information in Medicine.* 2010;49(2):105–120.
21. De Lusignan S. International informatics research, communication, episodes of care, evaluation and measuring outcomes. *Informatics in Primary Care.* 2012;20(1):1–2.
22. Dowding DW, Currie LM, Borycki E, et al. International priorities for research in nursing informatics for patient care. *Studies in Health Technology and Informatics.* 2013;192:372–376.
23. Alexander GL, Abbott P, Fossum M, Shaw RJ, Yu P, Alexander MM. The future of informatics in aged care: An international perspective. *Studies in Health Technology and Informatics.* 2016;225:780–782.
24. Bahri P, Dodoo AN, Edwards BD, et al. The ISoP CommSIG for Improving Medicinal Product Risk Communication: A New Special Interest Group of the International Society of Pharmacovigilance. *Drug Safety.* 2015;38(7):621–627.
25. Association AMI. *Journal of the American Medical Informatics Association,* About. 2016; http://jamia.oxfordjournals.org/about.
26. Methods of Information in Medicine, About. 2016; http://methods.schattauer.de/about/description.html.
27. Online Journal of Nursing Informatics. 2016; http://www.ojni.org/.
28. Telemedicine and e-Health, About this journal. *Telemedicine and e-Health* http://www.liebertpub.com/overview/telemedicine-and-e-health/54/.
29. Bashshur RL, Goldberg MA. The origins of telemedicine and e-Health. *Telemedicine Journal and E-Health: The Official Journal of the American Telemedicine Association.* 2014;20(3):190–191.

Chapter 7

The Importance of Volunteering

By Pamela V. Matthews

RN, MBA, FHIMSS, CPHIMS

Contents

Abstract

There is no greater sense of accomplishment than giving back to others. Identify the power of helping others both internally and externally to one's organization.

Keywords:

Volunteerism
Education
Mentoring

Career Development
Community Service
Community Engagement
Professional Engagement

Introduction

Volunteerism is part of today's fabric of society, with a wide variety of opportunities ranging from participation in professional societies, civic organizations, and nonprofit entities. One can focus volunteer activities around personal interests such as environmental conservation, animal welfare, or helping with local food pantries and building homes for those less fortunate. One may volunteer without a conscious thought or need of recognition, such as working with little league baseball, coaching a fellow colleague, giving monetary donations, or assisting with a local hospital, church, or community group. Many Fortune 500 companies provide Employee Volunteering Programs or Employer Supported Volunteering, which allow employees to volunteer during work hours. There are many benefits to companies that support these types of corporate citizenship programs including corporate image enhancement and improved employee retention. Regardless of company benefits, the most important benefit is the positive impact made from their employee volunteer activities [1].

April is National Volunteer Month in the United States, which began with the Presidential Proclamation 4288 signed by President Richard Nixon in 1974 [2]. Since the holiday's inception, a new proclamation is issued each year by the sitting American president designating April as National Volunteer Week to honor volunteers. Celebrations and news stories across the country focus on volunteer stories and emphasize their value. The President's Volunteer Service Award (PVSA) is the premier volunteer awards program, encouraging citizens to live a life of service through presidential gratitude and national recognition [3].

Volunteers provide a significant economic impact on American's economy. In 2015, 24.9% of the population, about 62.6 million people, volunteered according to the U.S. Bureau of Labor Statistics [4]. The 2015 Volunteering and Civic Life in America research, sponsored by the Corporation for National and Community Service (CNCS) and the National Conference on Citizenship (NCoC), indicated that over 62 million Americans volunteered 7.9 billion hours, which had an estimated value of nearly $184 billion of services! [5] Volunteering is for all ages. The U.S. Bureau of Labor Statistics reported in 2015 the median annual hours spent on volunteer activities ranged from a high of 94 hours for those age 65 and over to a low of 36 hours for those under 35 years old [4].

Clearly, volunteerism has a significant impact on today's society.

Volunteerism

According to the Meriam–Webster dictionary, a *volunteer* is a person who does work without getting paid to do something or is a person who voluntarily undertakes or expresses a willingness to undertake service [6]. In broader terms, *volunteering* is generally considered an altruistic activity where services are provided with no financial gain. Volunteering is also renowned for skill development, and often intended to promote goodness or improve human quality of life [7].

We do not know for sure when the volunteer phenomena begin. *Voluntaire*, originally from middle French, was used as early as 1600 to describe one who volunteers for military service. The non-military use of volunteer was first recorded as early as the 1630s. Also, the word volunteer has roots in Latin as *voluntaries*, meaning "voluntary of one's free will [8]." The word *volunteerism* was first officially noted in use as of 1844 to describe the act or practice of doing volunteer work in community service [9].

Healthcare and Volunteerism

Volunteerism intersected with health and medical care throughout history and played a significant role in forming today's healthcare industry. While this chapter is not intended to provide an historical account of healthcare, it is of interest to review a few examples where volunteerism in America help to shape today's industry.

The earliest origins of hospitals were primarily religious and charitable institutions caring for the sick rather than medical institutions for their cure. Those who worked in these institutions, mostly as volunteers, were typically bound with a common identity and strong communal character. The history of hospitals is distinctive for first primarily being for the poor and only later gaining a significant role in the scientific medical treatment of patients. The Pennsylvania Hospital became the first permanent general hospital in America in 1752. The New York Hospital was chartered in 1771 and Massachusetts General Hospital opened in 1821. These specific hospitals were called "voluntary" hospitals because they were financed by voluntary donations rather than taxes [10].

Physician's practice of medicine in America dates back to the early 1600s. Physicians where formally trained, often through apprenticeships, and may have held a university degree. The New Jersey Medical Society, chartered in 1766, was the first medical professional organization in the colonies which "form a program embracing all professional matters: the practice, apprentice educational standards, fee schedules and a code of ethics." These physician professional societies began regulating medical practice using examination and licensure as early as 1760. By the early 1800s, medical societies were charged with establishing physician practice standards and certification [11]. The turning point occurred on May 5, 1847, when nearly 200 delegates, representing 40 medical societies and 28 colleges from 22 states and the District of Columbia, met in Philadelphia, Pennsylvania. Out of this came the first session of the newly formed American Medical Association (AMA), where delegates adopted the first code of medical ethics and established the first national standard for preliminary medical education and the degree of Medical Doctor (MD) [12].

Hospitals, clinics, and other provider entities sprung up across America due in part to local communities, religious institutions and various forms of volunteerism. Only a few hundred hospitals were located across America as of 1870, which had closer connections to charity than to medicine [13]. While Florence Nightingale had reformed England's military hospitals, trained nurses before 1870s across America were generally not known or not organized. During the American Civil War (1861–1865), the United States Sanitary Commission handled most medical and nursing care of the Union armies. Dorothea Dix, who volunteered as the Commission's Superintendent of Army Nurses, convinced the medical corps of the value of women working in 350 Commission or Army hospitals. As a result, over 20,000 women were volunteers working in hospitals throughout the North and South during the Civil War.

America's driving need for highly skilled nurses paved the path for today's nursing profession, which came largely from volunteers—those who formed groups, charities and concern citizens focused on monitoring and development of the nursing profession [14]. Fast forward to the twentieth century: the American Society of Superintendents of Training Schools for Nurses and the

Nurses' Associated Alumnae of the United States, founded in 1896, merged in 1901 to form the American Federation of Nurses. This federation then joined the National Council of Women and the International Council of Nurses, which led to the formation of the American Nurses Association (ANA) in 1911 [15].

Clara Barton, who gained fame for her work in nursing, led efforts with her circle of acquaintances to establish the American Red Cross in Washington, DC on May 21, 1881. Barton first heard of the Swiss-inspired global Red Cross network while visiting Europe. Returning home, she campaigned for an American Red Cross. From the beginning, the American Red Cross activities included mobilizing volunteers for disaster relief operations, which can still be seen today. One of the first activities of the American Red Cross was in providing disaster relief to the victims of the 1889 Johnstown Flood [16].

These are just a few examples where volunteers and the roots of volunteerism provided the platform for dedicated people to advance the betterment of healthcare and the public's well-being that helped shape today's healthcare industry.

Healthcare Associations and Societies

Today's healthcare industry, like other industries, enjoys the benefits provided by many professional societies, associations, and other nonprofit organizations. Professional associations and professional societies are used interchangeability for the most part and are typically nonprofit. Societies represent individuals of a specific profession focused on a common goal of advancing their profession and their individual knowledge through a common identity and strong community character [17]. These societies provide their membership with tools, resources, information, and opportunities that their members may not otherwise have. They provide the environment for members to engage, stay connected, advocate with others, share experiences, and celebrate triumphs. Also, professional society engagement is a foundation for individual career growth and advancement. The result of active volunteerism in these types of organizations benefit the employer and the advancement of the industry at large, resulting in a "Win-Win" for all.

Individuals may even elect to participate in more than one professional society based on their job and career. When evaluating the benefits of a particular professional society, the following question should be asked: How will participation in the society support immediate job needs and assist in long-term career growth and development?

For more information on professional associations, see Chapter 6 of this book, Dr. Anthony Blash and JoAnn W. Klinedinst's "The Role of the Professional Association."

Benefits of Volunteerism

Volunteering in professional societies can be rewarding and beneficial regardless of where one may be in their career. It not only supports building and maintaining a current resume, but sends a signal to employers, colleagues, and other associates that one is dedicated to the profession and the industry while seeking career growth opportunities. Society members may even have a competitive advantage over others in the industry and stand out as a job candidate. A student having volunteer activities, even community-based activities, on the resume demonstrates their ability to handle commitments and achieve results while being actively engaged. Benefits from participation or volunteerism in a professional society are many [18]. Society membership provides access to:

- Unique opportunities to learn new skills and knowledge.
- Educational opportunities leveraging a wide variety of platforms, ranging from onsite programs to online and interactive vehicles.
- Latest news and developments while providing a broad perspective of the industry.
- Federal and state policy advocacy activities that that drive industry legislation, regulation and compliance activities.
- Networking events at the national, regional, local and affiliated chapter level.
- Colleagues and peers that energize and diminish the feeling of individual aloneness.
- National and influential industry leaders.
- Opportunities to serve on volunteer workgroups that sharpen team-building and management skills.
- Opportunities to "fill in professional gaps" with specific skills and leadership development that inadvertently may not be available with specific job positions.
- Job and career opportunities which may be exclusive to only society members.
- Opportunities that may lead to another career or profession.

The 2015 Healthcare Information and Management Systems Society (HIMSS) Individual Membership Satisfaction Survey results identified the top four motivating factors for professionals joining HIMSS as professional development, chapter involvement, annual conference discounted pricing, and availability of volunteer opportunities. Survey results identified the top four motivating factors for existing members to renew HIMSS membership as professional development, discounted conference pricing, volunteer opportunities and educational opportunities [19].

These driving motives can be drilled down into several services offered by societies that members find to be of great importance to volunteering their time and effort, including networking, education, mentoring, and career development.

Networking

Volunteerism, regardless if it is community based or professional, can expose one to a broad range of people with diverse backgrounds from many walks of life. One's circle of professional friends and colleagues can greatly expand through professional networking activities. Professional societies can offer unparalleled networking opportunities for members to connect with peers, mentors, and industry leaders. Meeting with others who are like-minded can be equally beneficial and rewarding through building a trusted community of those with similar interests. Professional societies provide this trusted environment for member networking opportunities to compare experiences, discuss best practices, brainstorm ideas, explore innovative ideas, and develop collaborations—all of which is pushing the profession and industry forward. Many societies support formal special interest groups and access to various social media and virtual platforms for membership to stay connected. Volunteer work group opportunities are another option for members to engage for networking purposes as well as skill development. Members may attend society-sponsored conventions, conferences, regional events, and workshops where collaboration discussions can begin and continue to be nurtured after the event. In addition, networking is an excellent way to sharpen interpersonal and communication skills with a diverse group of colleagues. There is limited evidence that people who actively volunteer tend to make more money due to their efforts with developing their professional network [20]. Above all, the ultimate benefit of networking is development of lifelong professional colleagues and friends that are forged only through active participation in professional societies throughout a career.

Education

Professional societies offer many opportunities that allow members to grow and develop through writing, presentation, and communication skills. Activities which support a volunteer's continuing professional development can be done through participation in educational events at the national, state, or regional level as well as with local affiliated chapters. These events may also provide opportunities for members to participate as speakers, honing their presentation skills. Volunteers may participate in planning groups whose purpose is identifying educational program topics and speakers or by reviewing submitted speaker proposals. A volunteer member may learn new skills and expand their use of communication and interactive tools with society-sponsored education delivered through virtual platforms and social media. In addition, volunteer members may sharpen their writing skills by developing articles or case studies to share with others in exclusive society publications or web-based content, including journals, podcasts, newsletters, DVDs, and online forums. The 2015 HIMSS Individual Membership Satisfaction Survey revealed the top three program and service opportunities that members participated in over the year was accessing information and content from the website, attending in person conferences and events and participation in virtual conferences [19].

Mentoring

Giving back to a profession—or paying it forward—is a key volunteer motivation factor for many experienced professionals. Mentoring programs, both formal and informal, provide an avenue for experienced professionals to share with those who are early in their career or with those who do not have extensive experience in a particular area. Likewise, those seeking mentors benefit from a mentor's experience that can be leveraged both immediately with current job positions and long term with careers. Mentors may share their experiences, assist with problem-solving, make industry introductions, as well as coaching with job interviewing, career planning, and skill development. This benefits not only the emerging professional but the industry at large. Volunteer mentoring is also a great opportunity for retirees to assist others through sharing their vast knowledge and expertise while staying engaged in the industry.

Career Development

Professional societies provide many volunteer opportunities focused on career development like professional certifications, where volunteers may be used in developing certification examinations and training materials as well as serving as training instructors. This helps the volunteer in staying current in their profession and industry while advancing their writing and presentation skills. Volunteers who become certified demonstrate that a standard level of industry proficiency and knowledge beyond academic degrees and work experience enhances career growth opportunities. Many societies offer advanced membership status such as fellowships, fellow member status, or lifetime member status. These status designations are based on active participation of a member's long-term volunteer service within the society and the industry. These are only a few examples of voluntary credentials that assist members in demonstrating their dedication to a profession while benefiting from continuous industry education and career development.

Societies may offer volunteer opportunities for members to participate in formal career planning services such as sharing guidance to members in job search strategies, resume writing, effective interview techniques, or salary negotiations. Volunteers not only hone their career planning efforts in helping the society provide these services, but they can gain new insights and guidance for the future. Volunteers who utilize exclusive job posting services offered through a society can benefit through finding new employment opportunities or determining their next position for career advancement. Likewise, a member seeking new staff may employ the society's job posting services to quickly seek out qualified candidates leading to faster fulfillment of opened positions. This can leave a positive impression on the member with their peers and employer leadership.

Professional development (including certification, career services and advancement) was the number one motivating factor in both joining HIMSS as a new member and renewal an existing HIMSS membership according to the 2015 HIMSS Individual Membership Satisfaction Survey [19].

In addition to the benefits derived from volunteering in professional societies, there are many benefits from volunteering based on personal hobbies, interests, and community services.

Personal Hobbies and Interests

Volunteerism can lead to new interests and may provide an outlet for pursuing hobbies and expanding one's horizons. One may have personal ties or experiences that lead to volunteerism, such as volunteering for a hospice organization after a loved one experienced cancer. Hobbies and interests can be an outlet for maintaining a work-life balance and may improve overall motivation. The sense of fulfillment and satisfaction that come from hobbies or interests may spill into the work life and minimize work-related tension. Pursuing these interests may open doors to learning new skills that can be leveraged professionally and even lead to a new career.

Community Service: Give Back/Pay It Forward!

The community one lives in can easily be taken for granted with daily pressures and balancing work with personal life. Also, communities can suffer from budget cuts and lack of skilled employees just like corporate organizations. Many mission-driven and community nonprofit organizations rely on volunteers to supplement paid staff in order to achieve their goals and mission. Examples range from libraries, museums, religious institutions, healthcare providers, and even government services such as local fire departments, as well as national organizations providing local community services. One's professional experience and skills can be of great need by these organizations and leveraged through volunteerism. Likewise, community service may benefit the volunteer by opening doors for a new job or assist in changing career paths.

Community volunteerism is another way of giving back where one sees the direct impact of their efforts in their community and with the residents. It also provides a great opportunity to stay informed and engaged with the local community. Most importantly, community volunteerism provides the opportunity to build one's network of friends and colleagues.

Health

Over the past two decades, there is a growing body of research that indicates volunteering provides individual health benefits in addition to social ones. The Corporation for National and

Community Service (CNCS) presented the report, entitled, "The Health Benefits of Volunteering," which established a strong correlation between volunteerism and individual health. This research shows that individuals who volunteer benefit from both psychological and physical benefits such as improved sense of belonging, lower blood pressure, greater sense functional ability and lower rates of depression [21]. This is most likely due to the fact that volunteering may take the focus off one's problems and creates a greater appreciation for work, family, and personal life. Volunteering may give one a greater perspective, increase positive self-awareness and enhance overall life fulfillment. Early involvement with volunteering tends to create a more meaningful and purposeful volunteer in later years that continues after career retirement [22].

Conclusion

Volunteerism supports communities as well as promoting the advancement of professions and industries while providing significant contribution toward the well-being of the volunteer and the general public.

Volunteerism can reflect the picture of the whole person—ranging from personal interests, community engagement to professional and industry achievements. Volunteerism demonstrates dedication and commitment as well as serving as an inspiration to others to get involved.

Why Volunteer? Regardless of the motivation, everyone can volunteer to "pay it forward" (or pay back) in some capacity to individuals, communities, professions, industries, and our society at large. Most important of all, the volunteer will equally be rewarded!

References

1. Boston College, Center for Corporate Citizenship, Carroll School of Management. Corporate Volunteerism. http://ccc.bc.edu/corporate-volunteerism.html.
2. The American President Project, 1974 Presidential Proclamation 4288 National Volunteer Week, 1974, http://www.presidency.ucsb.edu/ws/index.php?pid=77158&st=volunteer&st1=week.
3. The President's Volunteer Service Award, https://www.presidentialserviceawards.gov/.
4. U.S. Bureau of Labor Statistics. 2015 Volunteering in the United States. http://www.bls.gov/news.release/volun.nr0.htm.
5. Volunteering in America. Volunteering and Civic Life in America 2015: National, State, and City Information. https://www.volunteeringinamerica.gov/.
6. Merriam-Webster online dictionary. Volunteer. http://www.merriam-webster.com/dictionary/volunteer.
7. Benefits of Volunteering. Corporation of National and Community Service. http://www.nationalservice.gov/serve-your-community/benefits-volunteering.
8. Online Etymology online dictionary. Volunteer. http://www.etymonline.com/index.php?term=volunteer.
9. Merriam-Webster online dictionary. http://www.merriam-webster.com/dictionary/volunteerism.
10. Starr, P. 1982. *The Social Transformation of American Medicine.* New York: Basic Books, The Perseus Books Group, 145–150.
11. National Library of Medicine. Doctor of Medical Profession. https://www.nlm.nih.gov/medlineplus/ency/article/001936.htm.
12. American Medical Association. AMA History Timeline. http://www.ama-assn.org/ama/pub/about-ama/our-history/ama-history-timeline.page?.

13. Starr, P. 1982. *The Social Transformation of American Medicine*. New York: Basic Books, The Perseus Books Group, 25.
14. Starr, P. 1982. *The Social Transformation of American Medicine*. New York: Basic Books, The Perseus Books Group, 155.
15. American Nurses Association. ANA History. http://www.nursingworld.org/history.
16. American Red Cross. History. http://www.redcross.org/about-us/who-we-are/history.
17. Analytic Quality online Glossary. Professional Body. http://www.qualityresearchinternational.com/glossary/professionalbody.htm.
18. Reasons People Volunteer. Positive Force. http://www.positiveforce.com/12-reasons-people-volunteer/.
19. Horowitz, J. 2015. HIMSS individual member satisfaction survey. Informally published survey. Chicago, IL: HIMSS Analytics.
20. Benefits of Volunteering. World Volunteer Web. http://www.worldvolunteerweb.org/resources/how-to-guides/volunteer/doc/benefits-of-volunteering.html.
21. The Health Benefits of Volunteering: A Review of Recent Research. The Corporation for National and Community Service. http://www.nationalservice.gov/serve-your-community/benefits-volunteering.
22. Five Reasons Why You Should Volunteer. *Psychology Today*. https://www.psychologytoday.com/blog/the-third-age/201403/5-reasons-why-you-should-volunteer.

Additional Resources

Association for Healthcare Volunteer Resource Professions: www.ahvrp.org.
Association of Leaders in Volunteer Engagement: www.volunteeralive.org.
Corporation for National and Community Service: www.nationalservice.gov.
International Association for Volunteer Effort: https://www.iave.org/about-iave/.
The American President's Project: National Volunteer Week: www.presidency.ucsb.edu/ws/index.php?pid=77158&st=volunteer&st1=week.
The President's Volunteer Service Award: www.presidentialserviceawards.gov.
World Volunteer Web: www.worldvolunteerweb.org.

Chapter 8

Earning a Certificate to Demonstrate Competency

By John Eckmann
MPH, CPHIMS

Contents

Abstract

For health information technology (health IT) professionals who are interested in advancing their knowledge in a specific area, but are not ready to earn a certification, certificate programs can serve as a powerful alternative. The following is an overview of the importance of demonstrating one's competency with a certificate program.

Keywords:

Health IT landscape
Talent Shortage
Competency
Career Mobility
Professional Certificate
Professional Certification

Introduction

Many factors motivate health IT professionals to demonstrate competency by earning a professional certificate, like seeking gainful employment, or enhancing one's skillsets. Health IT professionals generally rely on a combination of experience and education to demonstrate competency. The broader field of *information technology* (IT) finds "practitioners" with mixed experiences and academic credentials. There are numerous examples of individuals demonstrating competency with four-year college degrees; others have careers based on experience alone; or a combination of both. Earning a professional certificate has merit too, and this chapter will explore "why." Very often, individuals explore university-level certificate programs as a powerful alternative to professional certification.

A prerequisite to understanding the compelling dynamics of health IT certificates necessitates defining the term health IT, as well as differentiating between professional *certificate* and professional *certification*. Many definitions of health IT exist. Generally, health IT describes the management and resources needed for exchanging of data among providers, payers, patients, etc. The health IT professional or "practitioner" is primarily concerned about obtaining, storing, and using data for the purposes of healthcare delivery. Subsequently, due to the dynamic nature of healthcare combined with the complexity of IT, health IT certificates often focus not only on the technical aspects of a healthcare setting, like managing computer networks, managing projects, fostering change through change management techniques, disaster recovery, and cybersecurity, but also on clinical topics relevant to informatics. This chapter will broadly consider a few factors that converge on how the health IT professional can embrace health IT certificates as a viable career enhancement.

Terms and Definitions

The definitions of the terms *certificate* and *certification* are unique when applied to demonstrating competency. The online Oxford Dictionaries provides the following definitions (https://en.oxforddictionaries.com):

- Certificate: (noun) An official document attesting a certain fact.
- Certification: (noun) The action or process of providing someone or something with an official document attesting to a status or level of achievement.

Too often, when a potential student is considering whether to earn a certificate or certification to demonstrate their competency, their tendency may be to simplify the choice. "On the surface" of the matter there are similarities between the two. However, because of the distinctive influences a certificate versus a certification might have to a health IT practitioner's competency, there is essential uniqueness. It is important to more fully understand and appreciate the uniqueness of earning a professional certificate; only then can differentiating certificate versus certification be understood. The definitions supplied by the Institute for Credentialing Excellence (ICE) will be used to further clarify *certificate* and *certification*, because the audience of interest is *health* IT. This chapter is exploring why earning a certificate to demonstrate competency is important to health IT practitioners, and ICE's sentinel background is in healthcare credentialing. ("ICE began in 1977, when in cooperation with the federal government, the National Commission for Health Certifying Agencies (NCHCA) was formed to develop standards of excellence for voluntary certification programs in healthcare."[1]) Understanding the differentiating aspects of a certificate will help the health IT professional when considering an assessment-based certificate as an alternative method for demonstrating their competency.

1. A *certification* program is designed to test the knowledge, skills, and abilities required to perform a particular job, and, upon successfully passing a certification exam, to represent a declaration of a particular individual's professional competence. In some professions, certification is a requirement for employment or practice.
2. In contrast to certification and licensure, an *assessment-based certificate* program is an educational or training program that is used to teach learning objectives and assess whether those objectives were achieved by the student.

Factors Influencing Earning a Health IT Certificate

One obvious reason to earn a certificate may be money: finding new employment, staying employed, being promoted, learning a new skill, etc. The health IT professional who enhances their skillsets are more attractive to prospective employers. Employers, when looking for health IT talent, are constrained by budgets, and therefore attempt to "strike gold" with experienced and certificate-proven health IT talent.

Another factor to consider is "time in career." Reasons for earning a certificate are somewhat diverse, perhaps more particularly evident when contrasting entry level individuals with mid-level or senior health IT professionals. Before proceeding, it is worth noting there is limited data available to conclude whether a certificate results in competency. Human Resource (HR) experts have observed a "mixed bag" in their study to "understand the awareness, perceptions, and value of HR and other professional certifications, certificates, and degree programs by organizations of varying sizes within the United States and outside of the United States."[2] The presumed benefit of a certificate is questionably observed elsewhere in healthcare too. It is safe to say, however, that health IT professionals who earn a professional certificate are adding to their "professional toolbox" by demonstrating competency, since a healthcare certificate is prescribed and understood as a "good dose of medicine."

Many colleges and universities offer certificate programs which deliver knowledge and skills anticipated to fill jobs for projected areas of economic growth. Certificate programs are a way of attending to students whether they are traditional full-time or part-time students. Often the certificate programs are available online to capture attention from students with a preference for this method of instruction delivery. The goals of certificate programs are to enhance an understanding of a body of knowledge that can serve students intending entry into the job market or to continue their education. The academic courses assembled for a certificate program, while fewer and focused, have equivalent learning objectives when the same courses are applicable for matriculating college degrees. While the certificate programs are a fraction of the cost of pursuing a college degree, there is always the option of applying the investment into pursuing a college degree.

An example of an area where institutions of higher education have developed certificate programs is information security. Because information security has been identified by the U.S. Department of Labor as one of the fastest growing professions, certificate programs are widely offered. Some of these programs are designed to address their learning objectives in as little as two semesters. The successful conclusion of a certificate program has merit for students wanting to enter a job sector, continue their education, advance their career, change careers, or put more simply: demonstrate their competency.

Admission requirements into certificate programs may have both business-centric and academic entry requirements: cover letter or statement of purpose highlighting goals, resume, letters of recommendation, and official transcripts from an accredited college or university. Almost without exception, certificate programs follow their host institution's academic calendar in as much as relevant start and stop deadlines apply. Because of the higher educational institution's influence on their certificate programs, most often the roster of courses comprising a certificate program are recognizable and transferrable. An example of a 12-credit hour *Graduate Certificate in Information Assurance, Security and Privacy*, offered by the University of North Carolina at Greensboro, is shown below, and illustrates a familiar collegiate classification of a certificate offering (http://bryan.uncg.edu/isscm/graduate/certificates/info-assurance/).

Required Courses (9 credit hours)

- ISM 671 Data Management (3 credit hours)
- ISM 673 Telecommunications and Networks (3 credit hours)
- ISM 676 Information Security and Privacy (3 credit hours)

Elective Courses (3–6 credit hours from the following or other approved courses)

- ISM 675 Business Analytics (3 credit hours)
- ISM 679 Special Topics in Information Systems (3 credit hours)

The health IT industry is fortunate to have numerous online certificate opportunities (see Table 8.1) where the certificate programs are valued both in the health care industry as well as related areas in higher education.

Certificates are often recognized and considered trusted, reliable, and as being consistent with the healthcare industry's standards of practice. The visibility of earning a certificate demonstrates a higher education accomplishment which further supports and contributes to best practice.

However, there is comfort in being "certified" too. It is worth noting that in 2013, the Office of the National Coordinator for Health Information Technology (ONC) unveiled their "mark" for Electronic Health Records (EHR) and other health IT products. ONC's certification mark was to serve as visual proof of an EHR's functionality, interoperability, and security. An ONC news release at that time suggested ONC's branding was a positive for providers: "The use of the ONC Certified HIT mark will help to assure them that the EHR they have purchased will support them in meeting the Meaningful Use requirements."[3] Although ONC's Certified health IT mark is about systems, similarly, comforting, competent assurance is the purpose applied to certificate programs which are celebrated too.

ONC Certified HIT   2014 EDITION

Patient safety has also been offered as a foundational reason health IT professional must demonstrate their competency. Health IT professionals are "electronic field medics" when considering the digital evolution in healthcare has generated a greater reliance on electronics and an expectation for real-time access to digital information. Because of their direct involvement when introducing technical innovation and subsequently supporting technology's evolution into the mainstream patient care settings, there exists legitimate concern as to whether health IT practitioners might

Table 8.1 Sample of Health IT and Related Graduate Certificates

George Mason University	The College of Health and Human Services	Quality Management and Outcomes Management in Health Care Systems, Certificate	In-person	http://chhs.gmu.edu/hap/ health-administration/certificate-quality-improvement-and-outcomes-management-in-health-care-systems.cfm
Johns Hopkins University	Carey Business School	The Business of Healthcare Graduate Certificate	Online	http://carey.jhu.edu/academics/ certificate-programs/ business-of-health-care/
University of Colorado Anschutz Medical Campus	College of Nursing	Nursing Leadership and Health Care Systems Certificate	In-person	http://www.ucdenver.edu/ academics/colleges/nursing/ programs-admissions/CE-PD/ Pages/ LeadershipSystemsCertificate. aspx
University of Massachusetts Boston	College of Advancing and Professional Studies	Healthcare Informatics Certificate	Online	https://www.umb.edu/academics/ caps/certificates/ healthcare_informatics
University of North Carolina Charlotte	The Graduate School	Certificate in Health Informatics	Online	http://hi.uncc.edu/ graduate-certificate
University of South Florida	Morsani College of Medicine	Graduate Certificate in Health Informatics	Online	http://www.usfhealthonline.com/ programs/certificate/ graduate-certificate/
University of Pittsburgh	School of Public Health	Health Care Systems Engineering	In-person	http://www.publichealth.pitt.edu/ health-policy-and-management/ academics/certificates

affect patient safety.[4] The Institute of Medicine observed: "It is widely believed that, when designed and used appropriately, health IT can help create an ecosystem of safer care ..."[4]

Other factors influencing the decision of health IT professionals to earn a certificate to demonstrate competency are to remain relevant by refreshing their understanding of a body of knowledge. This motivator is more common among mid-level and seasoned professionals. Similarly, because certificate programs are often offered by reputable academic centers, prestige can influence health IT professionals with extensive experience.

As key stakeholders, organizations rely upon health IT professionals for their innovation to not only construct the digital solutions necessary but also to supply the subsequent maintenance to sustain the technologies when they are implemented and operational to healthcare. According to a study earlier this year by International Data Corporation, thriving organizations will have the "ability to adjust to the speed and needs demanded by digitally empowered business transformation."[5] (*Thriving* is categorically familiar to healthcare; as a patient who is at risk as a *failure to thrive*.) In the IDC study, the IT organizations characterized as "thrivers" (% of respondents)[5]:

- Are highly responsive and collaborate in real time across the enterprise (53%)
- Have an IT culture that excels at experimentation in every part of the business (58%)
- Have a hyper focus on user experience as a differentiator from competitors (51%)

On October 9, 2016, *60 minutes*, the CBS news show, televised a segment stating "It might not be long before machines begin thinking for themselves—creatively, independently and with judgment sometimes better than ours." Perhaps for good reason—Will Rogers said, "Good judgment comes from experience, and a lot of that comes from bad judgment."

During this one-hour television show there was compelling information about artificial intelligence supplying benefit to healthcare. For years, health IT professionals have relied on academic programs and/or technical certificate programs to demonstrate their competency as technical experts—participating and contributing to the highly technical and digitized transformation the world of healthcare has experienced by supplying their expert judgment. Health IT professionals rely on learning to stay informed, and earning a technical certificate demonstrates both a commitment and understanding of the challenge.

Timing Is Important Too!

When should health IT professionals actively seek to earn a certificate? The short answer is constantly. As was previously discussed, some professionals are attempting to enter the field and find employment in health IT, and others are trying to advance their health IT careers. As a career, health IT is sufficiently complex and dynamic: earning a certificate is a reliable way to demonstrate understanding of a body of knowledge that is continually evolving.

Individuals who are seeking to enter the health IT profession often explore earning certificates to enhance their marketability and expedite their entry into the field of work. For individuals already employed as health IT professionals, their interest in earning a certificate may be to demonstrate their competency in a specialized technical area to enhance or broaden their skillset. Because the evolution of technology is fast-paced and ever changing, many times, health IT professionals will seek technical certificates to reinforce and refine their skills. By doing so, they position themselves as someone with a better understanding of contemporary and/or "cutting-edge" technologies. Health IT professionals recognize their investment in a certificate program has benefit to their career both in the short term and long term.

Equally interesting are government programs that influence the popularity of seeking a professional certificate by creating jobs. For several years, the U. S. Bureau of Labor Statistics has characterized the health IT "landscape" as needing additional skilled professionals capable of supplying technical skills. The Health Information Technology for Economic and Clinical Health (HITECH) Act, enacted as part of the American Recovery and Reinvestment Act of 2009, was signed into law on February 17, 2009 to promote the adoption and meaningful use of health IT. At that time, CMS established requirements for eligible professionals and eligible hospitals for the electronic capture of clinical data, including providing patients with electronic copies of health information in return for incentive payments. Due to the health IT talent shortage generated by the stimulus program, in 2010, there were government awards approximating $84 million to universities and community colleges to help support the training and development of more than 50,000 new healthcare IT professionals.[6] In the article, Gwen Darling, CEO, Health IT Central, went on to say: "Those of us who are involved with workforce development were pretty excited about this allocation of resources, as were the thousands of students who enrolled in the programs who believed a lucrative career in HIT would be waiting for them upon graduation."

Summary

Health IT professionals often demonstrate their professional competency by earning a certificate. The health IT certificate programs, widely available at universities and community colleges, teach to learning objectives and assess whether those objectives were achieved by the student. This type of learning is an attractive alternate to technical professional certification for several reasons: (1) The economy of supply and demand for trained health IT professionals is clearly a factor contributing to the viability of certificate programs; (2) The value perceived by prospective students and employers is a known motivator for training pursuits; and (3) The element of time is a consistent factor which attributes to motivating entry into certificate programs. Not surprising, patient safety is offered as a reason for demonstrating competency—do no harm.

One of the appealing reasons for demonstrating competency by earning a certificate via an assessment-based certificate program is its "shelf life." A common criticism of technical certifications is they usually have an "expiration date" and will expire if the individual does not maintain the certification. Maintenance of Certification (MOC) is an important consideration for health IT professionals when choosing between technical professional certification versus an academic professional certificate program. MOC must be factored into the overall cost and time commitment when making choices about demonstrating competency.

Observations and Conclusions

Although it is not an exhaustive list, the several reasons why health IT professionals earn certificates to demonstrate their competency include: patient safety, prestige, improve earnings, and career longevity. A more difficult conclusion, without further analysis, is discerning which of these is a primary motivator and which is secondary, etc. Money is an apparent primary motivator because, in theory, earning a health IT certificate to demonstrate competency has both macro and micro economic benefit. It is widely accepted that being more competent is a valued attribute to both employees and employers who are optimistic about career longevity. Certificates are observed to have positive effects on job entry and career mobility (changing jobs or promotion), too.

Health IT professionals may find themselves in careers with expectations to be generalists or highly specialized. Specialization, or the competency of understanding a body of knowledge about a specialized area, is the objective of certificate programs.

In the science fiction novel, *Time Enough for Love*, the character Lazarus Long supplied a list of competency for humans, suggesting specialization is for insects.[7] While the list does not include the competency of health IT practitioners, perhaps it did not consider a possibility where two worlds collide.

References

1. Institute for Credentialing Excellence Website, About Us. http://www.credentialingexcellence.org/p/cm/ld/fid=32.
2. Study Reveals Value Employers and HR Place on Professional Certification. http://www.employmentlawdaily.com/index.php/news/study-reveals-value-employers-and-hr-place-on-professional-certification/. Source: The survey was conducted by the HR Certification Institute (www.hrci.org) and B2B International (www.b2binternational.com) and was released on June 27, 2010 at the 2010 Society for Human Resources Management Annual Conference & Exposition, held June 27–30 in San Diego, CA; www.shrm.org.
3. ONC unveils new certification mark, Offers meaningful assurance for providers. By Mike Miliard, July 11, 2013.
4. Institute of Medicine (IOM), *Health IT and Patient Safety: Building Safer Systems for Better Care*, Washington, DC: National Academy Press, 2012.
5. IDC Helps CIOs Adjust to Business Demands of Digital Transformation with Leading in 3D, A New Leadership Framework. Press Release, March 22, 2016.
6. Healthcare IT Certifications. By Andrea Clement Santiago, August 09, 2016.
7. Heinlein, R. A., *Time Enough for Love*. New York: Ace Books (paperback edition, 1988), page 248.

Chapter 9

Differentiating Yourself with a Professional Certification

By Dr. Kay S. Lytle

DNP, RN-BC, NEacA-BC, CPHIMS, FHIMSS

Contents

Abstract

It's no secret that credentials enhance one's professional competency. This chapter helps you assess whether a professional certification will enhance your career.

Keywords:

Career advancement
Career ladder
Professional growth
professional certification

Introduction

Professional certification indicates an individual has voluntarily met a level of requirements or standards within a defined area (National Library of Medicine, 2016). Certification is specific to a defined role, area of practice, or body of knowledge. This chapter covers the benefits of certification, selecting a certification, preparing for certification, applying for certification, displaying your credential, and maintaining your certification.

Benefits of Certification

Individuals pursue professional certification for a variety of reasons. Sometimes professional certifications are an entry level requirement for a job or a preferred qualification. Professional certification may be an organizational requirement for career advancement along a career ladder. Getting a certification can boost your career options and can result in salary increases. Some organizations provide certification bonus payment to staff on achievement of the certification. Other individuals set certification as a professional goal and plan to meet for their own personal sense of accomplishment. Achieving certification can provide a professional challenge, offer professional growth, determine competence, validate knowledge, provide a source of professionalism, increase satisfaction, provide recognition, and increase one's professional credibility (Kaplow, 2011; McLaughlin and Fetzer, 2015.)

Employers vary in their support for professional certification. Some may offer financial support for review classes, provide free access to online modules for review, provide time for certification preparation, and/or pay the certification examination fees. Other organizations may defer reimbursement based on successful completion of the examination, provide a salary increase, or compensate with a separate bonus payment. Unfortunately some organizations provide no financial support directly for certification-related activities. Your supervisor or human resources representative can answer questions as you investigate. For many individuals the personal and professional gains of certification outweigh the costs.

Selecting a Certification

There are a wide variety of professional certifications available for the health IT professional. Determine your personal goals and review the options available to you. The choice may vary based on your current and intended career path. Most certification materials are available online. Start with a thorough review of the certification qualifications. Qualifications will vary by the specific certification and can include things such as education level, years of experience, and a specific type of experience (health IT, project management, leadership, etc.). Review the certification handbook that will provide details to you about the qualifications, cost, credential earned, and renewal process. While it may seem early to review the renewal process, it is important to be informed about the ongoing requirements so you can determine if you will be able to meet them (more on renewal later). Some certifying bodies offer an entry level certification and a more advanced certification; usually distinguishing with required education and/or experience. You may select a preferred professional certification that requires you to complete further education, get more years of experience, or have more targeted experience. Depending on the time involved, you can begin your certification review in parallel with meeting these basic requirements.

A variety of certifications exist based on your current or future desired health IT focus. Consider speaking with peers outside your organization by engaging with those in a professional organization (see Section II Establishing and Nurturing Your Career, Chapter 6: The Role of the Professional Association). A brief overview of a subset of the certifications is provided here including those offered by Healthcare Information and Management Systems Society (HIMSS), Project Management Institute (PMI), American Health Information Management Association (AHIMA), College of Healthcare Information Management Executives (CHIME), as well as those geared toward healthcare clinicians.

HIMSS offers two professional certifications, the Certified Associate in Healthcare Information and Management Systems (CAHIMS) and the Certified Professional in Healthcare Information and Management Systems (CPHIMS) (HIMSS, 2016a). The CAHIMS is the entry level certification, requiring a high school diploma or equivalent, and has no practice requirement. The CPHIMS is for experienced professionals and includes education and experience requirements. CPHMIS professionals include roles such as CIOs, VPs or directors of IT/IS, consultants, managers, system analysts, and project managers; and represent a variety of work sites such as hospitals, health systems, consulting firms, vendors, and governments (HIMSS, 2016b).

PMI offers a variety of certifications; the most well known is the Project Management Profession (PMP) for the experienced project manager (PMI, 2016a). PMI also offers the Certified Associate in Project Management (CAPM) for the entry level professional, in addition to other specialty-focused certifications (PMI, 2016a). AHIMA offers a variety of certifications through the Commission on Certification for Health Informatics and Information Management (CCHIIM), including a Certified Healthcare Technology Specialist (CHTS) as well as certifications for coding, health information management, and privacy and security AHIMA (2016b). CHIME offers a Certified Healthcare CIO (CHCIO) program for chief information officers and IT executives (CHIME, 2016).

The American Nurses Credentialing Center (ANCC) offers an Informatics Nursing certification using the RN-BC credential that requires a registered nurse hold a bachelor's degree and meet one of several practice requirements (ANCC, 2016b). ANCC reported 1,827 certified informatics nurses as of the end of 2015 (ANCC, 2016a). The certification is based on the scope and standards of practice for nursing informatics (American Nurses Association, 2015). Board-certified physicians may certify in the subspecialty of Clinical Informatics and take the examination through either the American Board of Preventive Medicine (ABPM) or the American Board of Pathology (ABP) based on their core certification (Detmer and Shortliffe, 2014). The Clinical Informatics subspecialty was first offered in 2013. The American Medical Informatics Association (AMIA) is establishing an Advanced Health Informatics Certification (AHIC) based on the same core content as clinical informatics with a phased approach to eligibility requirements for non-physicians (Gadd et al., 2016a,b; Gardner et al., 2009).

There are many other certification options available based on your career focus such as advanced information technology or computer certifications, training, business analyst, and others. See Table 9.1 for a partial listing of available certifications that may be pertinent to health IT professionals. You may easily identify a preferred certification to meet your goals. Others may need to select among several and weigh the career advancement and other benefits against the cost and renewal requirements. You can always talk with peers, seek out those already in the roles you desire, or work with a mentor (see Section III, Learning from Others; Chapter 11, The Mentoring Process). Select a certification that aligns with your personal and career goals.

Table 9.1   List of Certifications, Credentials, and Websites

Certification	Credential	Website
Advanced Health Informatics Certification (in development)	AHIC	https://www.amia.org/advanced-health-informatics-certification
Certification of Competency in Business Analysis	CCBA®	http://www.iiba.org/Certification-Recognition/CCBA-Certification.aspx
Certified Associate in Healthcare Information and Management Systems	CAHIMS	http://www.himss.org/health-it-certification/cahims
Certified Associate in Project Management	CAPM®	http://www.pmi.org/certification/certified-associate-project-management-capm.aspx
Certified Business Analysis Professional	CBAP®	http://www.iiba.org/Certification-Recognition/CBAP-Designation.aspx
Certified Coding Associate	CCA®	http://www.ahima.org/certification/CCA
Certified Coding Specialist	CCS®	http://www.ahima.org/certification/CCS
Certified Coding Specialist—Physician-based	CCS-P®	http://www.ahima.org/certification/ccsp
Certified Documentation Improvement Practitioner	CDIP®	http://www.ahima.org/certification/cdip
Certified Healthcare Chief Information Officer	CHCIO	https://chimecentral.org/chcio/
Certified Health Data Analyst	CHDA®	http://www.ahima.org/certification/chda
Certified Health Informatics Systems Professional	CHISP®	http://www.ashim.com/health-it-certification/
Certified Healthcare Privacy and Security	CHPS®	http://www.ahima.org/certification/chps
Certified Healthcare Technology Specialist	CHTS	http://www.ahima.org/certification/chts
Certified Professional in Electronic Health Records	CPEHR	http://www.healthitcertification.com/overview.html
Certified Professional in Health Information Exchange	CPHIE	http://www.healthitcertification.com/overview.html
Certified Professional in Health Information Technology	CPHIT	http://www.healthitcertification.com/overview.html
Certified Professional in Healthcare Information and Management Systems	CPHIMS	http://www.himss.org/health-it-certification/cphims

(Continued)

Table 9.1 (Continued) List of Certifications, Credentials, and Websites

Certification	Credential	Website
Certified Professional in Learning & Performance	CPLP®	https://www.td.org/Certification
Certified Professional in Operating Rules Administration	CPORA	http://www.healthitcertification.com/overview.html
Certified Technical Trainer	CTT+	https://certification.comptia.org/certifications/ctt
Clinical Informatics Subspecialty	BC	https://www.amia.org/clinical-informatics-board-review-course/board-exam
HealthCare Information Security and Privacy Practitioner	HCISPP®	https://www.isc2.org/hcispp/default.aspx
Healthcare IT Technician (Retired February 28, 2017)	–	https://certification.comptia.org/certifications/healthcare-it-technician
Informatics Nursing	RN-BC	http://nursecredentialing.org/InformaticsNursing
PMI Agile Certified Practitioner	PMI-ACP®	http://www.pmi.org/certification/agile-management-acp.aspx
PMI Professional in Business Analysis	PMI-PBA®	http://www.pmi.org/certification/business-analysis-pba.aspx
PMI Risk Management Professional	PMI-RMP®	http://www.pmi.org/certification/risk-management-professional-rmp.aspx
PMI Scheduling Professional	PMI-SP®	http://www.pmi.org/certification/scheduling-professional-sp.aspx
Portfolio Management Professional	PfMP®	http://www.pmi.org/certification/portfolio-management-professional-pfmp.aspx
Program Management Professional	PgMP®	http://www.pmi.org/certification/program-management-professional-pgmp.aspx
Project Management Professional	PMP®	http://www.pmi.org/certification/project-management-professional-pmp.aspx
Registered Health Information Administrator	RHIA®	http://www.ahima.org/certification/RHIA
Registered Health Information Technician	RHIT®	http://www.ahima.org/certification/RHIT

Preparing for Certification

Once you have selected a certification that meets your professional needs, it is time to start preparing. Start by reviewing the test content outline provided by the certifying body. This will include the subjects and topics on the examination, and may indicate the percentage of each on the examination. Most certifying bodies complete a role delineation study to determine the knowledge, skills, and activities that inform the test content outline (ANCC, 2013; HIMSS, 2015; PMI, 2016b). Take the practice or sample test provided; most certifying bodies offer a short set of questions for free. Some certifying bodies may also offer a more detailed practice exam for purchase. Identify your areas of strength and weakness. Identify gaps in your personal knowledge. Develop a plan to remediate the gaps.

A certification study plan may include a variety of activities such as self-study, online review courses, or instructor-led review courses. Review the list of references; these are used to develop the exam questions. Select one or two items that based on the table of contents provide the best coverage in your identified areas of weakness. Identify materials available in your personal library or available to you on loan from your local library, organizational library, or your manager (as an alternative to purchase). You may want to pursue more formal review options such as certification prep courses, many offered in person and online. Study options are often an extension of your personal learning preferences. Some individuals prefer self-study and others prefer study buddies or a study group. Plan time on your calendar and allow yourself a reasonable amount of time based on your areas of weakness, it may be six months or more. Set a goal for yourself and plan to meet it.

Once you have completed your initial review and preparation, plan to retake the provided sample exam questions. Most examinations have a standard format for their questions, including a stem sentence and multiple choice answers with one right answer, one close but incorrect answer, and two distractors. Typically certification exams will not use multiple-multiple choice answers or include stem sentences that state *all*, *not* or *except*. Read each question slowly so you are clear on what the question is asking. If you have improved and feel satisfied with your performance and preparation, then it is time to apply for certification.

Applying for Certification

The certification handbook will provide you with details needed to submit your application and contain additional information about the certification examination process. Timing will be important in relation to completion of your personal preparation, as most require scheduling of the examination within a defined time period, such as 90 days. Many certification exams are offered locally or within a short drive at regional testing centers that administer many different exams. If the location is not familiar you may want to get directions and consider a dry run, especially if this will help you feel prepared and reduce your anxiety. The certification handbook should have included the number of test questions and overall time allotted to take the examination. Consider the location logistics and your personal preferences for best performance as you schedule an examination date and time in the morning or afternoon.

Prepare yourself to be on your best performance by getting a good night's sleep, eating a healthy meal, dressing comfortably, and taking a few deep breaths. Allow for extra time and plan to arrive early; most examination centers do not allow for late starts. Be clear on the entrance requirements such as your candidate number and driver's license or other required identification documentation. Some testing sites provide onsite lockers and you may not enter the testing area with cell phones, keys, sweaters, or other personal items. Some certification bodies allow testing centers to provide your results at the end of the testing session, and others send notification via mail.

In the event you do not pass, give yourself some time before reconsidering. Based on your results, you may want to plan for additional study and review time and then retake the examination. Many examination scores will be broken down by areas of focus, so it may be clear that you need additional study in one or two areas. Some certification bodies provide for a shortened application process if you retake the exam within a defined time period such as 90 days. Other certification bodies limit the time period before you can retake the exam, such as 60 days, and limit the total number allowed with a year. The reexamination information is located in the candidate handbook.

Displaying Your Credential

Celebrate your success! Once you earn your credential you can display it with pride such as including it on your email signature line, business card, and on business letters or other formal communications. Each certifying body will identify the appropriate credential to use based on the certification achieved. The standard format for the order of credentials is your highest degree (if desired) followed by the certification credential. Some examples are:

- John Brown, CPHIMS
- Mary Jones, BA, CPHIMS
- Bill Smith, MS, CPHIMS

You may want to announce your certification accomplishment. The certifying body may provide you with a letter or announcement format that can be used with your employer, the local newspaper, or your professional organization. If your organization offers reimbursement, bonus payment, or career advancement, there may be additional documentation and paper work required. Take pride in your accomplishment!

Maintaining Your Certification

Maintaining your certification becomes the next step in the process. It is important to review the renewal requirements early. Certifications are normally renewed on a three- or five-year cycle, depending on the certifying body. Most renewals will have similar requirements as in the initial certification around ongoing experience or practice requirement, commonly in the specific area of the certification. There are frequently requirements for continuing education with a minimum number of hours to complete and many provide alternative options for some of the hours such as professional presentations, publications, academic credit, student mentoring, and the like. Be clear on the exact requirements; presentations may require a certain number of presentations, exclude those provided as part of your work, and may not allow for a repeat of the same content. Some options may include activities offering further professional development through services such as item writing for the examination. For continuing education, investigate any requirements for topics related to the test content outline or a percentage of the hours being by certain approved providers. Identify what materials you will need to submit at the time of renewal to validate that you attended, the material presented, and the continuing education provider. A continuing education certificate may be sufficient, but sometimes additional material such as the education outline from the session may also be necessary. Several months before the expiration of your certification, the certifying body will notify you via mail and/or email. At this time you can verify you have met the renewal requirements and prepare to submit the renewal application. Some provide online sites to track your continuing education in an ongoing basis, so it is easier to provide information about meeting the renewal requirements. For additional information on continuing education, see Section V, The Importance of Lifelong Learning; Chapter 24, The Many Facets of Continuing Education.

Check with your employer to see if recertification fees will be paid or reimbursed. Some organizations offer a recertification bonus payment, often lower than the initial certification bonus, to help defray the costs. Review the certification renewal requirements early so you can be prepared with all necessary requirements.

Conclusion

Certification provides validation that an individual meets a set of standards and provides one with a sense of professional accomplishment. Certification can help advance your career. Chose a certification that aligns with your personal and professional goals. Review the certification materials to verify that you meet the necessary qualifications. Review the test content outline to determine your strengths and weaknesses and develop an action plan for your gaps. Develop a plan to meet the gaps. Complete the application for certification, schedule your examination, and prepare for the exam day. Celebrate your certification success and proudly display your earned credential. Turn your eye to maintaining your certificate and review the ongoing requirements. Certification can foster your career success.

References

American Health Information Management Association (2016a). *CCHIIM*. http://www.ahima.org/certification/cchiim.

American Health Information Management Association (2016b). *Types of certification*. http://www.ahima.org/certification/exams?tabid=specialty.

American Nurses Association (2015). *Nursing informatics: Scope and standards of practice* (2nd ed.). Silver Spring, MD: Nursesbooks.org.

American Nurses Credentialing Center [ANCC] (2013). *2013 nursing informatics role delineation study: National survey results*. http://nursecredentialing.org/Certification/NurseSpecialties/Informatics/RELATED-LINKS/Informatics-2013RDS.pdf.

American Nurses Credentialing Center [ANCC] (2016a). *2015 ANCC certification data*. http://www.nursecredentialing.org/Certification/FacultyEducators/FacultyCategory/Statistics/2015-CertificationStatistics.pdf.

American Nurses Credentialing Center [ANCC] (2016b). *Informatics nursing*. http://nursecredentialing.org/InformaticsNursing.

College of Healthcare Information Management Executives [CHIME] (2016). CHCIO certification & CEUs. https://chimecentral.org/chcio/.

Detmer, D. E. and Shortliffe, E. H. (2014). Clinical informatics: Prospects for a new medical subspecialty. *JAMA*, 311, no. 20: 2067–2068.

Gadd, C. S., Williamson, J. J., Steen, E. B., Andriole, K. P., Delaney, C., Gumpper, K., LaVenture, M., Rosendale, D., Sittig, D. F., Thyvalikakath, T., Turner, P. and Fridsma, D. B. (2016b). Eligibility requirements for advanced health informatics certification. *J Am Med Inform Assoc*, 23, 851–854.

Gadd, C. S., Williamson, J. J., Steen, E. B., and Fridsma, D. B. (2016a). Creating advanced health informatics certification. *J Am Med Inform Assoc*, 23: 848–850.

Gardner, R. M., Overhage, J. M., Steen, E. B., Munger, B. S., Holmes, J. H., Williamson, J. J. and Detmer, D. E. (2009) Core content for the subspecialty of clinical informatics. *J Am Med Inform Assoc, 16*: 153–157.

HIMSS (2015). *HIMSS CPHIMS Certified professional in healthcare information & management systems: Candidate handbook and application.* http://www.himss.org/health-it-certification/cphims/handbook.

HIMSS (2016a). *Health IT certifications.* http://www.himss.org/health-it-certification.

HIMSS (2016b). *Who is CPHIMS certified?* http://www.himss.org/health-it-certification/cphims/who-cphims-certified.

Kaplow, R. (2011). The value of certification. *AACN Advance Critical Care*, 22, no. 1: 25–32.

McLaughlin, A. and Fetzer, S. J. (2015). The perceived value of certification by Magnet® and non-Magnet nurses. *JONA*, 45, no. 4: 194–199.

National Library of Medicine (2016). *Medical subject headings.* https://meshb-prev.nlm.nih.gov/#/record/ui?ui=D002568.

Project Management Institute [PMI] (2016a). *Certifications.* http://www.pmi.org/certification.aspx.

Project Management Institute [PMI] (2016b). *Project management professional (PMP) handbook.* http://www.pmi.org/-/media/pmi/documents/public/pdf/certifications/project-management-professional-handbook.pdf.

Chapter 10

Seeking an Advanced Professional Designation

By Selena Davis

PhD(c), PMP, CPHIMS-CA

Contents

Abstract

While certificate programs and professional certifications can contribute to continuing competence, advanced professional designations represent another dimension of demonstrating professional competency.

Keywords:

Qualifications
Lifelong Learning
Professional Designation
Competence
Competency
Achievement
Continuing Professional Development

Introduction

An increasing number of people are looking to establish, advance, or nurture their career and as such many more people today are earning professional designations than ever before. Simply put, for employers, a professional designation brings comfort and for employment seekers it brings confidence. Such qualifications identify an individual as: (1) having reached the highest standard of professional knowledge and skills; (2) actively participating in a professional practice which is guided and informed by ethical standards, and the norms and global language of the related domain; (3) belonging to a community of highly educated and skilled professionals, organizations, and experts worldwide; and (4) committing to continuing professional development.

The idea of cultivating one's career and voluntarily seeking further qualification often arises from a desire for personal recognition, increased income, inherent drive for lifelong learning, and/or to perform a job to the best of one's ability. The process of seeking an advanced professional designation in and of itself offers numerous informal possibilities to nurture one's career and expand one's network by way of exploring and investigating continuing learning opportunities, both virtually and face-to-face with experts in the profession. More formally, seeking an advanced qualification is most associated with certificate programs, professional certifications and professional designations.

The literature and the industry tend to describe certificate programs easily but blur the terms professional certification and professional designation, perhaps because by definition a certificate program may be simpler to characterize than the other two. A certificate program is distinguished as a set of course work or curriculum completed within a set period of time for a specific field of study that results in a certificate of completion. Such programs are often prerequisite education requirements for licensure or for a specific industry's professional certification or designation.

The terms "certification" and "designation" are usually used interchangeably and while there are many similarities among the terms such as formal training, specific body of knowledge, examinations, membership and fees, and code of ethics and professional conduct, it may be reasoned that the difference is that an advanced professional designation associates with a professional governing body, which establishes a nationally or internationally accepted level of knowledge and skill that must be regularly demonstrated through maintenance requirements to represent ongoing competency. In this way, the maintenance requirements of a professional designation support a reduction in the risk of professional obsolescence—i.e. the discrepancy between a professional's level of proficiency and the current state-of-the-art standards in the field required for successful performance (Setor et al., 2015). A professional certification (e.g., PMP, CPHIMS) is typically defined as a formal recognition of professional or technical *competence* (Lysaght and Altschuld, 2000). It validates that an individual has attained the knowledge and skills necessary for competent practice in a particular profession. A professional designation (e.g., CRNBC, FRCPC) conveys a *continuing competency* as measured by the issuing national or international professional governing body and as managed by the individual on a regular basis.

Professional Competence

The term competence has been described in the literature in numerous ways with no generally accepted definition. Further, and in many cases, the terms competence and competency are not necessarily synonymous. That is, competence has been referred to as a potential ability and/or a capability to function in a given situation, whereas competency focuses on one's actual performance in a situation. According to Schroeter (2008), this means that competence is required

Table 10.1   List of Components in Competence Conceptual Framework

Competence Dimension	What Is It?	How Is It Achieved?
Know	Theoretical knowledge, judgment, and reasoning	Formal and on-the-job training and continuing professional development
Can	Ability to perform a task in a structured setting under observation	Application of theoretical knowledge to a task
Do	Ability to perform a task in daily practice unobserved	Practical experience
Share	Ability to communicate knowledge and build competence in others	Distribution of knowledge, mentoring others, and peer review contributions

before one can expect to achieve competency. Other authors have described competence as involving the implementation of combined knowledge, know-how, and behavior (Bennour and Crestani, 2007) or as a cross-functional integration and coordination of one's ability to exploit its resources or building blocks of competence (Torkkeli and Tuominen, 2002). Still other authors have described competence as the habitual and judicious use of communication, knowledge, technical skills, clinical reasoning, emotions, values, and reflection in daily practice for the benefit of the individual and community (Epstein and Hundert, 2002).

The nature of professional competence is multi-dimensional. To simplify, a list of the key components of competence are synthesized into a conceptual framework (Table 10.1) and described based on the work of several authors (Capece and Bazzica, 2013; Lysaght and Altschuld, 2000; Epstein and Hundert, 2002).

Characteristics of Competency

Competency too has been defined in a few different ways. For example, competency has been described as a set of characteristics (knowledge, skills, and abilities), which are relatively stable across different situations (Ley and Albert, 2003) or as the degree to which individuals can apply the skills and knowledge associated with the profession to the full range of situations that fall within the domain of that particular profession (Lysaght and Altschuld, 2000). Irrespective of the differences in definition, and fundamental to the understanding of the close relationship between ability and the "work" of the profession, the key characteristics of competency have been summarized in the literature as an individual's ability to

- ■ Combine various resources where their value arises from more than the simple possession of these resources.
- ■ Support the way the activity is performed by way of a cognitive structure that organizes the way the activity is performed and is relatively stable across a full range of situations.
- ■ Construct an action such that each time it is called upon, it may be improved, enriched, and developed in order to be adapted to the changing features of the situation (Capece and Bazzica, 2013).

The literature holds that one's competence can become a competency once it has been built over time and not easily exceeded. That is, one's capability to integrate knowledge, skills, and experience in a given situation may become, over time, a proficient application of such characteristics in the full range of situations that fall within a given profession. Ultimately, the collection of one's competencies that are widespread become one's core competency (Torkkeli and Tuominen, 2002). For example, as a health information technology (IT) professional certified in healthcare information and management systems (CPHIMS), numerous competencies are required to collectively hold a core competency in the profession. For example, some key competencies include information management and IT, project management, system analysis, system evaluation, clinical health services, and leadership and organizational management.

Giving shape to the work of various authors (Capece and Bazzica, 2013; Lysaght and Altschuld, 2000), a professional competency model (Figure 10.1) illustrates how the continuous collection of theoretical knowledge ("Know"), application of skill in a structure setting ("Can"), performance in daily practice over a wide range of situations ("Do"), and sharing the information, skill and wisdom with others ("Share") leads to competency. With the continued development and application of knowledge and skills, a reduction in the risk of professional obsolescence is supported.

It may be argued that the highest level of competence relates to the "Do" and "Share" dimensions as they are dependent upon the proficiency at the "Know" and "Can" levels. In this way, knowledge and skills performed in a structured setting are a necessity, but insufficient condition of competency (Lysaght and Altschuld, 2000). Subsequently, it may be rationalized that the professional designation may be distinguished and valued from the professional certification through well-structured, up-to-date maintenance requirements established by a related national or international professional governing body, which includes the demonstration of the "Do" and "Share" dimensions of professional competence and results in a reduction of the probability of a discrepancy between a professional's level of proficiency and the current standards in the field required for successful performance.

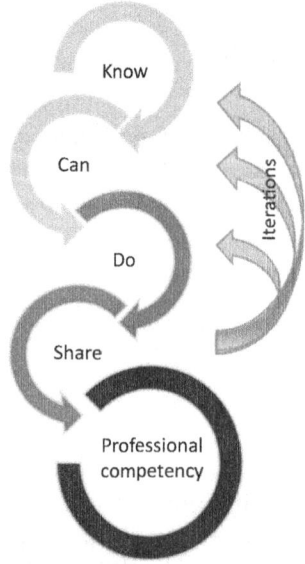

Figure 10.1 Professional competency model.

Benefits and Barriers

Many professional designations are used as "post-nominal letters", meaning that they are included after the person's name (e.g., Janet Smith, ABC). Top-level professionals across a broad spectrum of sectors have unequivocally agreed that a few letters after a name can make a difference in one's career (Schonfeld, 2010; Human Resources Professionals Association, 2012). Simply stated, possessing a professional designation proves beneficial both personally and professionally, as well as to the public (Foubister, 2003; Williams and Counts, 2013).

Benefits

For the individual, a professional designation provides personal recognition, opportunities to increase one's professional network, access to emerging tools and continuing professional development courses both in-person and online, increases job satisfaction, and often comes with an increase in income and career advancement (Kaplow, 2011). In practice, retaining a professional designation leads to empowerment by way of an increased confidence for the effective execution of domain knowledge and skills, as well as enhancing collaboration (Wade, 2009; Fritter and Shimp, 2011). It also is associated with positive in-practice peer assessments (Wenghofer et al., 2014).

For the organization that employs experts with a professional designation, it leads to higher retention rates, a sense of pride and achievement, and a higher level of professional service (Fritter and Shimp, 2011; Kaplow, 2011). It also has benefits to other stakeholders. While empirical evidence of outcomes is limited for the customer, studies in healthcare of providers who retain their professional designation have identified an increased adherence to evidence-based best practices (Kaplow, 2011). For the profession itself, an increased confidence in the service provided by its professionals is most celebrated.

Intrinsic and Extrinsic Motivating Factors

Different factors motivate different professionals to pursue and maintain advanced qualifications like professional designations or certifications. Two distinct groupings, described as intrinsic and extrinsic factors in the literature, offer insight into the motivators for an individual to personally and professionally grow. The intrinsic factors, or rewards, relate to the internal motivators while the extrinsic rewards are typically motivators supported externally. Table 10.2 lists the main internal and external motivators associated with the value of an advanced qualification (Niebuhr and Biel, 2007).

Challenges and Issues

For many professions, despite the evidence that there are benefits and intrinsic rewards for obtaining and maintaining advanced qualifications, the lack of strength of the extrinsic value makes it challenging and less attractive to seek or keep the professional designation. Considerations to address barriers by organizations, administrators, and employers in general should be made to increase such things as opportunities for recognition and greater compensation (Wade, 2009). In fact, financial concerns over the cost of examination and the costs to maintain the designation are frequently reported in studies as two of the most significant barriers (Williams and Counts, 2013; Fritter and Shimp, 2011). Table 10.3 lists the barriers identified in the literature to obtaining an advance qualification in order of strongest barrier (Niebuhr and Biel, 2007).

Table 10.2   Internal and External Motivators

Internal Motivators	External Motivators
Enhances feeling of personal accomplishment	Promotes recognition from peers
Provides personal satisfaction	Promotes recognition from other professionals
Validates specialized knowledge	Increases marketability
Indicates professional growth	Promotes recognition from employers
Provides professional challenge	Increases public confidence
Enhances professional credibility	Increases salary
Provides evidence of professional commitment	
Indicates attainment of a practice standard	
Enhances personal confidence in abilities	
Provides evidence of accountability	
Indicates level of professional competence	
Enhances professional autonomy	

Table 10.3   Barriers to Certification

Cost of examination
Lack of institutional reward
Lack of institutional support
Lack of access to preparation courses or materials
Discomfort with test-taking process
It costs too much to maintain the credential
Lack of access to examination site
Lack of access to or availability of continuing education
I did not pass the examination when I took it
No desire/no interest in certification
Not relevant to my practice

Beginning Your Search

Whether you are just establishing your career or are a seasoned professional, the best place to begin your search for the right professional designation is with your professional association or governing body. When it comes to the health IT professional, the best place to start is with the Healthcare Information and Management Systems Society (HIMSS), an international professional governing body (http://www.himss.org/ProfessionalDevelopment).

The key for those seeking an advanced professional designation is to look for a(n)

- Requirement of specific level of knowledge and experience as a prerequisite.
- Academically rigorous and comprehensive credentialing process.
- Program to support continuing professional development.
- Requirement of adherence to a professional and ethical code of conduct.
- Necessity for maintenance of professional competency—i.e. "Know-Can-Do-Share"—to a prescribed standard.
- Condition for removal of the credential if professionals are not compliant with the outlined standards.

Maintaining Your Professional Designation

Given the rate of change in most fields, many would argue that the legitimacy of professional governing body—and by extension, the professional designations they confer—rests in their commitment to: (i) test the knowledge of an individual before granting the designation; (ii) require a regular demonstration of professional competency; and (iii) be willing and able to discipline, and even revoke the designation of, those who break rules or fail to meet stringent standards on an ongoing basis.

Competence planning, monitoring, and maintenance activities play an important role in building a professional competitive advantage. In reality, competencies are considered resources which need to be identified, measured, and managed and in fact, studies indicate a significant positive relationship between competency and one's ability to create and sustain a competitive advantage (Capece and Bazzica, 2013). Maintaining and renewing an advanced qualification with the governing organization supports professional competency and the notion of competitive advantage. It is contingent on one's commitment to undertake continuous professional development so as to maintain and advance their ability to apply the current knowledge and skills of the profession.

Before and once a professional designation is obtained, an individual should review the national or international governing body's maintenance requirements. Many governing organizations now have online systems for tracking and managing credentialing of their professionals who hold an advanced qualification. It is strongly recommended that the online system be utilized to document the fulfillment of requirements on an ongoing basis. At the very minimum, engaging with the system well in advance of the renewal date of the designation is prudent.

To maintain a professional designation, and in addition to the annual membership dues, professionals must most commonly:

- Submit details of their activities which maintain competency according to the prescribed standards of the professional governing body.
- Submit fees for renewal of the designation.
- Commit to the code of ethics and standard professional conduct.

Conclusion

In the fast-paced field of health informatics, many health IT professionals may seek a professional designation as an aspect of lifelong learning to ensure they have the professional competency to advance initiatives that positively impact patient care. This worthwhile endeavor must be considered carefully to ensure that the benefits resonate and there exists an ongoing commitment to oneself and the profession. Ultimately and once obtained, the more you use your professional designation, the more its meaning will be recognized as a symbol of highest professionalism.

References

Bennour, M., and Crestani, D. (2007). Using competencies in performance estimation: From the activity to the process. *Computers in Industry*, 58(2), 151–163.

Capece, G., and Bazzica, P. (2013). A practical proposal for a "Competence Plan Fulfillment" key performance indicator. *Knowledge and Process Management*, 20(1), 40–49.

Epstein, R. M. and Hundert, E. M. (2002). Defining and assessing professional competence. *JAMA*, 287(2), 226–235.

Foubister, V. (2003). Tales of success. Certification proves beneficial, both personally and professionally. *Materials Management in Health Care*, 12(6), 33–36. Retrieved from http://www.ncbi.nlm.nih.gov/pubmed/12854208.

Fritter, E. and Shimp, K. (2016). What does certification in professional nursing practice mean?. *Med-Surg Matters*, 25(2), 8–10.

Human Resources Professionals Association. (2012). *The Value of a CHRP: More Promotions and Better Pay*. Retrieved from https://www.hrpa.ca/Documents/Designations/The-Value-of-a-CHRP.pdf

Kaplow, R. (2011). The value of certification. *AACN Advanced Critical Care*, 22(1), 25–32.

Ley, T. and Albert, D. (2003). Identifying employee competencies in dynamic work domains: methodological considerations and a case study. *Journal of Universal Computer Science*, 9(12), 1500–1518.

Lysaght, R. M., and Altschuld, J. W. (2000). Beyond initial certification: The assessment and maintenance of competency in professions. *Evaluation and Program Planning*, 23(1), 95–104.

Niebuhr, B., and Biel, M. (2007). The value of specialty nursing certification. *Nursing Outlook*, 55(4), 176–181.

Schonfeld, G. R. (2010). Privilege of peerage: The value of professional designations. Retrieved June 26, 2016, from http://post.nyssa.org/nyssa-news/2010/04/privilege-of-peerage-the-value-of-professional-designations.html

Schroeter, K. (2008). Competence literature review. Retrieved from http://www.cc-institute.org/docs/default-document-library/2011/10/19/competence_lit_review.pdf?Status=Master

Setor, T., Joseph, D., and Srivastava, S. C. (2015). Professional obsolescence in IT: The relationships between the threat of professional obsolescence, coping and psychological strain. In *Proceedings of the 2015 ACM SIGMIS Conference on Computers and People Research* (pp. 117–122).

Torkkeli, M., and Tuominen, M. (2002). The contribution of technology selection to core competencies. *International Journal of Production Economics*, 77(3), 271–284.

Wade, C. H. (2009). Perceived effects of specialty nurse certification: A review of the literature. *AORN Journal*, 89(1), 183–192.

Wenghofer, E. F., Marlow, B., Campbell, C., Carter, L., Kam, S., McCauley, W., and Hill, L. (2014). The relationship between physician participation in continuing professional development programs and physician in-practice peer assessments. *Academic Medicine*, 89(6), 920–927.

Williams, H. F., and Counts, C. S. (2013). Certification 101: The pathway to excellence. *Nephrology Nursing Journal : Journal of the American Nephrology Nurses' Association*, 40(3), 197–209, 253. Retrieved from http://www.ncbi.nlm.nih.gov/pubmed/23923799.

LEARNING FROM OTHERS

Chapter 11

The Mentoring Process

By Joseph J. Wagner
MPA, FHIMSS

Contents

Abstract

As a Mentor, sharing one's challenges and opportunities is an excellent way to contribute to the success of others. Identify whether mentorship is right for you as either a Mentor or Mentee, or both.

Keywords:

Mentor
Mentee
Experience
Advice
Guidance
Development
Coach
Goals

Introduction

Mentoring—just what is mentoring? Well, it is defined by Webster's as:

> To teach or give advice or guidance to (someone, such as a less experienced person or a child): to act as a Mentor for (someone)*

We acquired "Mentor" from the literature of ancient Greece. In Homer's epic *The Odyssey*, Odysseus was away from home fighting and journeying for 20 years. During that time, Telemachus, the son he left as a babe in arms, grew up under the supervision of Mentor, an old and trusted friend. When the goddess Athena decided it was time to complete the education of young Telemachus, she visited him disguised as Mentor and they set out together to learn about his father. Today, we use the word Mentor for anyone who is a positive, guiding influence in another (usually younger) person's life.[IBID]

In this chapter, we discuss what it means to be a Mentor or a Mentee, the value of both, and some effective methods to employ as the Mentor or Mentee.

The Mentor

Being a Mentor is an important responsibility and one that can be very rewarding. The Mentor role is similar to being a teacher in that you provide instruction to someone who is less knowledgeable than yourself. Yet mentoring goes further than that because as a Mentor you also provide your work and personal life experiences, things that can only be learned through daily interactions with others. A perfect example is the real-time knowledge that is gained through actual experiences of a seasoned project manager. For example, a project manager will lead a team of resources from many different departments comprised of staff from all levels within an organization. The project manager and this group of individuals are formed to deliver some type of solution. Initially, the project manager may start out with a small project and over time be given more complex projects. Learning how to deal with multifaceted issues that involve multiple stakeholders comes with the experiences gained by working on increasingly challenging projects over time.

The role of the Mentor is to educate or pass on the knowledge that was gained from working on these more complex projects. Describing the "gotchas," sharing best practices, and explaining how to deal with difficult human resource issues are experiences that cannot be fully learned from books. The seasoned project manager should consider himself or herself an important mentor.

As a Mentor, you should focus on the development of your Mentee by coaching them and providing counseling on their projects and the issues they may encounter. When you meet with your Mentee, your initial discussion should be a time for introductions. What is the Mentee looking for in terms of guidance? What are their aspirational goals? What are their career plans? During this meeting you will explore these details which will determine if you have the correct background and experiences to be a good Mentor to them.

With this information, you can then focus on the areas where the Mentee is deficient in certain skills or experiences. You should always be looking for places that you can push the Mentee beyond their current skillset so that there is ongoing, continuous development.

---

* Merriam-Webster, Online Dictionary, www.merriam-webster.com.

When deciding to be a Mentor, you must be sure that you have the time and energy necessary to work with your Mentee. Make sure that you can commit to the time it takes to be a good Mentor.

The Mentee

A Mentee is often thought of as a younger person; however, this is not always true. Throughout your career you will have many opportunities to meet well-educated and highly experienced people. Your work may span several different technologies, skillsets, and required experience. Take technology as an example. With so much new technology being introduced into the healthcare environments today, many times the younger person has been exposed to the technical requirements in early learning situations, training sessions, or actual work. Regardless of age, the Mentee is the person that will be learning form the Mentor.

The role of a Mentee is to gain as much knowledge as possible from their selected mentor. Meetings should be scheduled and dedicated to time for the Mentor and the Mentee to share experiences and discuss how they were handled so that they can be analyzed to determine if there is room for improvement. The Mentee should take note of issues that arise that are difficult or unusual so that they can be discussed with their Mentor. It is important to have regularly scheduled meetings so that your progression in skills is continuous and relative to your time with the organization.

It should be mentioned that throughout your career you will probably have several Mentors. As you progress in your career and become more knowledgeable and experienced, your Mentors will change. It is also common for someone to have more than one Mentor due to the diversity of their role with the organization. Some people will require education from Mentors that have human resource skills, technical skills, and specific skills related to your chosen course of study.

Selecting Your Mentor

The Mentor is someone who has more experience, education, or training than other people in the organization with similar or more novice roles. The concept of mentorship is to have the Mentor teach, train, or share the wisdom they have gained from the additional experience, education, or training. This is done to help the more amateur person to learn from the Mentor. This helps the person to become proficient in their role faster, by assimilating this knowledge without having to experience it independently through more formal methods or having to wait to have similar experiences that may come much later in their life.

It is important when selecting a Mentor that you choose someone who has the prerequisite skills and experience that you are seeking. One way to get this information is to check with your human resources department. Representatives should have an understanding of the requirements and roles that each potential Mentor possesses. You can also use the Internet as well. One particularly popular site that is frequently used to gather information on people is LinkedIn.* Many professionals use LinkedIn to create their professional profile. By reviewing the professional profiles for individuals in your company or city you can create a list of potential mentors.

---

* LinkedIn is a business-oriented social networking service which can be accessed at: https://www.linkedin.com.

When beginning your career in health IT there will be many areas where only real-life experiences will give you the depth and breadth of knowledge that is required to become a truly successful employee. Some roles in health IT may require that you become a subject matter expert— an example being when you work with clinical application systems e.g., Lab, Pharmacy, Radiology or others. Large-scale hospital clinical information systems have many supporting ancillary systems, each requiring a different set of skills. The same is true for Integration applications that are used in hospital and Health Information Exchanges (HIE). Programming, development skills, project management, support services, and strategy development are just a few of the areas you may be considering. It will be important for you to find a Mentor that has experience in the specific area you are considering for yourself.

If you are not quite sure of what you wish to pursue, then you should select a Mentor that has managed or supported several different areas you are interested in or select more than one Mentor so that you can better understand each of the various areas. In addition to the methods described above you can check with local career counseling agencies, like the Career Counselling Consortium (www.careercc.org), as they may have local mentorship programs available for you to solicit. Most stated have several counseling centers that can be easily found on the Internet.

The one area that is typically universal in every healthcare field is human resource management. Working with people from all different departments and levels of an organization takes solid resource management skills. As you progress in your career, you will undoubtedly be required to manage your own resources as well. The human resource management department typically has clearly written policies and procedures; however, managing people cannot always be governed by what is written. It is important to consider having a strong Mentor that you can turn to for advice when a situation arises. This can be a human resources person, or someone who is managing a large group of people.

There are two different scenarios when it comes to healthcare organizations and mentorship. Some organizations have a formal mentorship program while others have not embraced these programs and you will have to structure a mentorship program on your own.

Formal Mentorship Programs

Formal mentorship programs are becoming more common in the workplace. The formal program ensures that there is some type of process to set up people that wish to be Mentors. Typically the Mentors will have their mentoring skillsets listed so that selecting your Mentor is made by simply identifying the person(s) that have the experience you are looking for. Most programs have published policies and procedures that are to be followed by the Mentor/Mentee. These programs typically limit the number of Mentees a Mentor can accept so that the Mentor has the proper amount of time for his Mentees. Policies set up guidelines for meeting schedules, roles of the Mentee and Mentor, and an evaluation process.

Even if you work for an organization that has a formal program with a list of potential Mentors, it is still important that you speak to several possible Mentor candidates to be sure that you are selecting the best resource. You should treat your first meeting with a potential Mentor as an interview. Spend time interviewing him/her to be sure that they have the skills and experience that you wish to gain. Have the Mentor speak of their previous experiences mentoring and how those people are now doing. Be sure to ask how much time per month they have available for your sessions. During these interviews you will probably find that you feel more comfortable with a particular person. You should take this into consideration because the mentoring process should be comfortable and engaging with honest and open conversations.

Once you have decided on your Mentor be sure to create an outline or list of goals and expectations. Review this with your Mentor so that they have input to your mentorship. You want to be sure that you both agree on what will be accomplished during your mentorship to ensure that you have the best possible experience.

Informal Mentorship Programs

Organizations that do not have a formal program for assigning Mentors will require you to search out and select a Mentor on your own. Not having a list of Mentors and their skillsets will require you to do some research on your organization's leaders. This should not discourage you from proceeding. There are several simple methods to use to gain the required information you need to get the right person for you.

Start with your human resources department. Obtain an organizational chart for the company and sit down with your human resources representative and discuss the levels in the organization, positions, and job responsibilities. Remember that your Mentor may come from a department that is not closely related to your own.

Set up meetings with the potential Mentor candidates and discuss with them your desire to have a Mentor. Clearly define what you would expect from them using the details provided in this chapter. Be sure that the person understands and is ready to commit to the time and effort it takes to make the mentorship a valuable use of time for both of you.

Other Considerations When Selecting a Mentor

As mentioned, it is not cast in stone that you have just a single mentor. Different people offer varying experiences that can provide a significant benefit to you. It may seem most appropriate to select a Mentor from your current place of employment; however, there are many other places you should also consider. You can break down your development goals into many different categories. Here are just a few to illustrate where you may consider seeking a Mentor:

Human Resources: Human resource management is a very important part of your education. Learning the policy and procedures of the organization is important, but their experiences when dealing with resource issues will be invaluable.

Project Managers: Large, complex project leaders possess significant work experiences and may have relative industry-accepted certifications you may wish to consider, such as, Project Management Professional (PMP), Agile, or Black Belt.

Technical skills: If your work is technical in nature it will be helpful to identify a System Matter Expert (SME) that has the technical skills you will need to acquire. Look within your organization, check with vendors, and search the Internet for relative user-support blogs.

Future Educational Considerations: Undergraduate, Graduate, and PhDs should all be considered when mapping out your development plan. Higher education is quickly becoming the norm for many healthcare careers. Seek out managers within your organization that have graduate or doctoral degrees for their advice. Set up a meeting or attend an orientation with local colleges and universities to better understand what your opportunities may be.

Volunteering: Volunteering should also be part of your career plan as it offers a great way to network and "give back" at the same time. Speak to your managers and directors about possible volunteer opportunities in the healthcare field.

Conclusion

Finding a strong Mentor should be part of everyone's development plan. The process will provide you with many benefits. Over the course of your relationship with your mentor(s), you have the opportunity to increase your understanding and skills related to human resources, technical skills, managing complex projects, handling change management, and increasing your professional network.

Sun Microsystems compiled the following metrics associated with mentoring*:

- Both Mentors and Mentees were approximately 20% more likely to get a raise than people who did not participate in the mentoring program
- 25% of Mentees and 28% of Mentors received a raise—versus only 5% of managers who were not Mentors
- Employees who received mentoring were promoted FIVE times more often than people who didn't have Mentors
- Mentors were SIX times more likely to have been promoted to a bigger job

The statistics speak for themselves. As you progress in the development of your skills and gain experience, you should consider being a mentor. The mentoring experience can be a rich and rewarding way of giving something back to the healthcare community. Bestowing your life experiences and skills on a Mentee ought to be part of your own career plan.

---

* Quest, Lisa Forbes, October 31, 2011, How becoming a Mentor Can Boost Your Career, http://www.forbes.com/sites/lisaquast/2011/10/31/how-becoming-a-mentor-can-boost-your-career/#735fee75662a.

Chapter 12

Managing by Walking Around

By Jason Bickford
MCSE

Contents

Whether you are rounding for bedside clinical care, or simply to gain a better perspective of your customer, the opportunities to recognize where a small change can have a large impact may never be realized if you are restricted to the confines of an office or desk. Jason's personal adoption of the MBWA strategy enabled him to quickly recognize an opportunity to transform direct access to electrocardiographic tracings within the electronic medical record from a poor-quality reference image to a high-value addition for physicians with near diagnostic quality results!

Joel McAlduff, M.D.
Vice President and CMIO, MedStar Health (former CMIO at Banner Health)

Abstract

There is much to be learned by leaving one's office and experiencing the challenges and opportunities faced by employees in the care setting.

By getting out from one's department and engaging with others in the patient care setting, lots can be gleaned to improve health IT services for all stakeholders.

Keywords:

Patient Care Delivery
Personal Brand
Empowerment
Workplace Culture
Building Relationships
Creating Relationships
Visibility
Employee Engagement
Job Satisfaction
Leadership Effectivenesss
Retention and Commitment

Introduction

Healthcare Professionals are confronted with trying to find a balance in improving the quality of care while decreasing medical errors. This ongoing challenge and tightrope that is being walked also includes reducing costs with fewer resources. The role of a health information technology (health IT) Professional is not only to provide support to providers, nurses, and ancillary departments so they can provide exceptional patient care, but also to support systems and technologies that do so too. The pinnacle of a health IT professional is to contribute to improving patient care outcomes and/or enabling the business to provide exceptional patient care through the use of technology. One style of business management that can foster a productive workplace culture and help you reach pinnacle career success is Managing by Walking Around (MBWA).

The Concept

The concept of MBWA, also known as management by wandering around, has been around for decades and can be traced back to management practices that were deployed by Hewlett-Packard back in the 1970s (https://www.mindtools.com/pages/article/newTMM_72.htm). MBWA involves leaders stepping away from their offices or desks in order to roam around the workplace to solicit staff feedback, observe processes and workflows, build relationships, and show visibility and appreciation for the work that is being done.

The Benefits

The benefits of MBWA for a Healthcare IT Professional can be very rewarding as well as enlightening. William Edwards Deming, who was an American engineer, statistician, professor, author, lecturer, and management consultant, once shared that "If you wait for people to come to you, you"ll only get small problems. You must go and find them. The big problems are where people don't realize they have one in the first place" (http://itmanagersinbox.com/1687/management-by-walking-around-mbwa/).

MBWA, when used consistently, can make you more approachable and helps build trust so that everyone is empowered to share their ideas and problems with you. The additional healthcare process and business knowledge that can be gained will help to connect the dots and see the big picture as well as the finer details. This process can also accelerate decision-making and information sharing. MBWA can also create accountability and lessen that perception that when you're out of sight, you're out of mind. MBWA may improve employee morale by increasing employee productivity, engagement, and job satisfaction, which may also impact the retention of talented employees. Organization morale or workplace culture can be an influence when an employee's voice is being heard and their trust is earned. It can also help foster a collaborative workplace culture through the sharing and exchange of ideas that could improve productivity and creativity, and create cost-saving measures.

Strategies and Suggestions

There are numerous MBWA strategies and suggestions, offered in the upcoming paragraphs, that can help you achieve many desired outcomes, but the most important for sustained achievement is that your walking around excursions must have results that matter. There must be follow through on action items, commitments, and communication. MBWA can be a consistent part of your routine for general rounding, for a one-on-one discussion, as part of project planning, or event solution brainstorming. *MBWA is less about having the right answers and more about having the right questions.* You need to be able to listen to feedback that is shared and then, in turn, provide timely follow-through or your credibility will be lost. MBWA should be a process of active listening, soliciting feedback, prompting suggestions, and developing ideas that create an opportunity to identify and resolve issues. The process must enable active problem-solving, increasing the ability for Health IT Professionals to act on improvement suggestions, but with a balance between gathering more suggestions and prioritizing them, versus implementing existing ones that have already been identified. A lack of balance and not allowing enough time for reflection will create challenges for yourself and those you are leading. MBWA is also an opportunity to be social and share communications on current opportunities as well as giving updates on upcoming changes. A Health IT Professional can become the bridge between business and clinical teams and help create dialogue across leadership lines, resulting in an improved workplace culture. If an in-person MBWA format is not possible then try a virtual means by connecting through video, chat, or a phone call.

Implementing MBWA

As a Health IT Professional, you may be wondering how you can implement your own MBWA routine. I offer you a few tips to get started, but first, you must have your own goal or purpose defined. Whether it's to discover process improvements, create new ideas, or build upon lessons learned, it is valuable to have a cause.

1. *Reserve Time*: Block your calendar for 1–2 hours either bi-weekly or monthly
2. *Create an Identity*: You should be yourself, be curious, be genuine, and be transparent

3. *Relax*: Keep it informal but bring something along to take notes
4. *Inquire*: Listen, observe, ask open-ended questions, and solicit feedback
5. *Praise*: Recognize those that are making positive changes and contributions
6. *Actualize*: If you say you're going to do something, find an answer or ask a question; make sure you respond within a few days or be ready to answer the next time you round
7. *Build*: Relationships, business knowledge, and process improvements

In today's healthcare landscape many organizations are challenged with managing rapid change. A regular MBWA routine can transform Health IT Professionals in becoming more approachable. This routine will encourage staff to speak up and share. If the purpose is aligned with improving outcomes and is a collaborative process aimed at uncovering gaps in policies, procedures, and technology usage, the results should yield the creation of best practices and development or refinement of standard operating procedures.

As a Health IT Professional, you can be respected and sought after for your technical skills and subject matter expertise and habits formed through MBWA. You can also avoid becoming too distant and disconnected. The more connected you are and the more relationships you build, the better you can anticipate your customer needs.

MBWA Major Considerations

There are three major components that you should consider when Managing by Walking Around in a Health IT setting. They are: (1) getting to know the people; (2) the process; and (3) the technology that is involved. Peter Fine, President and CEO of Banner Health, often shares with his staff that "visibility breeds credibility, credibility breeds trust; so if you want to be trusted, you have to be visible." This quote and message that Peter shares from one of his mentors is a great reminder that inspires my own MBWA excursions.

Improving Patient Care Delivery with MBWA: An Example

There are many examples and stories that can be shared about the benefits of MBWA and also having a mindset that everything takes people, process, and technology. I would like to share one that is personal to me. Dr. Joel McAlduff, former CMIO at Banner Health, shared with me that physicians were frustrated with interpreting EKG's that were being scanned into the Electronic Medical Record due to image degradation after being scanned. As an ambitious Health IT Professional I made it my mission to make the process better. My approach was to first understand the entire process, the people involved, and the current technologies in place. I contacted the Head of Radiology and asked for permission to observe an EKG technician while the technician was conducting an EKG test with a patient. The patient was accommodating while I observed the technician connecting wires to a patient from a mobile cart. The technician conducted the test and then rolled the cart into a room where it was connected to the network for transmitting to the EKG server for later printing of the EKG on specialized paper. Using a desktop scanner, a preliminary report was scanned into a Document Imaging solution that indexed and released the EKG report to the patient's chart but, of course, with less-than-desirable quality. I attempted to improve everything I could with the scanner and scanning software, but it only resulted in marginal improvements to the image quality. I consulted an external vendor resource that supported the Document Imaging solutions to see if there were other possibilities. He suggested a computer output to laser disk (COLD) feed process using technology that we owned but had not yet implemented. A COLD feed is an older term that refers to the scanning or importing of documents and making the images available in another source system. I researched the software and started exploring its capabilities in order to feel comfortable with its potential before moving on to the next steps. One requirement of the software was importing the EKG output as an XML or PDF document. This required me to engage the EKG application owner, who was an individual that worked in Technology Management, since that was a clinical system. I shared the complaint from the CMO and the potential of the COLD feed software that could possibly unalter the EKG report and deliver an exceptional provider-viewing experience. The Technology Management leader was receptive to converting the EKG to a PDF, but it required an upgrade and some configuration as well as report formatting standardization in order to populate required fields such as patient Medical Record and Encounter numbers, which were necessary for routing to the correct patient's chart. These formatting changes required us to present them to a steering committee and once approved we were able to move forward with non-production testing. We engaged a Healthcare Informatics Leader to help us in coordinating the change process and procedures as well as getting hospital leadership support. Once we were satisfied with our testing efforts we scheduled an implementation date and time. I arrived onsite in the Radiology department and waited patiently for the first EKG report to be generated and then exported as a PDF for the COLD feed software to pick up and route to the patient's chart. It was truly an exciting and rewarding experience to visualize the results and then share them with CMO. The result was an improvement in the patient care process and the clinician's voice was heard. In this accomplishment, I knew that the people that I learned and worked with, such as the Radiology department Head, EKG Technician, Technology Management and Informatics Leaders and the Chief Medical Officer, all contributed to the success. The CMO, sharing his frustrations with a poor process, and myself, observing the process from beginning to the end, helped inspire me to find a better process and to learn about a technology that significantly improved workflow and cost savings since expensive EKG paper was no longer required. The new process not only resulted in a better image for clinicians to view, but the time it took to post the chart was reduced by hours, thereby improving patient care.

Summary

MBWA was not a concept I was familiar with during the EKG project, but I somehow knew it was going to be essential for me to go beyond my office cubicle in order to facilitate necessary change, as well as earn stakeholder support. The visibility I created did indeed earn credibility and, in turn, trust with peers. MBWA was created for management but there are clear benefits for health IT professionals that are leading projects or providing technology support. There have been many advancements in technology that have allowed teams to meet virtually, but truly effective meetings, planning, collaboration, and most importantly engagement, in my opinion, are typically done in person. That is the spirit of MBWA.

Conclusion

One of your most important commodities, besides your health, is how you spend your time. I believe that MBWA is worthy of adopting, but only if you are clear with purpose and intent and can invest the necessary time, effort, and consistency. MBWA-related communications and managing expectations will also need to be carefully balanced between daily duties and trying to please everyone. Engage and build relationships with people. Ask questions to clarify the process and determine why specific things are done a certain way. Understand the function of technology and to expand its benefits in reaching a maximum outcome. As part of your MBWA initiative, if you're always mindful of the people, process, and technology components and diligent about creating consistency in delivering purpose, value, and outcomes you'll be on your way to becoming a health IT professional rock star! MBWA can create an opportunity for you to develop your own personal brand and style for delivering organizational value, influencing workplace culture, and aligning yourself with strategic initiatives that can signify you as a subject matter expert, rising star, future leader, or be considered for a promotional leadership opportunity.

Chapter 13

Experiencing a Job Exchange

By Deborah Newman
FACHE, FHIMSS, MBA

Contents

Abstract:

One way to appreciate both one's current position and a colleague's position is to experience another position. Identify ways to participate and take advantage of an effective job exchange experience.

Keywords:

Job Exchange Process
Insights
Experience
Leadership

Clinical Care
Clinical Professional
Clinical Support
Administration
Mentor
Mentoring
Cross Train
Cross Training

Introduction

How do you describe job exchange? And how do you have an understanding of what a job exchange is? It is not as uncommon as you might think. There are benefits toward a job exchange that are not always evident with the initial thoughts of this job growth activity.

The key components of the job exchange process create a structure that takes the initial idea through to ensuring a successful experience (Figure 13.1). The beginning of the process involves identifying the potential job that would be part of the job exchange. A job exchange has many benefits to both parties, so there must be a commitment and understanding of the benefits for each person. The next important step is to document the proposal, including risks and benefits to each participant as well as the organization.

Multiple levels of approval must be obtained for the job exchange to occur. The hierarchy of approvals follow the natural approval process beginning with the immediate supervisor through to Vice President approval. After support is obtained for the job exchange, Human Resources (HR) must be involved to ensure all labor laws and competencies are aligned prior to the experience.

After the job exchange, documentation of the experience will ensure appropriate communication to all interested parties as to the benefits and lessons learned. This documentation should be communicated to all interested parties, including management and Human Resources. This documentation also forms the basis to "pay it forward" and paves the path for others to experience this rewarding and career-enhancing activity.

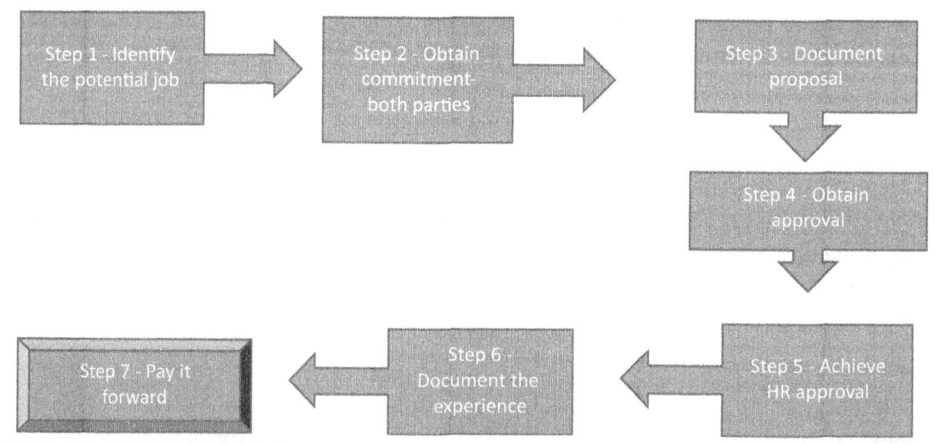

Figure 13.1 Job exchange process flow.

Job Exchange Process Step 1: Identify the Potential Job

When determining the job that you would like to experience with a job exchange, it is important to ensure there is an alignment with your current job. One way to identify this is to look at your supervisor's scope of responsibilities. In healthcare, departments are typically categorized under top leadership in four basic areas of Clinical Care, Clinical Professional, Clinical Support, and Administration.

Clinical Care Leadership Area

The first employee category is Clinical Care, which includes physicians, nursing, clinical departments (such as the emergency department, surgery, acute care nursing) and clinical care support staff such as CNAs (certified nurse aide), and secretaries. This category of employees has the most interaction with patients and documentation in the Electronic Health Record (EHR). Many of these employees are required to have a certain degree (RN, CNA, MD) which is a constraint on which roles would be available for a job exchange. A job exchange in this category is usually between one department and another (such as the ED or ICU) or one location and another (such as a surgical center or urgent care center).

Clinical Professional Leadership Area

The second job classification category is Clinical Professional, which includes departments such as physical therapy, respiratory, rehabilitation, radiology, and laboratory. Clinical Professional employees also have interaction with patients, but may also have other administrative responsibilities to ensure the care received by the patient is the most appropriate. A Clinical Dietitian may round in the mornings and interview patients, but then has a portion of their day monitoring test results and patient diagnoses which affect the diet for the next day. These employees have a key role in documenting in the EHR, and also tend to document specific areas of the EMR that require specific training prior to working in their role. This specific documentation requirement can be a constraint on which roles would be available for a job exchange, and may require additional EMR training prior to the job exchange. With this employee category, a job exchange would typically occur between different locations.

CLINICAL CARE JOB EXCHANGE EXAMPLES

- A CNA who just received his CNA degree experiences a 3-week job exchange as a Unit Secretary to achieve an understanding of the work flow and the role of the CNA in the patient care process.
- An ICU RN experiences a 1-month rotation in the Oncology Clinic to better understand the cancer disease process from the onset of diagnosis.
- The Unit Secretary in the Orthopedic Office experiences a 2-week job exchange as a Unit Secretary in the Surgical Center and another 2-week experience in the Orthopedic Inpatient Unit to better understand the course of a patient's surgical experience.

CLINICAL PROFESSIONAL JOB EXCHANGE EXAMPLES

■ A Clinical Dietitian in the Nursing Home experiences a 1-month job exchange with a Clinical Dietitian at the Acute Care Hospital to better understand the patient transfer process between the two settings.
■ The Physical Therapy Department Director has a program in place to have a 2-week job exchange for all PT Technicians between the outpatient clinic, the acute care hospital, and the nursing home.
■ An Orthopedic Office Radiology Technologist experiences a 1-month rotation at the acute care hospital to obtain educational experience toward an advanced certification.

Clinical Support Leadership Area

The Clinical Support area is the third job category section that includes departments focused on the patient indirectly such as patient accounting, quality management, risk management, patient accounting, and Health Information Management. Employees in this category may interact with patients, but it is not an interaction that is key to the delivery of care. Some of these employees may have a degree or certification required for the position, such as a Registered Health Information Administrator in Medical Records, but these certifications may not be required prior to performing the job. Healthcare organization's HR policies often allow these employees to gain experience in their role in anticipation of an upcoming certification exam. Employees in these positions have a greater flexibility in choosing a job exchange position without the constraints of having a certification or degree prior to the exchange. The document required in these positions are not typically in the EMR, but are in a separate software specifically designated for the process they are responsible for. These could be separate modules within the EMR (Patient Complaint Module, Quality Management Module, Patient Accounting Module) or separate software that may or may not be interfaced with the EMR (Patient Billing Software, Care Management & Discharge Planning Software, Surgical Quality Software).

CLINICAL SUPPORT JOB EXCHANGE EXAMPLES

■ A Quality Management Specialist experiences a 2-month job exchange with a Risk Management Specialist to better understand the overlap between the two functions.
■ The Patient Accounting Representative dedicated to Outpatient Clinic billing gains a better understanding of the revenue cycle process by shadowing the Outpatient Clinic Coding Specialist for 1 week and then a job exchange for 2 weeks.
■ The Director of Health Information Management obtains approval for a 1-month job exchange with the Director of Risk Management to explore a potential career change.

Administration Leadership Area

The remaining departments constitute the Administrative areas that are not focused directly on the patient such as accounting, marketing, administration, facility engineering and HR. These departments tend to have a very focused set of skills specifically geared to the job that is performed, and although there are some required degrees & certifications, much of the job expertise is obtained on the job and through continuous training and education. These employees have the flexibility to experience a job exchange without extensive prior preparation. The work instructions tend to be robust in these categories lending them ideal for a job exchange. The work balance in Administrative areas does depend on some computer software systems, but also has a manual or hands-on component such as filing, pipe repair, interviewing, press announcements, and auditing. These are excellent departments for a job exchange when a person is interested in a career change in the future and can experience the job prior to an educational commitment.

ADMINISTRATIVE JOB EXCHANGE EXAMPLES

- The Executive Secretary to the President experiences a job exchange with the nursing home secretary prior to going to school for her Certified Nursing Assistant degree.
- An HR Specialist is interested in Public Relations and arranges a 2-week job exchange with a Marketing Specialist to better understand the overlap in their customers.
- An Accounting Secretary experiences a job exchange with the Patient Accounting Secretary to understand the differences between the two financial processes.

Once you determine the general leadership category, review the requirements of each department within that category. Some departments require a clinical certificate such as an RN license or a certified respiratory technician. Other departments require a certain level of education such as an MBA, or a certain number of years in a field. Evaluating the job requirements will be important to ensure you are identifying a reasonable potential job to exchange with. With this analysis, you will determine if you will be qualified for the job exchange. Job requirements can be found on the job description located in HR for the role or job of interest. Documentation of the job requirements will include the physical requirements, degree or certification requirements, years or settings of past experience, and behavioral responsibilities of the position.

Another approach for a job exchange is to assume the responsibilities of the job that you would like to exchange with, but have the job owner sign off on the work or tasks that you perform. This is an effective way to experience a job exchange that you may not be qualified for, but are able to perform some of the duties to experience the job. This is a good job exchange option when you are investigating if you are interested in the other job as a viable new job that you would be interested in obtaining additional education or experience for in order to advance to the desired new position.

Job Exchange Process Step 2: Obtain Commitment from Both Parties

A job exchange process is dependent on two parties essentially agreeing to the process and benefits of the job exchange. The person interested in the job exchange will typically have the innate commitment from a personal and professional perspective. This person initiating the job exchange will have already processed their personal pros and cons related to the job exchange. The person who is receiving the request for a job exchange may have not yet had a chance to think through the pros and cons of the job exchange. Often, the person initiating the job exchange will have multiple conversations with the person receiving the job exchange request to deliberate and discuss the benefits to ensure the activity will benefit both parties.

This is a key time to collaborate with the job exchange parties to organize a trial period where there is a limited time of a few days to see if a longer time period job exchange will work out for both parties. During this trial period, both parties can determine what activities are appropriate for the job exchange and what the aspect of the job exchange proposal will be. This is an ideal situation in which both parties can determine the content of the job exchange proposal and the contents of that activity.

As a result of this commitment from both parties, it is important to ensure there is a documented commitment statement from both parties prior to working on the job exchange proposal. The healthcare organization may permit certain job exchanges, while denying others, for various reasons. Despite the benefits, the current workloads of the departments and/or organization may be too much to allow for the learning curve during the job exchange. If the job exchange is with the same position, but in different areas, these are typically easier to get approved. The commitment statement does not need to be formal, but should be documented in a fashion such as an email or memo to file indicating the commitment by both parties to the job exchange experience and the positive benefits that are desired from the activity. This documentation is important for the next step of documenting the job exchange proposal.

Job Exchange Process Step 3: Document the Job Exchange Proposal

There are perceived benefits and challenges with a job exchange arrangement. The proposal should outline the benefits in addition to the potential challenges and the actions or plans to address the challenges. One benefit for the organization is that the job exchange will empower the parties to understand the specific challenges of the other party. For example, if a Quality Professional in a rural area has a job exchange with a Quality Professional in an urban area, they will be able to achieve a better understanding of the issues in a different environment. Another benefit for the organization is related to cross training of team members and the ability to assume the other person's job with minimal orientation. One good example is where a medical/surgical unit nurse participates in a job exchange with a critical care/intensive care nurse. This nurse is now able to cover both settings depending on the staffing needs after an effective job exchange arrangement.

The job exchange proposal will also have a benefit of a positive effect of fostering a positive collaboration and relationship between colleagues. When there is a structured job exchange, there are intangible benefits for both parties which manifest themselves in a mutual respect for the other person's job tasks and challenges. For example, in an urban neighborhood, it is more common to have patients arrive at the hospital with guns and knives on their person. In a rural neighborhood, it is a rare experience to have a gun or knife in the facility. Those two arrival methods may require different policies and procedures, and the job exchange can enlighten one person as to inherent risks that may not have been evident in current policies.

The proposal should include a series of responsibilities, and those responsibilities need to be well documented. If the job exchange is a full exchange where one person is doing the activities of another person, that expectation should be outlined in detail so all parties understand the scope of the job exchange. On the other hand, if only a selected set of duties are encompassed in the job exchange, those need to be documented with explicit areas of responsibilities assigned.

The job exchange proposal should encompass the disadvantages of the interaction, such as the productivity of both parties and the salary of cross training. The more important part of the proposal needs to focus on the positive aspects of the job exchange, which should include achieving a job freshness, appreciation of associated colleagues, and a level of awareness of other colleague tasks. Another advantage is to understand the perspective of another industry, such as a nursing home RN working as a hospital intensive care RN. A personal satisfaction perspective is also achievable through a job exchange as the individuals are learning, growing, and exploring an enjoyable and fulfilling personal experience. The experience is likely to be extremely satisfying and personally fulfilling and any personal thoughts and perceptions to include in the proposal would be helpful for ensuring a complete and comprehensive job exchange proposal.

Job Exchange Process Step 4: Obtain Initial Approval

When a person is interested in a job exchange experience, it is important that the request is supported by the person to whom you directly report. A job exchange proposal should be written that describes the scope of the job exchange, the length of the experience, the benefits for the individual, and the benefits for the organization. An example is provided in Appendix 13.1. This approval should be obtained with a tiered approach, beginning with an initial verbal exchange of the idea and ending with a job exchange proposal document that solidifies the discussions with your supervisor about the experience. If an organization has a formal job exchange program through HR, this document and process may be further defined in a policy or form.

During the initial approval process, the work reassignment details must be addressed. This is related to the work reassignment of both parties. The person who wishes to have a job exchange experience must document the plans for coverage of current work duties while they are experiencing the job exchange. This could entail a temporary reassignment to others on the team, or procurement of a temporary position to cover the assigned tasks. Thought also has to occur for the person that is sharing the job exchange and if that person will serve as a mentor or will be temporarily reassigned to other tasks. It is ideal if the person will serve as a mentor to ensure the job exchange tasks are well understood and communicated.

A job exchange experience is considered a temporary opportunity to experience another position in the company, and should have a specific time limit assigned to the experience. A typical experience is 2–4 months in length and requires a formal report to the direct supervisor as to the information or experiences accomplished during the experience.

When initial approval is achieved, it is imperative to document this approval in a formal fashion. See Appendix 13.1 for an example of formal approval. Evidence of approval could be documented as a memo to file, official contract, or other cosigned document agreeing to the specifics of the job exchange.

Job Exchange Process Step 5: Achieve Human Resources Approval

After initial approval is received from your direct supervisor, the next step is to have HR review and approve the job exchange proposal. The Fair Labor Standards Act and other employment laws govern how an organization can manage employee work accommodations and payment. The HR Department will review the job exchange proposal and ensure all legal regulations are satisfied and that the pay rate for the time spent during the job exchange is appropriate. Depending on the local market (rural, urban, inner city, country, etc.) there is a difference in the pay that is appropriate for time spent. Reimbursement can be affected by different countries, states, etc. and these items need to be negotiated and included in the agreement. This information should also include travel expenses incurred in the provision of services, including international considerations such as passport or other travel considerations.

Job Exchange Process Step 6: Documenting the Experience

When a job exchange experience concludes, it is important to document the experience. An example can be found in Appendix 13.2.

Documentation of the experience should include the date, time spent, and the activity. It should also include information related to general comments, positive observations, and opportunities for improvement. The date and time spent information will justify and document the length of the experience, and also indicate when your current job responsibilities were covered by others. General comments should include information such as the people that were involved in the activity (such as a mentor, a supervisor, or a committee) and other specifics about the specific interaction. Positive observations should include thoughts on how the process worked well, how a meeting was run, or how a task seemed effective. This information is subjective and should be worded in a professional manner indicating it was a brief observation of a complex process. Opportunities for improvement are typically a result of conversations with the job exchange team member about significant ideas that could affect the job process in a positive fashion that is actionable and agreed upon. It is advisable to document a daily log of time spent with participants, including executives and other participants that you interact with. This job should include the participant, the essence of the interaction, time spent with each activity, and action items or follow-up items. Interactions with patients or other stakeholders should also be documented as a part of the job exchange to ensure the time spend with the other job is effective and efficient and satisfies the qualifications of the job exchange proposal.

Job Exchange Process Step 7: Pay It Forward

A job exchange experience is one that can be very valuable for the job exchange personnel. Many job exchange personnel ensure that documentation and job proposal information is well documented so that another person will be able to experience the same valuable experience with another individual. If you are able to document the proposal, and the documented benefits of a job exchange, you can set up the situation for another person to experience a similar set of events, which will further the quality and positive aspects of the job that you are realizing—and the job that you are working on. Excellent documentation of a job exchange experience will ensure another person will be able to have a job exchange experience that will further their career and job experiences.

Conclusion

A job exchange is an excellent way to experience other positions in a variety of settings. It is important that HR policies are followed when setting up job exchanges. Participants can gain valuable insights into positions of interest without leaving one's current position. Participating in a job exchange experience can be a rewarding exercise that benefits both participants, as a great way to appreciate both one's current position and a colleague's position is to experience another position.

Appendix 13.1: Job Exchange Proposal Sample Template

[YOUR ORGANIZATION]
JOB EXCHANGE PROPOSAL
[Select Date]

OVERVIEW

1. Job Exchange Background and Description
2. Job Exchange Scope
3. Advantages & Disadvantages
4. Deliverables
5. Affected Parties
6. Affected Business Processes or Systems
7. Implementation Plan
8. High-Level Timeline/Schedule

APPROVAL AND AUTHORITY TO PROCEED

We approve the job exchange proposal as described above, and authorize the team to proceed.

Name	Title	Date

Approved By   Date   Approved By   Date

Appendix 13.2: Job Exchange Summary & Report Sample Template

[YOUR ORGANIZATION]
JOB EXCHANGE SUMMARY & REPORT
[Select Date]

OVERVIEW

1. Job Exchange Background and Description

2. Job Exchange Scope

3. Deliverables – Summary of Achievement
   - Activities
   - Time Spent
   - Observations

4. Affected Business Processes or Systems-Observed Effect

5. Timeline/Schedule Analysis

6. Positive Observations

7. Opportunities for Improvement

8. General Comments

Report Author Approval	Date	Report Author Approval	Date

Page 1 of 1

Chapter 14

The 360-Degree Assessment

By David Lafferty

CHCIO, CPHIMS

Contents

Abstract

Providing and receiving honest, peer-focused feedback can have a transformational impact on one's career. Done correctly, a health IT professional can learn from others and make corrections to enhance his or her skillsets and abilities.

I am not a product of my circumstances. I am a product of my decisions.

(Steven R. Covey)

Keywords:

Assessment
Perception Disparity
Human Behavior
Group Dynamics

Human Behavior
Job Performance
Fundamental Attribution Error

Introduction

The Center for Creative Leadership describes the 360-degree assessment as a method of systematically collecting opinions about an individual's performance from a wide range of co-workers. This could include peers, direct reports, the boss, and the boss's peers—along with people outside the organization, such as customers. This form of assessment has grown in popularity due to its ability to help individuals discern differences within their own perception of their performance (self-perception) compared with the perception of others that they work with. Often, the disparity in these two viewpoints is vastly different, something that psychologists refer to as Fundamental Attribution Error. But before we get into the particulars of the finer points of perception disparity, let's first understand a bit about where this feedback approach originated, and how it can have a transformational impact on the career of today's health IT professional.

Where Did It Come From?

One of the fundamental ideas of the 360-degree assessment, to understand and contrast self-perception with how others perceive you, is rooted in the studies of Kurt Lewin, an American-born social psychologist*. Lewin proposed that human behavior is influenced largely by its environment, with variations in the norm being a function of tensions between the self and the environment. Later on in his research, Lewin went on to develop his theories into what he called group dynamics; where he theorized that groups alter the individual behavior of their constituents.

Looking through the lens of Lewin's theories today, it's easy to view a number of examples in today's healthcare environment. Certainly you're familiar with the term "The leaders set the tone." This concept memorializes the fact that a team, department, or even an entire organization's attitude and work performance is directly influenced by the behaviors and attitudes of the senior most leaders in that organization. In fact, the same holds true when considering the behaviors and attitudes of peers in the organization as well. Quite simply, it's an example of modeling behaviors. Now let's look at just one practical example illustrating the effects of behavior modeling in a healthcare setting.

In 2014, a study was conducted to determine whether or not peer influence hand any effect on hand hygiene in the hospital setting. The study focused its observations on a 20-bed medical intensive care unit at a large university study. This study found that when a worker was alone, meaning no recent contact with other healthcare workers, the observed adherence rate to hygiene protocols was 20.85%. In contrast, when other healthcare workers were present, the observed adherence rate increased to 27.9%. The study found that this increase was statistically significant and was measurable at various times of the day and in a variety of social context settings. As a result, the study concluded that the presence and proximity of other healthcare workers can be associated with higher hand hygiene rates (Monsalve et al., 2014).

---

* Kurt Lewin, September 9th 1890-February 12th, 1947 (brittanica.com).

Fundamental Attribution Error

So we've established that the behavior of others can influence one's own behavior; exactly as Lewin had theorized. However, the example of the hygiene study clearly shows how one reacts to the situation. It doesn't really give us any insight into how or why individuals reacted the way they did. Did the sole healthcare workers make a conscience decision to change their hygiene habits on their own? Or, did they perhaps worry about how others might perceive the quality of their hygiene habits, endeavoring to make their hand hygiene more visible to their peers?

Now, put yourself in the shoes of one of the sole worker's peers—do you automatically assume that the sole worker has substandard hygiene adherence, or do you consider the very real possibility that their hygiene adherence is perhaps more compliant than your own? Maybe it's simply a matter of you not observing your peer as frequently as they are practicing their hygiene behind the closed doors of a patient room.

Often we make assumptions that the problem is the person and not that the situation, or environment, may be contributing to the problem. This very human response illustrates the basic concept of fundamental attribution error, or cognitive bias. Fundamental attribution error suggests that people often attribute the behavior of others to dispositional causes rather than situational (Reeder, 2015).

Now let's look at how cognitive bias factors into the situation of the sole healthcare worker's hand hygiene. As a peer, do you assume that that this person just doesn't wash their hands because you never observe it? Do you consider that this person doesn't wash their hands because there are not sufficient hygiene stations placed throughout the hospital? Or, as suggested earlier, do you even consider the possibility that this person's hygiene is exceptional?

By now, it's easy to establish that one's environment, the observations of others, and one's own perception of what others will think have a clear and measurable impact on job performance.

Traditional Feedback Methods

So it's clear that one's environment has a direct influence on job performance. In addition, it's also clear that fundamental human nature often causes us to assume that the person is the problem. Lastly, simple human nature predisposes us to react differently when we are being observed by others; either consciously or unconsciously.

One of the primary benefits of the 360-degree assessment is that it provides a mechanism to capture the impact of fundamental attribution error on an individual's job performance. It effectively contrasts the various differences in how others perceive the person's performance with how that individual perceives their own performance. Moreover, the 360-degree assessment also presents an individual with performance-related feedback derived from the observations of others. To better understand the differentiating benefits of the 360-degree assessment, it helps to contrast this with what is typically evaluated in the traditional performance review process.

Research

Probably one of the most fundamental challenges with the traditional performance review it that it has historically employed a top-down approach, with feedback flowing from manager to subordinate. This method is really an artifact from the days when managers were tasked with force-ranking individual employees from best to worst performance, the intent being that the lowest performers would be managed out of an organization. However, this feedback method poses at least three questions which, it can be argued, are more effectively addressed using the collaborative and peer-based approach of the 360-degree assessment:

1. Is that manager directly involved at the daily task or assignment level with the employee, or, are they too far removed from the day-to-day that their assessment of performance lacks true evidence?
2. Does the manager perhaps rate the employee that they hired as a better performer than the employee they did not hire—otherwise known as rater bias? (Sutton, 2006)
3. While the traditional top-down performance review might assess individual performance, what does it do in the context of evaluating (or improving) team performance?

In today's health IT climate, the need for instant feedback, solid collaboration, and effective interdisciplinary teamwork are tantamount to quality patient care. Yet, traditional performance/feedback mechanisms don't address team performance and, more likely than not, are not conducted with the necessary frequency so that an individual's performance can be coached and improved on a regular basis. Dare we say that the "Annual Performance Review" leaves many gaps and opportunities on the table for both individual and team performance improvements?

Administering the Assessment, Who Should Participate?

So how can we begin to close these gaps and utilize a mechanism more reflective of today's team-based goals and one which surfaces very real observations and perceptions of one's performance? To start, it's essential to determine who will participate in the 360-degree assessment process. With the many models that are available today, it's important to know that there is not just one answer. In fact, organizations may even employ a model where the stakeholders participating in the assessment may change as the employee travels higher up the org chart (Figure 14.1).

The most common methods of 360-degree assessment include a component of review from a supervisor(s), peer, and subordinate. However, many models also include a review component from an individual outside of the organization. This may be comprised of a customer, vendor, service provider, or similar party. This suggests that a minimum number of reviewers (feedback

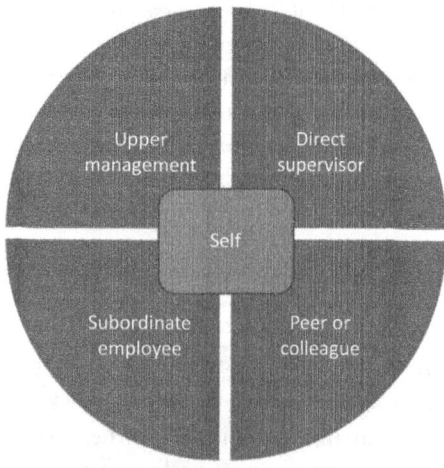

Figure 14.1 Possible feedback sources for a middle management employee.

sources) might begin with three to four individuals. However, larger organizations might select multiple representatives for each of these roles, and may end up with seven, ten, or more.

According to the United States Office of Personnel Management, studies have shown that feedback results are more accurate and credible when multiple feedback sources are utilized (United States Office of Personnel Management, 1997). However, it's also important to consider feedback sources (individuals) that are within the sphere of influence of the employee who is being assessed. So while there is no magic number of feedback sources, selecting the right feedback sources—those that the employee influences—is a critical aspect of achieving a good 360-degree assessment. Failure to do this effectively yields the same poor feedback result as that when the high-level manager administers the top-down annual performance review to a lower level employee.

Administering the Assessment, Rating Criteria

To implement a 360-degree assessment does not necessarily equate to having to completely redesign and develop new performance criteria. While we've already discussed some of the gaps presented by a traditional performance review process, what's important is that an organization has a mature and consistent process of some sort. Job performance criteria should be clearly spelled out and be related to the job description and duties of the employee being rated.

To design a 360-degree assessment from the ground up is truly beyond the scope of this chapter. There are a number of performance management companies and performance management toolsets that can be employed to build a comprehensive performance review tool. But again, if the organization already has a performance tool, often this existing tool can be adapted from the traditional approach and become the basis for a highly effective 360-degree assessment.

Let's look at an example of a traditional, top-down, annual performance review. Figures 14.2 through 14.4 depicts a portion of the annual performance review for a nurse at a large, nonprofit post-acute care provider.

This portion of the review deals with specific criteria related to the regular job duties of a nurse in the organization. Performance in each area (goal) is weighted as each item contributes to an overall score for the employee's review. The reviewer scores each item using a Likert (Jamieson, 2016) scale rating of 1–5 with 5 being exceptional and 1 indicating that improvement is needed.

Now, consider how this review might be adapted for use in a 360-degree assessment. Consider how the nurse's case manager might evaluate his or her performance of how well they perform patient assessment and develop effective care plans. In an interdisciplinary setting, consider for a moment how various members of the patient care team (i.e., physician, social worker, LPN, CNA, ARNP) might view the nurse's performance. In certain care settings, patient/family satisfaction surveys are required in order to satisfy regulatory quality requirements. How might the patient or family members perceive the performance of the individual nurse? When these various viewpoints are considered as a whole, it begins to portray a much more comprehensive picture of an individual's performance. Again, we have to remember that a key benefit of the 360-degree assessment is that it provides not only a means to rate the individual, but also can improve team performance dynamics as well.

So in the case of our example review document, two minor changes could be effected which would easily adapt this conventional top-down review into our desired 360-degree review. First, it is helpful to understand the role of the reviewer. In this case, adding a section for the reviewer to indicate their level of participation with the individual being reviewed (peer, subordinate, manager, other) is helpful. This becomes a determinate factor in how closely the reviewer interacts with the individual being reviewed. This is illustrated in Figure 14.5.

Performance Objectives
Performance Period: July 1, 2015 thru September 30, 2016

Competency/Core Value	Results Achieved	Rating	Weighted Rating
Compassion Understanding the emotional state of another; sympathetic consciousness of others' distress, together with desire to alleviate it.			5.00%
Respect An assumption of good faith and competence in another person or in the whole of oneself; a high special regard, the quality or state of being esteemed.			5.00%
Integrity Firm adherence to a code of moral values; honesty; basing of one's actions on an internally consistent framework of principles.			5.00%
Teamwork People working together to accomplish a common goal.			5.00%
Communication A process by which information is exchanged between individuals through a common system.			5.00%
Development The process of growth; to make active or promote the growth of another person or oneself.			5.00%
Stewardship The careful and responsible managing of something one does not own such as property or financial affairs.			5.00%

Figure 14.2   Example of a Performance Objectives Worksheet.

Lastly, it is likely helpful to look at the rating scale choices to ensure that they are better reflective of the individual performance. Remember, earlier we discussed rater bias. Providing a rating scale with choices ranging from "Unacceptable," "Successful," or "Meets Criteria" may not offer a suitable choice for a peer reviewer, especially one who is not a capable manager. The unintended result is rater bias, as the peer reviewer chooses a rating that is non-confrontational or overly positive. So it's important to select rating criteria that lends itself to the varied participants in the 360-degree review process, for example:

■ Consistently demonstrates behavior or skill
■ Sometimes demonstrates behavior or skill
■ Rarely demonstrates behavior or skill
■ Almost never demonstrates behavior or skill

In this way, the reviewer can select more accurate ratings that provide a more realistic picture of the individual performance.

Performance Goals
Performance Period: July 1, 2015 thru June 30, 2016

Performance Goal #1	Performance Goal and Due Dates	Results Achieved	Rating	Weighted Rating
Assessment and care planning, essential job requirements	1. Assesses the impact of the terminal diagnosis on the patient's physical, functional, psychosocial, spiritual and environmental needs. 2. Develops an individualized plan of care specific to the identified needs, reevaluates the plan, updates the plan of care when the need arises. 3. Demonstrates the ability to assess the need for symptom management and communicates with the physician and other team members in an effort to alleviate the distressing symptoms. 4. Completes ongoing assessments of the patient's terminal diagnosis and accurately evaluates eligibility for recertification using the local coverage determination (LCD) criteria. 5. Assesses for the need to change the level of hospice care as appropriate. **Measurement:** CD chart audit, discussion at IDG meeting, interaction with and feedback from CD and other team members.			35.00%

Performance Goal #2	Performance Goal and Due Dates	Results Achieved	Rating	Weighted Rating
Compliance	1. Follows standards of practice of hospice nursing as well as legal, and regulatory requirements. 2. Utilizes point of service for documentation to ensure accuracy and timeliness. 3. Determines and meets appropriate frequency with scope of services. 4. Adheres to company policy and procedures and follows these in all work related activities. **Measurement:** EMR documentation and missed visit report; Clinical director chart audits; service recovery reports.			15.00%

Performance Goal #3	Performance Goal and Due Dates	Results Achieved	Rating	Weighted Rating
Communication and teamwork	1. Coordinates the needs of the patient and family with other interdisciplinary team members using the case management approach to meet the changing needs of the patient and family. 2. Exhibits flexibility, time management skills, and dependability as it relates to all internal and external customers. 3. Consistently demonstrates all core values **Measurement:** IDG meeting and team member discussion, EMR scheduler and time log, feedback from internal and external customers, facilities, patients, and family members.			15.00%

Figure 14.3   Example of performance tactics to achieve performance goals.

Performance Goals
Performance Period: July 1, 2015 thru June 30, 2016

Competency/Core Value	Results Achieved	Rating	Weighted Rating
Compassion Understanding the emotional state of another; sympathetic consciousness of others' distress, together with desire to alleviate it.			5.00%
Respect An assumption of good faith and competence in another person or in the whole of oneself; a high special regard, the quality or state of being esteemed.			5.00%
Integrity Firm adherence to a code of moral values; honesty; basing of one's actions on an internally consistent framework of principles.			5.00%
Teamwork People working together to accomplish a common goal.			5.00%
Communication A process by which information is exchanged between individuals through a common system.			5.00%
Development The process of growth; to make active or promote the growth of another person or oneself.			5.00%
Stewardship The careful and responsible managing of something one does not own such as property or financial affairs.			5.00%

Figure 14.4   Example of a form to document performance goal achievements.

Time spent	Every day	A few times a week	A few times a month	Every few months	NA (Never)
Your interaction with employee					

Role	Supervisor/ manager	Peer	Subordinate	Patient	Family member
What is your relationship with the employee?					

Figure 14.5   Example of documenting time spent and role of interaction with employee.

Practical Applications

Evidence has shown that an effective 360-degree survey, combined with employee coaching, does have a marked effect on patient satisfaction measures (Michiel, 2015). While it may be feasible to easily adapt an existing, traditional review tool for use in a 360-degree approach, a larger, more complex organization may require a much more formalized and structured approach that takes into account the many complex relationships and factors of physician–patient interaction in a large healthcare setting.

The Pulse360 survey tool (Physician's Universal Leadership-Teamwork Skills Education), was developed by the U.S. Department of Health and Human Services to serve as the benchmark for quality healthcare. It serves as a tool to provide for patient feedback based on their experience with staff and clinicians. With Medicare-based compensation becoming closely tied to patient satisfaction measures, survey tools like this will become more critical to gauge and assess employee performance across the episodic healthcare experience.

When Conducting 360-Degree

In an outpatient setting, the value of including patient and family member evaluations in the 360-degree process becomes even more insightful. In this case, the vastly different perceptions of performance between the healthcare professional and the patient or family member becomes even more pronounced. In 2010, a study was conducted comprised of over 800, 360-degree evaluations for pediatric residents over a five-week period (Nicole, 2010). This study concluded that while overall performance of the medical residents was rated very highly from the healthcare team, the ratings were consistently much lower when viewed from the standpoint of the patient and family members. Had the input of the patients not been considered, it would seem that the overall performance of these residents was considered very positive; perhaps not requiring any further coaching or development. However, with the patient feedback included, now more specific and meaningful aspects of performance are brought to light; aspects that may have a much greater bearing on patient quality measures and overall satisfaction. This is just one example which truly illustrates the benefits of the 360-degree approach. A conventional top-down performance review not only would have excluded any feedback from the patient, but very likely may not have even rated the residents as good performers compared to the feedback that was received by the other members of the healthcare team.

No System Is Perfect: What the 360 Does Not Do

Despite the numerous benefits found in the 360-degree assessment, it is clear that there is no perfect performance-rating system. Any attempt to apply a precise measure of performance against the imprecise and complex concept of job performance can never yield a perfect result.

While it's highly insightful to gain a complete view of performance for the individual, oftentimes poor performance in one area might garner more attention and concern compared with the broad context of performance from the various raters. Conversely, overly positive feedback from many raters may hide or minimize the impact of perceived poor performance in one particular area. While these issues can be mitigated, the possibility should always be considered when evaluating the complete performance picture.

For example, an employee that does not frequently deal with patients certainly should not have a patient or family member participate in the 360-degree process. Similarly, a senior level executive should not participate if he or she does not have the benefit of some degree of close interaction with the individual being rated.

One of the other significant risks in the 360-degree assessment is the potential for the emotional or political motives of the rating participants. Consider a peer reviewer that stands to make personal or professional gain, creating a quid-pro-quo* situation. "You scratch my back and I'll scratch yours" or "I'll rate you highly if you do the same for me." Similarly, consider the disgruntled employee: "I'm going to get back at so-and-so so I'll give them a bad review." The distinct possibility of these very real issues makes it even more important to effectively select the appropriate rating sources for the employee.

In order to ensure that the assessment process is used effectively, it's important that these factors are considered within the context of the overall review. Managers (reviewers) must strive to understand the underlying causes of individual, and perhaps incongruent, areas of performance, and work to either evidence or discount that particular behavior. Similar to the well-known concept in statistical analysis where the top and bottom measures are discounted, the manager should be versed enough in the inner workings of the various departments and reviewer roles to effectively factor in (or out) these potential outliers in performance.

Conclusion

A 360-degree assessment can have a dramatic and transformational effect on employee performance. Understanding how others perceive an individual's performance can often cause a level of introspective improvement that is more powerful than a manager simply discussing an issue with the individual. In today's highly collaborative and complex healthcare environment, adapting performance tools to positively shape individual and team performance can positively affect patient outcomes and quality of care. In this way, the individual can become more a product of their decisions and not their environment.

References

Chandler, N., Henderson, G., Park, B., Byerley, J., Brown, W. D., and Steiner, M. J. (2010). Use of a 360-Degree Evaluation in the Outpatient Setting: The Usefulness of Nurse, Faculty, Patient/Family, and Resident Self-Evaluation. *Journal of Graduate Medical Education*, 2(3), 430–434.

Hagemen, M. G. J. S., Ring, D. C., Gregory, P.J., Rubash, H. E., and Harmon, L. (2015). Do 360-degree Feedback Survey Results Relate to Patient Satisfaction Measures? *Clinical Orthopaedics and Related Research*, 473(5), 1590–1597.

Jamieson, S. (2016, May 10). *Encyclopedia Brittanica*. Retrieved from: https://www.britannica.com/topic/Likert-Scale.

Monsalve, M. N., Pemmaraju, S. V., Thomas, G. W., Herman, T., Segre, A. M., and Polgreen, P. M. (2014, October). Do Peer Effects Improve Hand Hygiene Adherance among Healthcare Workers? *Infection Control and Hospital Epidemiology*, 35(10), 1277–1285.

Reeder, G. D. (2015, May 8). *Fundamental Attribution Error/Correspondance Bias*. Retrieved from Oxford Bibliographies: oxfordbibliographies.com/view/document/obo-9780199828340/obo-9780199828340-0114.xml.

Sutton, J. P. (2006). *Hard facts, dangerous half-truths & total nonsense*. Boston: Harvard Business School Publishing.

United States Office of Personnel Management. (1997). *360-degree Assessment: An Overview*. Washington, D.C.: Performance Management and Incentive Awards Division.

---

* *Quid pro quo:* something that is given or taken in return for something else; substitute (dictionary.com).

Chapter 15

Professional Coaching

By Joyce A. Zerkich

PMP, CPHIMS, ACC, MBA, MSBIT

Contents

Abstract

At times, it is helpful to have an external, third-party resource to provide guidance. Explore the benefits and opportunities when using a professional coach to help identify opportunities and challenges and position oneself for success.

Keywords:

Coach
Coaching Session
Self-awareness
Job Performance
Mindfulness
Time Management

Personal Effectiveness
Trust Building
Mental Models
Honest Insight
Aspirations

Introduction

So you've decided you want to take more responsibility for your career, but are not sure what to do next.

A professional coach enables one (referred to as a "client") to more clearly define their desired future, take an honest view of their current situation, analyze the gap between both, and define a plan to move toward their desired future. The coach asks key questions which enable the client to gain insight into what the client really wants as well as plan next steps.

Some companies offer coaching to their employees. MetrixGlobal published results of coaching in a Fortune 500 company with participants from the United States and Mexico. Merrill C. Anderson reports that the results were positive, with 77% of the 30 respondents indicating that coaching had significant or very significant impact on at least one of nine business measures: "Coaching sessions were rich learning environments that enabled the learning to be applied to a variety of business situations." Other results yielded increases in employee satisfaction and productivity: "Employee satisfaction was viewed both in terms of the respondents being personally more satisfied as a result of the coaching as well as the being able to increase the employee satisfaction of their team members [1].

The bottom line is that coaching benefits the client both personally and professionally, which in turn increases the client's employer's effectiveness.

Why Work with a Coach

Among many reasons to use a coach for professional insight, those planning their career path can explore self-awareness, current job performance, long-term career planning, and professional relationship enhancement. Coaching also helps a client work on personal effectiveness such as skillful communication, listening, social and emotional intelligence, mindfulness, trust building, time management and mental models.

At times our own mental models hold us back because there is a gap between reality and our understanding of reality [2]. In the fable about the little girl who was frightened away by a spider, her mental model was to be afraid of spiders. In contrast, the reality is that spiders do help decrease the fly population and not all spiders are poisonous. In business terms, one may have developed a mental model to keep quiet at meetings which may have been reinforced by a previous boss or employer. So now when their boss asks them to speak up in meetings, they do not speak up, which causes their boss to question their performance. Their mental model is that the spider may bite them, but in reality the spider is not harmful. A coach can ask questions to help them look at their mental model and determine the gap between it and reality: It helps them to look at the spider differently. In a constantly changing business environment, coaching helps clients explore their connection to the world today.

A great example of a coach is the sport coaches in the United States. A baseball player's coach learns the player's aspirations (become the best pitcher in the country), strengths (fast ball pitch), and weaknesses (pitching to left-handed batters) by working with them. It is through understanding the baseball player that the coach can provide feedback to enable the ball player to plan the next steps to reach their aspirations. Similarly, a career coach looks to understand the client's aspirations (such as an improved resume, or confidently speaking up in meetings), strengths (dependability, education, personality), and perceived weaknesses (patience with staff, making presentations, interviewing for a job, making a career move). Just like the baseball player, a career coach can work with the client to help them focus on moving toward their ambitions. Both the sports and career coaches provide honest insight to help the ball player/client ground themselves in reality, yet see how to remove barriers themselves to reach their goal.

What to Expect in a Coaching Journey

A baseball player and a coach are successful if the both the ball player and coach are dedicated. During each session, the coach must be fully present and attentive to the player and the player must actively listen, examine their performance, clearly articulate their desired result, and understand the gap between their performance and desired result. The ball player must take responsibility after the coaching sessions to follow through with the planned next steps because they encompass the player's journey to greatness ("greatness" as defined as whatever the ball player's aspiration is) just as the coaching sessions. Excellent ball players practice hours to skillfully master a technique they have been coached on. If a client is committed to making a change, one of the first steps can be working with a coach; however, it is not the only step. It is one of the many steps in the journey to reach one's aspirations. Commitment to a plan as well as taking the responsibility to follow through is essential for the client undergoing career coaching.

Engage a career coach if you have time for homework in between coaching sessions. The coach will usually ask questions that require the client to spend some time reflecting, writing, or even researching ideas. The homework is intended to help the client dig deeper to reveal the client's truth. Some busy clients schedule monthly coaching because they want time to absorb the information as well as do the homework. Others are anxious for a change and dive right into weekly appointments. Either way, the level of client satisfaction is dependent upon the effort the clients puts into the sessions and homework. For example, one client of a professional coach was very well-educated and detail-oriented. He was looking for a job change. He used the coaching time to help him define his "perfect" job. Part of his first set of homework was to list what he did and did not want in his next position. This required undisturbed time for him to reflect on what was most important to him (which ended up being autonomy in an IT position requiring deep thinking), what would be nice to have (work in the healthcare industry), and what he could not tolerate in a job (sales, a lot of phone calls, a lot of interruptions, supervising staff). After several coaching sessions, he found that becoming a data scientist would meet his goals and aspirations. He could leverage his experience and education only needing one or two college classes to move into that position.

Summary: Work with a coach when you are committed to taking active responsibility for your future.

What to Expect in a Coaching Session

Coaching usually encompasses several sessions. Each coaching session lasts about 50–60 minutes. The purpose of the sessions is to solely focus on the client's need. If the client wants the session to be effective, the client cannot multi-task during the coaching sessions. It is time set aside in one's schedule to stop all other stimuli and focus purely on the topic at hand: The client's agenda.

The coach will begin by asking the client to sign a confidentiality contract, meaning that the coach will reveal none of the discussion to anyone else unless the client provides written permission. Trust is important in a client–coach relationship, so this document lays the trust foundation. Without trust, the client cannot feel free to explore and reveal their truth—which is what the coach needs to understand in order to help the client.

During the session, the coach asks exploratory questions with the intent to better understand the client's truth: Who they are, what is important to them, and what is keeping them from moving ahead. These types of questions can help the client see what is standing in their way of reaching success as well as the steps needed to move ahead. Good coaches are skilled at asking powerful questions which inspire a new awareness in the client: About their life, job, relationship, or anything they want to work on. Questions such as 'What is important to you?", "What does that help you with?", "What is it costing you to continue to hold back?", "What will happen if you do nothing?", or "Why is this true for you?" are among the many questions that help the client obtain clarity. A person can ask themselves these questions, but it takes a coach to listen to the client and ask non-judgmental questions to help the client dig deeper so the client can understand their deeper truth and needs.

What Coaching Is Not

Coaching is not therapy: Coaching assumes the client is whole and has all the answers within; the job of the coach is to help the client see their truth so the client can move ahead. Also, coaching focuses on the future: In contrast, therapy focuses on what happened in the past.

Coaching is not mentoring: The coach's job is to help the client uncover what is best for the client. The coach assumes each individual has a unique purpose within our global community. While mentoring is typically a mentor helping another individual follow the same path that the mentor has walked, coaching is helping the client find the client's unique truth and path. The mentor explains the mentor's truth so that the mentee can copy or mirror the path of the mentor in order to be successful.

In contrast, the coach asks powerful questions so the client can determine the client's own course of action: The client travels their own path toward fulfilling their goals.

The Focus of Coaching Sessions

Career coaching sessions do not all take the same path. There is no written formula because each path is unique and determined by the client. Some clients want feedback on written business documents such as resumes or cover letters. Others seek to understand how to move ahead at their current employer. Others are not sure which way to proceed next and are looking to define what career success really means to them before deciding on next steps.

As an example, one client contacted a coach looking for coaching on their resume. After a few sessions, it became apparent to the client that they actually preferred staying at their current employer, but felt stuck, not knowing what they wanted to do next. The coaching sessions helped the client determine their truth, which was the need to better their team dynamic skills, become more comfortable speaking up at meetings, and prepare for their next desired career move. Over the span of several coaching sessions, role-playing helped the client increase their confidence speaking up at meetings, while deeper reflection into the client's passion about their profession helped guide specific career move preparations and next steps.

Other clients have already accepted a new job, and are looking for coaching to help them exude confidence from day one and forward. They want to start on the right foot to ensure the first impression was the best impression they could make. Still others want coaching on how to work with their boss or colleagues so they can move ahead toward their goals.

In the end: The focus is on whatever the client needs.

Benefits of Coaching

The focus is on what is right for you and no one else. Coaching sessions initiate a path of personal discovery tailor made for the client. A coach will make no judgments, which frees up the client to explore and challenge norms, unwritten rules, and assumptions. These sometimes hold clients back from developing their aspirations.

The one hour of coaching time is sliced and pulled out of the 24-hour pie of the day. Both the client and coach solely dedicate the coaching time to concentrate on the client and develop a tactical plan. The coach's attention and effort for that hour is dedicated on what the client needs so the client can move closer to the client's aspirations. So much of our time is spent on taking care of work for others: Coaching sessions focus on doing the work that benefits the client.

A leader once said "You don't know what you don't know because you can't see it." He believed that in order to facilitate positive change, he needed others to provide honest, respectful, direct feedback so he could grasp through their eyes what he could not observe. The world is waiting for and needs the client to travel the journey toward his aspiration(s) because by doing so, the client fulfills himself by giving back to the global community in the form of his skills, talents, and expertise unique to him and no one else. We have no one else but each other: Each distinctively gifted member of the human society is all that the world has and we all need every ability and talent to make our world the best place.

Opportunities Coaching Brings

Utilize a coaching relationship to dig deep into what is preventing you from being successful. Understand what is really standing in your way, what you have control over, and what you can take responsibility for changing. Just like the baseball coach who asks questions and works with the pitcher to help the pitcher learn how to pitch to left-handed batters, coaches ask a lot of questions to help the client dig deep into what surrounds the client to keep the client from taking action. It usually takes a few coaching sessions to obtain clarity on your decision of what to move ahead on. Don't be afraid to challenge your preconceived notions about assumptions: Coaching is the safe time to explore why your assumptions exist as they do today.

Be accountable to yourself by using a coach to focus on yourself and what is best for you. In the mad-dash craziness of life, take time with a coach to be sure you are focused not only on what you need to do now to maintain, but also what to do in the future to plan your success. One client asked to focus on work-life balance. She wanted a coach to help her dig deep into why her life seemed out of balance and help her plan to be more successful. She asked for a quarterly coaching session to help her keep digging into her challenges as well as ensure she was steadily progressing. Quarter by quarter she kept herself true to the balance and came to realize boundary setting was a skill she was working on in order to maintain that balance.

The coaching session is all about your agenda so ask for the help you need. Although, don't be surprised if you go into a coaching session believing the focus of your discussion will be on one topic and after a few minutes, you decide it would greatly benefit you to concentrate work in a different area. As we peel back the layers of the onion of who we are, our unique talents, attributes, and skills are better revealed. Just like the ball player who concentrates his efforts to better his pitching skills may find skills in other areas, the client may find he possesses other talents and skills which were beforehand hidden to his perception. Similarly, as a client explores his long-term career plans, he may find that other jobs may interest him that he had not considered before the coaching.

How to Know If a Coaching Session Was Successful

After a few sessions, ask yourself if through the coaching you have learned anything new about yourself, changed the way you approach a situation(s), better defined your future, became more comfortable in a situation(s), taken an active role in moving toward your definition of career success. Since the coaching sessions focus on what you want to accomplish, what it really boils down to is did you learn more about yourself, your path, and your responsibility to see that journey through.

How Do I Find a Coach?

As stated before, some companies fund professional coaches for employees. Ask your colleagues and friends to recommend a coach they have used. The International Coach Federation, https://www.coachfederation.org/ [3], has a list of coaches. Additionally, many have attended coaching training given by professional coaches at Blue Mesa who in addition provide coaching services: http://bluemesagroup.com/ [4].

How to Select a Professional Coach That Is Right for You

References from other people are a great place to start. But, to make sure you select the right coach for you, the President of Blue Mesa, Professional Coaching Company, provides these tips [4]:

- The coach offers a complimentary introductory session and does not pressure you to work with them and clearly cares that you find the right coach
- You have clear agreements with your coach regarding cost, logistics, and how you will best work together
- It is a partnership of equals; the work together is a co-creation (the coach is not directing your actions or giving advice)
- The coach creates a trusting environment where it feels comfortable to reveal a full range of feelings
- The coach attends to your agenda (i.e., the things that are important to you)
- The coach does not judge you or recriminate you for choices you have made
- You feel that the time spent with your coach is well spent
- You are encouraged to articulate and achieve your desired outcomes
- The coach is comfortable giving you direct necessary when it is appropriate [4]

Conclusion

In conclusion, life is your Journey: Find a coach to help when you are stuck so that you fulfill your full potential.

References

1. Anderson, M. (2014). Leadership Coaching Return on Investment (ROI), Available at http://www.findyourcoach.com/roi-study.htm.
2. McMillan, Micki (2010). Blue Mesa Group, Micki McMillan, MCC, "Mental Models: Why a Straight Line Isn't Always the shortest Distance between Two Points" 2010.
3. https://www.coachfederation.org/, The International Coach Federation (ICF) is the largest world-wide resource for professional coaches, and the source for those who are seeking a coach. We are a nonprofit organization formed by individual members-professionals who practice coaching, including Executive Coaches, Leadership Coaches, Life Coaches and many more, from around the world. Formed in 1995, today ICF is the leading global organization, with over 20,000 members, dedicated to advancing the coaching profession by setting high professional standards, providing independent certification, and building a network of credentialed coaches.
4. Barlow MMC, Pat (August 2016) from Blue Mesa Group; Personal Interview.

THE ASPIRING
LEADER

IV

Chapter 16

Developing as a Leader

By Christopher B. Harris
FHIMSS

Contents

Abstract

Leadership can take many forms in the workplace. Deciding to become a leader, or not, is a very important decision that should be made early in one's career. Receive guidance on the opportunities and challenges of choosing a technical versus leadership track.

Keywords:

Engagement
Leader Development
Career Development
Management Styles
Career Paths
Personality Traits

Business Traits
Communication
Problem Solving
Strengths
Weaknesses
Accomplishment
Emotional Intelligence
Attitude
Empathy

Introduction

The need for leadership has never been greater. Indeed, federal incentives to accelerate the adoption and meaningful use of health information technology continue to evolve and challenge our capabilities to deliver. The American Recovery and Reinvestment Act of 2009 (ARRA) includes the Health Information Technology for Economic and Clinical Health (HITECH) Act, which specifies three main components of Meaningful Use:

1. Use of a certified electronic health record (EHR) in a meaningful manner, such as e-prescribing
2. Exchange of health information to improve the quality of care
3. Submission of clinical quality and other measures

Simply put, "Meaningful Use" means providers need to show they're using *certified EHR technology* in ways that can be measured significantly in *quality* and in quantity. The standards that providers must meet to qualify as meaningful users are introduced in three stages. As regulations increase in specificity over time, incentive payments decrease until penalties begin.

While a significant majority of health provider organizations have implemented EHR technology, the healthcare landscape continues to change. The introduction of the Medicare Access and CHIP Re-Authorization Act of 2015 (MACRA) is accelerating the transition to at-risk payment models, which means increased focus on developing capabilities to manage populations and creating differentiated customer experiences. Enabling digital and analytics technologies is creating the foundation for competing differently for customer, physician, and care provider stakeholders.

Developing as a leader and managing your career development in these dynamic and changing times means considering and addressing the following three questions:

1. How well do you know yourself?
2. How do you develop performance potential in others?
3. How do you create the opportunities to grow your leadership?

This chapter will provide perspective and suggestions on these questions as you consider your development as a leader. An important note before proceeding: There is no right or wrong set of answers to these questions. You will find literature on leadership replete with examples about all kinds of different people, management styles, personality traits, and career paths to leadership. What matters, is what you do with the information, knowledge, and passion you have.

How Well Do You Know Yourself?

There are a variety of different personality or business trait type tests that you can take to further understand key characteristics about how you process information, communicate, solve problems, and respond to external stress and/or ambiguous situations. This is important because people who become leaders use this information to navigate the opportunities they decide to pursue and to manage to their strengths, understand their own "blind spots" and influence their teams to achieve the desired outcomes. These personality type assessments will also provide insights and actionable considerations on how to identify and assess those you interact with in a similar manner. There will be insights and tips about how to adapt your management style to motivate and engage the teams and people you interact with. Some examples of these kinds of personality tests include:

- Myers-Briggs Type Indicator
- The Color Code
- Business Chemistry

These kinds of assessments should give insights into your management style and preferences, but also strengths and weaknesses. The definitions of strength and weakness are, perhaps, different than traditionally understood. Strengths are understood to be natural capacities that we yearn to use, that enable authentic expression, and that energize us (Govindji & Linley 2007).

Strengths

- Make you feel like you can do it over and over again without feeling tired
- Cause you to lose track of time
- Leave you feeling successful or fulfilling a need
- They are harder to not do than to do

A weakness, on the other hand, "is a shortage or misapplication of talent, skill, or knowledge that causes problems for you or others (Brim 2007).

Weaknesses

- Drain you
- Cause you to procrastinate because you dread doing them
- Take you longer to do than someone strengthened by those activities
- Feel like a weight until you do it and you do not feel relief

You are best the judge of your strengths. No one can tell you what is uniquely your own strength, however, through engaged dialogue with your co-workers or superiors you can learn how you might be able to apply your strengths each week. You define what strengths you will use and how you will utilize them to meet the goals and expectations of your work each day and each week. Leaders understand that they will get the greatest return on their investment by developing strengths, not weaknesses. However, you do need to address any fatal flaws and meet performance expectations, then from there, focus on growing your strengths. You will learn and grow the most in areas where you are already strong. Developing strengths will provide exponential improvement.

Action tip for identifying strengths:

1. Consider the best day you had at work recently. What made it so good?

   This question is intended to help you identify what defines accomplishment for you. When you have a strong feeling of accomplishment, is it related to personal interactions, solving technology issues, managing an activity such as requirements definition, or testing?

2. I loved doing what activity?

   When you realize your accomplishments, what is the activity within those accomplishments that really excited you? For example, is the activity building relationships such as in sales? Is the activity focused on delivering a project? Is the activity interacting with a specific kind of technology?

3. Did you care about what the subject or topic of the activity was?

   This question is trying to understand the role process plays within your accomplishments. It may not matter the specific subject, but solving complex problems with certain kinds of people may be key.

4. Did you care about who you did the activity with, to, or for?

   Does the "who" matter in your most exciting accomplishments?

5. Did you care about the objective or desired outcome of the activity?

   This question helps identify process importance versus being outcomes driven. Answers to these questions starts to build a profile that indicates where you find your passion, energy, and drive. The challenge, as a leader, is to then make decisions about the kind of career opportunities you will pursue. Consider how you can best allocate your time each day or week to engage these strengths and recognize how to manage the teams and people around you to shore up your weaknesses.

Action tip for identifying weaknesses (Moran):

1. Notice what you are avoiding

   What are the things on which you are spending your time? And what are the things you are avoiding? If you are actively putting off the same important tasks on a regular basis and there is no compelling reason why, it could be a good indication that you have not mastered those activities.

2. Look for patterns in feedback

   Think back on your performance review history and other feedback from managers and colleagues. Does that information reveal patterns? If you have a history of different people telling you the same thing, it is worth investigating whether you need work in that area.

3. Find someone who doesn't hold back

   It is critical to find people in your professional and personal lives who will tell you the truth, even when it is difficult. They do not necessarily have to be your best friends—but they do need to be honest, trustworthy, and unafraid to tell you when your efforts just are not cutting it.

4. Get to the punch-line

   If you are often the butt of jokes about your disorganized approach or inability to be on time, it could be a clue that these are issues the people around you are trying to correct through humor. Listen to the people around you for clues about the things that really bug them, then analyze whether they are areas that could potentially hold you back.

5. Find past failures

No path to success is all just wonderful steps forward in the sunshine. You cannot get better until you look honestly at your past failures and figure out why they happened. It is not pleasant. But if you can look at the situation honestly, you can assess the role you played. That gives important insight into areas that might need work. Then, you can reframe them from "weaknesses" or "shortcomings" to the next areas you want to build in your skillset.

Another important element to consider in developing as a leader is your emotional intelligence. Emotional intelligence is the capacity to be aware of, control, and express one's emotions and to handle interpersonal relationships judiciously and empathetically (Maignan). The ability to lead is critically dependent on ability to lead *people*. An obvious statement, perhaps, but one worthy of self-reflection about how well you deal with other people in a variety of business or even personal situations. Indicators of when you need to work on emotional intelligence (Maignan):

- You often feel like others do not get the point and it makes you impatient and frustrated
- You are surprised when others are sensitive to your comments or jokes and you think they are overreacting
- You think being liked at work is overrated
- You weigh in early with your assertions and defend them with rigor
- You hold others to the same high expectations you hold for yourself
- You find others are to blame for most of the issues on your team
- You find it annoying when others expect you to know how they feel

Ms. Wilkins goes on to describe several strategies for working on developing your emotional intelligence through soliciting feedback from coaches and mentors, developing an awareness of the gap between intent and impact of your words, understanding when to pause in the moment and prevent negative behaviors, engaging in active listening.

How Do You Develop Performance Potential in Others?

Gallup is well known for its surveys and research into defining the characteristics of high-performing organizations and teams. Over the course of many years, Gallup organization has surveyed 2.2+ million employees across 190+ organizations, 40+ industries, and 30+ countries (Gallup 2013). One question accounted for 79% of engagement of high-performing teams: "At work, I have the opportunity to do what I do best every day." The results of team members who "strongly agree" they have the chance to play to their strengths every day:

- 38% higher productivity
- 44% higher client satisfaction scores
- 50% greater employee retention

Enabling your teams to play to their strengths every day is a critical success factor in driving high-performance teams. The key to developing this potential rests in the ability to listen, engage, and create clarity with your teams.

Actively Listening

The same exercise noted above to determine your strengthening and weakening activities can be done with your team members. Each team member is asked to share their strength findings. Ask questions to clarify understanding but never make judgments. The key outcome of this is an understanding by you as a leader and your team regarding team member strengths. In fact, it may be very helpful to categorize or organize the strengths to create a Team Capability Map. This map consists of identifying the key capabilities that your department or team must provide to its customers, either internal or external. These capabilities may be grouped or organized as you clarify your thinking. These required capabilities are matched against the strengths that emerge from this exercise. At the intersection of each strength and capability is either an "x" or a team member name. This allows you to see where you have gaps based upon required capabilities. It is also helpful to guide your thinking about how best to delegate and manage your team based upon their strengths. Figure 16.1 illustrates this concept.

As team members better understand the key strengths that each wants to "play" to each day, they can utilize this knowledge to help each other complete activities and tasks. You are seeking to create an understanding by each team member that enables a clear answer to: Do the people on my team know where they can rely on me the most?

It is also important to understand and document how the team prefers recognition. How will the team celebrate success and how does each person like to be recognized when they do a great job? As a leader, you will need to follow through on celebrating key successes and milestones in a manner that your team values. This leads to reinforcing positive behavior and being actively engaged with your team.

Engaging

As a leader, you will enjoy much more success with your teams by accentuating the positive and recognizing the individual contributions that each team member makes. Engagement is created as a result of many things; however, having a leader that recognizes the specific, positive individual contributions that are made on a regular basis is far more motivating than constantly highlighting negative behaviors and focusing only on individual improvement needed discussion. Gallup will

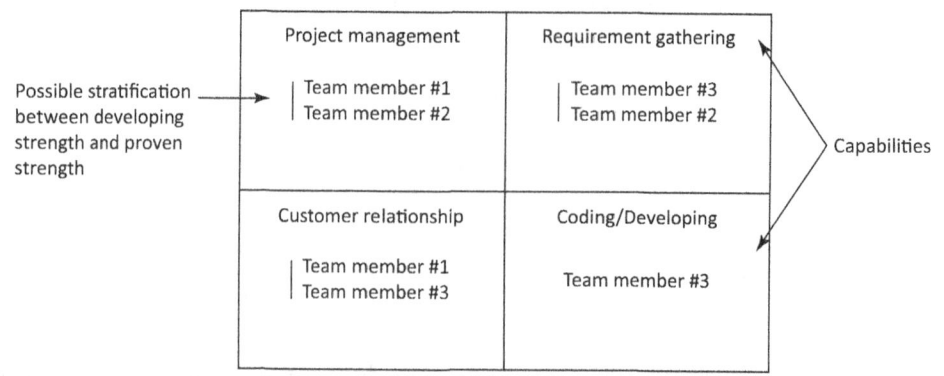

Figure 16.1   Sample team strengths to capabilities matrix.

refer to a survey question that asks: Has my supervisor or leader provided positive feedback to me in the past 7 days?

As a leader, you need to nurture and develop the team and team members each and every week through being consistent in the vision and objectives of the work to be done and working with your team members to establish expectations for individual work. This leads to creating clarity.

Creating Clarity

It is important to make sure your teams and team members understand what is expected of them at work. This means taking the time to discuss and document expectations. Expectations can include:

1. Roles and responsibilities: Defining and documenting a RACI matrix of Responsible, Accountable, Consulted, and Informed individuals for specific activities can help provide clarity between team members.
2. Behavior and etiquette around such things as meeting management, email responses, working hours: For example, establishing standards for meeting agendas, notes, timeliness to meetings, and engagement at meetings. Also, it is important to provide your full engagement in a meeting and not show disrespect or lack of engagement by interacting with your laptop or phone. For more information on workplace manners, please see Section IV, The Aspiring Leader; Chapter 19, Minding Your Manners in the Workplace and Beyond.
3. Work product or deliverable: It is important to describe and document the expectations for the work output. A whiteboard session is usually most helpful for driving to a level of common understanding and clarity.
4. Identifying key metrics that will be tracked for a work activity: Regardless of the metric, establishing a clear, shared understanding of how it is calculated and the source of data or information used is important for team member alignment.
5. Communications between and among team members: Defining expected work hours, work location and responsiveness to emails, phone calls, and pages helps to clarify appropriate use of these tools and others for collaboration.

Making sure your team members understand what is expected of them, creating shared understanding of strengths and working consciously to utilize those strengths, and recognizing individual team members as well as teams for their positive contributions in ways that meet their needs will create the environment your teams need to drive high performance. As a leader, you establish the vision, the goals and expectations for success. Empower your team to generate the great ideas needed to realize success and provide them the guidelines take action. A great leader taps into this natural power and guides the team without needing to review and control every detail.

This brings us to the topic of creating the opportunities to develop your leadership.

How Do You Create the Opportunities to Grow Your Leadership?

Creating the opportunities to grow your leadership skills is about how you take advantage of the role you currently perform and make it much more than was ever expected.

The keys to this are attitude, empathy and action.

Attitude

Attitude is a mindset and approach to how you interact with the work and people needed to execute your job. A key part of attitude for a leader is how you model it each and every day. Leaders establish principles concerning the way people (constituents, peers, colleagues, and customers alike) should be treated and the way goals should be pursued. They create standards of excellence and then set an example for others to follow. Because the prospect of complex change can overwhelm people and stifle action, they set interim goals so that people can achieve small wins as they work toward larger objectives. People unravel bureaucracy when it impedes action; they put up signposts when people are unsure of where to go or how to get there; and they create opportunities for victory (Kouzes and Posner 2016). In short, demonstrating an "I own it" mentality in everything you do will create progressively more career growth and leadership opportunities.

Empathy

Empathy, the leader's ability to put others before themselves, to seek to understand and build rapport, and to show concern for direct reports impacts the ability to build an environment based on trust, enabling people to reach their full potential (Blanchard n.d.). Your capacity to be empathic goes a long way in your ability to garner assistance and support from other people. Indeed, empathy is among the most human of all abilities, playing a profound role in being able to make meaningful connections and building quality relationships. Understanding and sharing the feelings of others enables you to interpret people's viewpoints effectively.

Recent research underscores just how valuable this is now and will be in the future. Since 1980, the labor market's growth in jobs requiring social skills outpaced the growth in jobs requiring routine skills, even routine analytical skills. Equally important, the jobs requiring good social skills are higher paying than those that don't require them. Although jobs requiring both high cognitive and high social skills are at the top of the earnings list, jobs requiring high cognitive skills but low social skills pay less than those requiring high social skills (Deming 2015).

When your team members feel you understand their challenges, you gain credibility to engage the discussion on how to address the challenges at hand. Questions that help create that empathy should be open ended and can include things like:

- How is this affecting you?
- What have you tried?
- What is your desired outcome?
- What are the criteria for evaluating the solution?
- What did you learn or we learn?

The intent of the questions above is to create a deeper more reflective discussion. It is in these situations that new or innovative solution ideas can emerge, empowering both the team member and the developing leader.

Action

The accelerant for attitude is action. As health IT professionals, we are inundated with data every day and yet are often challenged to find the right information and context to make informed decisions. Volume of email, ability to store ever larger amounts of data and the constant "on" access to the internet are examples of the data stream that can cause lack of clarity and raise more questions than provide insights. This can create barriers to taking timely action. Leaders focus first on the determining the right objective, then on understanding how the data and information inform approach and action. Data becomes information when you interpret and assess or provide context. Context can mean organizing and interpreting the data in terms of the overall objective of the plan currently in place. Further, analysis of risk, cost/benefit, options, and recommendations are helpful tools for the leader to divine the right thing. This can be confusing and, at times, overwhelming. The information becomes impactful when you choose what *action* to take with it. A quote may be illustrative of the point:

> *"I think Lee's army, and not Richmond, is your true objective point…Fight him when opportunity offers. If he stays where he is, fret him, and fret him."*—Abraham Lincoln's response to Gen. Joe Hooker, who'd asked for permission to advance on the Confederate capital rather than engage the enemy in combat—June 10, 1863 (Phillips)

The elements of attitude and action combined are powerful, but also need to be guided by several factors. These factors include organizational mission, project guiding principles, business or clinical imperatives for the service being provided. Understanding the business or clinical mission of your organization, department and work unit bound by guiding principles for the work is important. It is this framework that enables the ability to assess risks and barriers and mitigation strategies for the work that needs to be accomplished with your colleagues in support of the customers you serve. During the initiation of large projects, there are often guiding principles established that are used to inform project participants and stakeholders about how decisions will be made and the enterprise rational behind the project, i.e., the desired outcomes. Similarly, understanding and assessing risks and mitigation strategies associated with complex decisions helps frame the options for action and make clearer what is acceptable to the management of the business enterprise.

Bring It All Together

Growing your leadership skills and capabilities is about taking advantage of the opportunities to be proactive within your current role, modeling leadership behavior and seeking counsel and advice from people with diverse skills and capabilities. Establishing trust and credibility with your team means demonstrating empathy, truly seeking to understand your team member's concerns, challenges, strengths, and passions. Developing those relationships provides valuable insights into the actions needed to meet and exceed expectations, solve problems, and influence the people around you.

As you begin to put this all together for yourself, there is no right or wrong or single formula; rather, it is about how you assemble these elements into a package that makes most sense for who you are and where you want to go. Creating an action plan is a great next step in this process.

Conclusion

Our healthcare industry is changing at an ever more rapid pace and this presents many leadership opportunities. Developing as a leader means developing an understanding of yourself, including assessing your management style, strengths, and weaknesses. Also important is developing performance in others through listening, engaging, and establishing clarity in expectations. Listening and engaging others, as Gallup research identifies, is about tapping into the strengths of your team and harnessing those strengths every day and celebrating successes. Finally, we discussed approaches to finding opportunities to develop your own leadership through attitude, empathy, and action.

References

Ken Blanchard, Critical Leadership Skills, Key Traits That Can or Break Today's Leaders, n.d., http://www.kenblanchard.com/img/pub/pdf_critical_leadership_skills.pdf, as viewed August 28, 2016.

Brian Brim, Debunking Strengths Myth #1 October 2007; www.gallup.com/businessjournal/101665/debunking-strengths-myths.aspx, as viewed August 7, 2016.

David J. Deming, The Growing Importance of Social Skills in the Labor Market, National Bureau of Economic Research, Working paper # 21473, August 2015, http://www.nber.org/papers/w21473, as viewed August 28, 2016.

Gallup, State of The Global Workplace 2013, http://www.securex.be/export/sites/default/.content/download-gallery/nl/brochures/Gallup-state-of-the-GlobalWorkplaceReport_20131.pdf.

Reena Govindji and P. Alex Linley, Strengths use, self-concordance and well-being: Implications for strengths coaching and coaching psychologists, *International Coaching Psychology Review*, Vol. 2, No. 2 July 2007.

James M. Kouzes and Barry Z. Posner, *Learning Leadership: The Five Fundamentals of Becoming an Exemplary Leader*, San Francisco, CA: Wiley Books, May 2016.

Muriel Maignan Wilkins, Signs That You Lack Emotional Intelligence, *Harvard Business Review*, December 2014, https://hbr.org/2014/12/signs-that-you-lack-emotional-intelligence, as viewed August 7, 2016.

Gwen Moran, The Importance of Finding (And Facing) Your Weaknesses, www.fastcompany.com/3026105/dialed/the-importance-of-finding-and-facing-your-weaknesses; as viewed August 7, 2016.

Donald T. Phillips, *Lincoln on Leadership, Executive Strategies for Tough Times*, New York: Warner Books, 1992.

Chapter 17

Nurturing Inter-Personal Skills Development

By Dr. John R. Zaleski
Ph.D., CAP, CPHIMS

Contents

Abstract

In a health IT environment, a collaborative worksite is the norm: Rarely is anything done without the input of a team approach. Review the competencies needed to excel in this type of environment.

Keywords:

Transparency
Effective Management
Interpersonal Communication
Softskills
Mutual Respect
Honesty
Integrity

Inter-disciplinary Thinking
Collaboration
Focus
Respect

Section Acronyms

CIS	Clinical Information System
EHR	Electronic Health Record, Electronic Health Record System
Health IT	Health Information Technology
MDI	Medical Device Integration
PPE	Positive Practice Environment(s)

Overview

The healthcare enterprise involves many individuals in many roles, both on the front lines of the hospital, in the form of the care providers, and those staff supporting the various information technology systems, facilities, housekeeping, and medical devices used in patient care. As with most large and complex enterprises, the hospital represents a system of systems, in which many individuals in many roles are brought together to achieve a common objective: caring for the patient. Thus, hospitals are representative of a system of systems, each part of the whole and interactive within an ecosystem. The patient and his or her care is the object. Each member of the team caring for the patient and providing various support services for those directly interacting with and caring for the patient should know that their actions are directly related to quality of patient care: this is not solely reserved for the clinicians operating on the front line.

The ability to work harmoniously and efficiently as a team and promote positive work environments was developed into a worldwide campaign, the Positive Practice Environments (PPE) Campaign, to "… introduce and maintain improved working conditions and environments within health systems."* A collaborative effort was initiated by the International Council of Nurses, The International Pharmaceutical Federation, the World Dental Federation, the World Medical Association, the International Hospital Federation and the World Confederation for Physical Therapy. Among the various aims, some elements of positive practice environments are:†

- Fair and manageable workloads
- An organizational climate reflective of effective management and leadership practices
- Safe staffing levels
- Support, supervision and mentorship
- Open communication and transparency
- Access to adequate equipment, supplies, and support staff

---

* Global Health Workforce Alliance "Positive Practice Environments Campaign." URL: http://www.who.int/workforcealliance/about/initiatives/ppe/en/accessed July 4th, 2016.
† Positive practice environments for health care professionals Fact Sheet. Copyright © 2008 International Council of Nurses, International Hospital Federation, International Pharmaceutical Federation, World Confederation for Physical Therapy, World Dental Federation, World Medical Association.

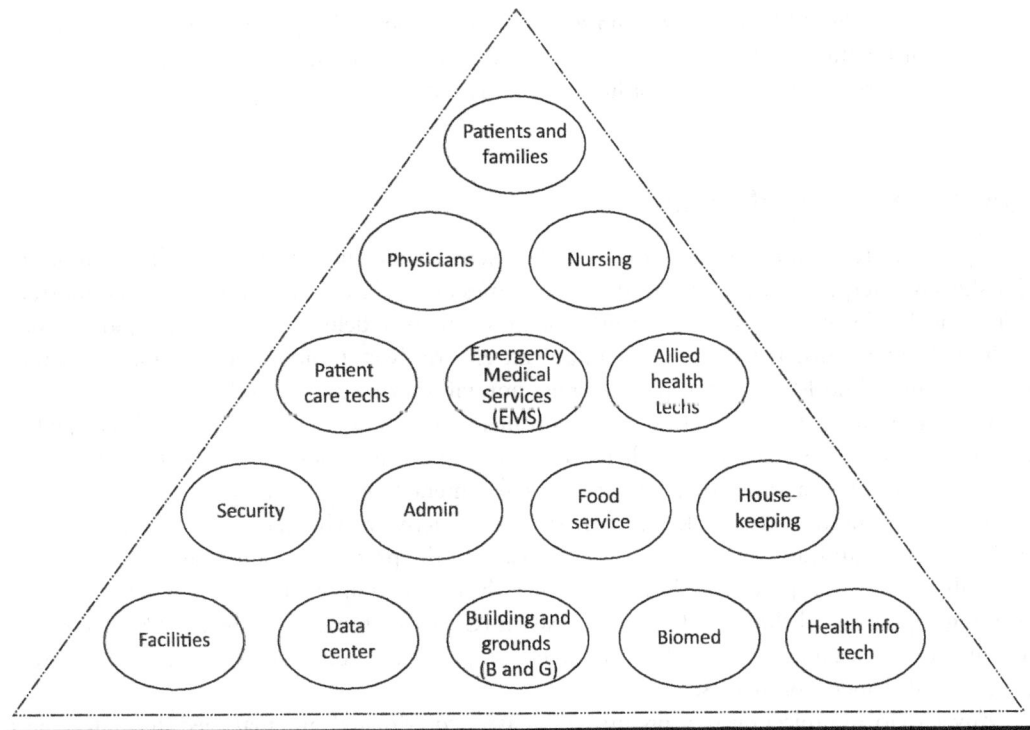

**Figure 17.1 Visualization of roles and competencies within the healthcare "Eco-Pyramid,"
with the patient at the pinnacle. Each role or competency is an important component of the
healthcare system in which individual members are part of the team.**

In this section, a review of the competencies needed to interact harmoniously and to succeed
in this type of environment will be conducted.

Health Ecosystem Team

In a healthcare environment, the various roles of individuals comprise what can truly be identified
as a team, with many competencies and roles participating according to functional or operational
areas, education, and needs. One way to visualize the various roles and competencies is through
a diagram that depicts the patient as the pinnacle of a triangle, as illustrated in Figure 17.1. The
patient is identified at the top of the pyramid (here termed an "eco-pyramid" because the representation also comprises the healthcare ecosystem).

Each functional role is essential in the Eco-Pyramid. Clinical personnel, such as physicians, nurses, and allied health providers (including therapists, emergency medical technicians,
and technicians) form the backbone of the healthcare operational environment, as they are the
frontline to the patient and meet their needs. Supporting individuals including administration,
health information technology, facilities, housekeeping, network management personnel, buildings and grounds, food service personnel, security personnel, and others provide the necessary
and supporting roles that are necessary for the ecosystem that is the healthcare enterprise to
operate.

Importance should be placed on those skills that are not only specific to unique functions, such as treating illness, managing data centers, food service, buildings and grounds, and facilities, but also to the soft skills necessary for human interaction.

Key Team Competencies

Perhaps there are no more important key competencies than communication and listening skills. The skills of interpersonal communication (sometimes referred to as "soft skills") are as important as technical skills in terms of cooperating as team members to deliver efficient and rapid care of a high-quality standard. The ability to communicate effectively is essential since without communication, technical skills will not be passed along, nor will they be understood.

Communicating and interacting with team members is a key interpersonal skill required in all aspects of our personal and work lives. They are equally as important for health information technology planning and deployment as they are for interaction with patients.

While communication is a key skill regardless of activity, whether communicating with a patient or communicating as part of a project team in the process of rolling out new hardware, new software, or new processes. As relates to health information technology, selecting or implementing departmental clinical information systems (CIS), electronic health record systems (EHR) and medical device integration (MDI) are three examples where communication and organization are essential elements of success.

Any activity or project must be organized, focused, coordinated, and managed through project planning functions headed by a project manager who calls regular meetings, chronicles minutes, follows up on action items and manages the project schedule. Furthermore, with regard to project meetings, a regular schedule should be established and adhered to. This is where laser focus on an end objective is key to preventing disarray. To this end, managing group interaction through regularly planned and conducted meetings is an important competency.

Project meetings are an essential vehicle for communication. Yet, effective meetings require planning, identifying an objective while consuming the minimum amount of time.[*] An empirical timeframe for a project meeting of one-hour duration is a reasonable outside target, as meetings of longer duration are often difficult to schedule and attention spans begin to deviate, particularly around the busy schedules of individuals, and have diminishing returns in terms of productivity, particularly with increased attendee participation.[†] If more in-depth meetings are required, these should be taken offline and scheduled as individual deep-dives into particular topics, the results of which can then be reported at the regular project meetings.

All regular meetings within the scope of the project will undoubtedly create action items. These must be tracked and identified with a single responsible individual. Report-outs on actions should occur at every regular project meeting.

Project teams, and project meetings, need to be respectful gatherings that nurture positive, complete, and unrestrained communication. To this end, listening is a key skill that should be cultivated. All members of the project team should be treated as equal participants. This includes vendors who are invited to participate.

---

[*] "Running Effective Meetings": https://www.mindtools.com/CommSkll/RunningMeetings.htm.

[†] Williams, Ray, Why Meetings Kill Productivity. *Psychology Today*. April 15th, 2012: https://www.psychology-today.com/blog/wired-success/201204/why-meetings-kill-productivity.

Organizational boundaries need to be removed to facilitate necessary communication. The points of view of all participants need to be respected in order to work together toward a successful solution. Poisonous environments wherein there is political angling, repression of facts, or oppression of individuals or necessary communication, is certain to result in failure and bad will and can result in wider-ranging impacts on the overall organization. This leads to the next key attributes: mutual respect, honesty, and integrity. Communicate openly and directly with people, honestly communicating all facts as they are pertinent to the topic at hand. Do not engage in rumor or unprofessional behavior, such as maligning individuals or talking behind people's backs. Integrity involves representing yourself and information honestly, without bias, and without participating in blame or "the search for guilt." Avoid seeking blame. Focus on the problem and identify actions to measure progress and performance. Respect for all individuals, their experiences, and their talents and gifts as individuals serves both the project and objective as well as all individuals participating. Everyone has experiences that make them unique as individuals, and everyone has value to add. It is up to the talents of the facilitator or team leader to seek and nurture the talents of all participants.

Turn frustrations into group solutions—don't sit and stew on problems. Enunciate your frustrations in a calm and clear way and solicit assistance in solving a problem. Sometimes uniting two or more individuals in the cause of solving a technical or business issue can elicit new ideas or approaches. Hence, open communication often serves the purpose of initiating the finding of a solution—expressing a problem openly serves to start the process of problem solution. Involve all stakeholders up front and communicate the importance of seeking their participation. Identify and delineate roles and intentions clearly.

Relative to staff with less overall experience, such as student interns, or trainees, make opportunities to mentor these less experienced staff. Sometimes this can be perceived as an impediment because it can be seen as taking time away from problem solution. Yet, as stated above, often involving other people can enable one to view the problem less myopically. Furthermore, mentoring is a critical function for an organization of any size as it promotes education and learning and brings forward the next generation of employees. Ensuring best practices are communicated forward is an essential aspect of mentoring.

Knowing how to separate one's own emotions from a problem or situation at hand is also a key skill. People can be defensive, particularly regarding their own ideas or projects. While a natural response, defensiveness promotes boundary creation and closed-mindedness. It can be difficult to look objectively at situations if one is bound to the situation or project in some way, such as the original creator, developer, or manager of a particular endeavor. Promote brainstorming of ideas and the creative process: Encourage participants to suggest solutions. Each participant should take responsibility for their tasks and action items. Oftentimes there are as many personalities present as there are individuals involved in a project. Some people are natural leaders, others wish to be led. While some people are tolerant and considerate of others, still others are not. If problems or issues arise with certain individuals as part of the group dynamic, and these issues rise to the level of disruption, then discuss with them privately offline.

Fostering the Creative Process

One view of an approach to interdisciplinary thinking is expressed through the four-stage model of the creation process:*

---

* Orviz, AF, "Effective Collaboration in Multi-Disciplinary Teams." © Copyright Angela Fernandex Orviz. MDes Design Innovation, Glasgow School of Art 2010. www.academia.edu, Page 10.

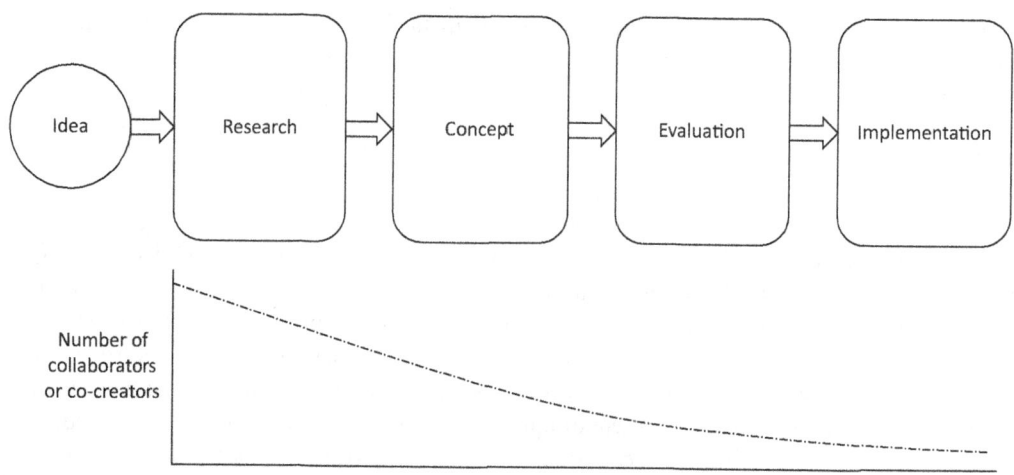

Figure 17.2   Suggested model of co-creation (project, implementation, offering, etc.) illustrating qualitatively how the number of collaborators in a multidisciplinary collaboration team may evolve over time: from many at the beginning of the process involved in defining the goals and framing the activity, to a relatively fewer number later on once the project has solidified and more specialization and logistics are needed to bring the project to fruition.

- Research
- Concept
- Evaluation
- Implementation

This model, modified from the source and represented with a relative scale of number of collaborators, is illustrated in Figure 17.2. Number of collaborators corresponds to co-developers, co-inventors, or co-creators. Oftentimes at the beginning of the creative process, many are involved in the birth and initial creation. That is, there are a larger number of collaborators present.

Ideas beget innovation resulting from a creative process, as everything that is created starts as a thought. The idea may be the brainchild of just one person, several people, or a group or committee. The idea may be related to a business objective, improvement project, or cost-saving effort or the result of a motivating event. The idea may be born of external motivators, such as regulatory requirements or patient safety objectives, cost-saving initiatives, the need for acquiring new equipment, hospital realignments, etc.

The research process involves seeking as much information as possible related to the concept as can be found. Most general collaboration occurs up-front in the research and conceptualization stages (i.e., "*ideation*"). Conceptualization can involve creating a straw-form of the idea—a model, or test artifact or implementation, such as a pilot project or limited rollout of the objective.

The evaluation stage seeks to bring recommendations and conclusions together from the various collaborators and create an objective method for establishing a decision process that can be translated into a crisp implementation. Implementation represents an actionable or operational phase which requires the carrying out of the creation identified in the first two stages. For example, if the enterprise is engaged in selecting a new electronic health record system (EHR), the decision-making process would consist of many disciplines up-front during the research and concept phases. The evaluation phase would be culled to a smaller number of specific and dedicated team members and the implementation phase would consist of an even more specialized team.

General Teamwork Obstacles

> True collaboration … means a work culture where joint communication and decision making among all members of the healthcare team becomes the norm … [is] an ongoing process that grows over time.

Ramon Lavandero*

The working dynamics among individuals vary almost as much as the number of people involved in a project. People can and will be passionate about ideas and, if not appropriately channeled, this passion can lead to arguments, lack of understanding, or the domination of the process by certain strong-willed individuals.

Listening can become difficult if you believe as a participant you have a better idea, or your ideas are not being heeded. Yet, listening can be more important at times than getting your ideas across, particularly if you can assimilate other ideas into your response so as to convey your interest in what others are saying as well as demonstrating that you are indeed listening to them.[†]

As such, a facilitator is oftentimes necessary to channel the energy of many individuals participating within the team ecosystem. As part of this, identifying, and recognizing the value of member contributions is essential. All members of the team have talents, knowledge, wisdom, and agendas and it is important to coordinate and clearly define the objective at each stage of the creative process to set the project objectives to guide and channel energies at the outset.

Individuals involved in a project have different capabilities ("gifts") that can be brought to bear and at different times during the project's evolution. Thus, at certain stages of project evolution, some individuals may have more to offer or more burden of responsibility. Human dynamics at each stage of a project need to be managed to ensure that all participants are equally valued for their individual contributions. As stated earlier, there may be some individuals who stand out more—who are more outgoing or gregarious than others. It is important to ensure that all voices are heard, and those who have something important to offer but yet are, perhaps, shy, are made to understand that their contributions are just as important. Thus, part of the role of project management is to manage the organizational dynamic of many individuals having differing personalities. These differing personalities result in stylistic and interactive differences among individuals that need to be managed to ensure the group is pulling together.

Furthermore, differences in "history and culture, coupled with historical interprofessional and intra-professional rivalries, complicate the establishment of effective collaborative care teams."[‡]

Self-perception of contributions versus external perception is important for effective collaboration as well. Hence, it is important for a facilitator or project lead to balance the objectives of the project with the talents and personalities of participants. While objective metrics for participation should be established up front by the facilitator—clearly identifying project objectives and

---

[*] Debra Wood, Collaborative Healthcare Teams a Growing Success Story. *Healthcare News.* AMN Healthcare. April 25th, 2012. URL: http://www.amnhealthcare.com/latest-healthcare-news/collaborative-healthcare-teams-growing-success-story/.

[†] The Importance of Interpersonal Skills, © 2010–2016 Saylor Academy. Page 1: https://learn.saylor.org/course/bus209.

[‡] Canadian Medical Association (CMA) Working Group, Putting Patients First®: Patient-Centered Collaborative Care: A Discussion Paper. July 2007. Page 2.

boundaries—expectations of participation as "good citizens" of the project should also be set forth to establish guiderails for expected behavior in participation.

Collaboration in Operational Healthcare Environments and Improved Patient Outcome

A suggested working definition of collaboration is to "function effectively within intra- and interprofessional teams, fostering open communication, mutual respect, and shared decision-making to achieve quality patient care."[*]

Of the key essential competencies for collaborative partnerships,[†] a suggested set of key competencies adapted from the source reference are as follows:

1. Know your capabilities, biases, strengths, weaknesses, and values.
2. Respect and value diverse opinions.
3. Resolve conflicts constructively and impersonally.
4. Seek to create resolutions and situations that allow everyone to win something in the end.
5. Recognize that collaboration requires integrating many different viewpoints and this is akin to systems of systems thinking. Contextualize the solution from the perspective of the integrated total of what the project objectives are in light of the participants and their talents.
6. Recognize that to be an effective contributor, you need not be correct 100% of the time. Mistakes are part of the process or journey of creation. Acknowledge errors and mistakes and treat them as opportunities to learn as improvement opportunities.
7. Take advantage of opportunities to seek multiple creative inputs and critiques.
8. Recognize that every collaborative effort need not require formal organizing and planning.
9. Provide people with enough flexibility to balance autonomous versus unified action as a group. People operate and function differently: some require strict direction and highly organized control. Others prefer to operate autonomously or individually and express themselves more effectively when unfettered by "groupthink". Respect all individual approaches and seek to integrate their contributions into the overall effort.
10. All decisions need not be made as a group. Don't over-engineer decisions and mandate an over-developed solution that needs multiple tiers of decision makers when solution with fewer individuals is appropriate.

Perhaps a good metric of interdisciplinary collaboration and communication in the healthcare environment can be reflected through the culture and behavior of its operational staff: In particular, the nursing staff. In one study of 100,000 nurses across 9 countries, burnout, job dissatisfaction and communication failures have been documented in large multiple-country studies as impacting more than 20% of nursing, and close to half of nursing lacked confidence that patients could care for themselves post discharge.[‡]

---

[*] Joanne Disch, Teamwork and Collaboration Competency Resource Paper. University of Minnesota School of Nursing. http://www.qsen.org (Quality and Safety Education in Nursing). Page 2.

[†] Deborah B. Gardner, Ten Lessons in Collaboration. *The Online Journal of Issues in Nursing* 2010; Volume 10, Number 1.

[‡] Linda H. Aiken et al., Importance of Work Environments on Hospital Outcomes in Nine Countries. *International Journal for Quality in Health Care* 2011; Volume 23, Number 4: pp. 357–364.

In other studies[*,†], clinical staff members of intensive care units (ICUs) with mortality rates lower than anticipated perceived their teams as functioning in better harmony and as being more trusting than did staff members of units with higher mortality rates. Finally, it is suggested that a positive link exists between healthy and positive clinical staff interaction and coordination (i.e., physicians and nurses) and improved patient status outcomes.

In yet another study from 1986,[‡] treatment and outcome in 5,030 ICU patients at 13 tertiary care hospitals was performed. Patients were stratified by individual risk of death using diagnosis, indication for treatment, and APACHE II scores. Actual and predicted death rates were compared as the standard. One hospital had 69 predicted but 41 observed deaths, while another had 58% more deaths than expected. These differences occurred within specific and unique diagnostic categories, and were related principally to the interaction and coordination of ICU staff, unit administrative structure, and treatment specializations.

Example Project Team: Rolling Out Medical Device Integration Solutions

Rolling out an enterprise medical device integration (MDI) solution requires a cooperative multi-disciplinary team involving the talents from the data center and information technology staff, clinical staff, biomedical engineering, networking and data center staff, and facilities.[§] The MDI system facilitates charting patient care device data in support of anesthesia information management systems, ICU documentation, medical–surgical units, post-anesthesia care units, and others involving the real-time or near-real-time hemodynamic, pulmonary, and cardiovascular monitoring of patients. Medical device data are required for patient care management and are an essential adjunct to clinical charting in EHR.

Figure 17.3 illustrates the high-level scope of an MDI rollout, with patient care medical devices transmitting data from the point of care (left-hand side); MDI middleware in the center; and EHR (right-hand side). Shown in this diagram are three separate components:

■ Point-of-care patient care devices (i.e., medical devices that collect patient care data from the patient bedside)
■ MDI middleware (i.e., the hardware and software that communicate data from the patient care devices to the EHR
■ EHR that receives the data and provides the user-interface to the operational end user (i.e., clinician)

The implementation of an MDI solutions represents one example of a multi-member team comprising different stakeholder members of the healthcare enterprise having different, sometimes

---

* Susan A. Wheelan, et al., The Link Between Teamwork and Patients' Outcomes in Intensive Care Units. *American Journal of Critical Care.* Novembers 2003, Volume 12, Number 6: pp. 527–534.
† Joanne Disch, Teamwork and Collaboration Competency Resource Paper. University of Minnesota School of Nursing. http://www.qsen.org (Quality and Safety Education in Nursing). Page 4.
‡ William A. Knaus, et al., An Evaluation of Outcome from Intensive Care in Major Medical Centers. *Annals of Internal Medicine* 1986; Volume 104, Number 3: pp. 410–418.
§ J.R. Zaleski, Connected Medical Devices: Integrating Patient Care Data in Healthcare Systems. Copyright © 2015 HIMSS. Pages 73–74.

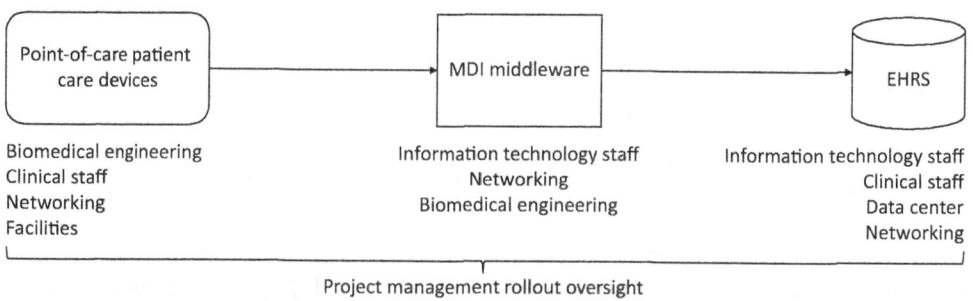

Figure 17.3   High-level view of point-of-care medical devices communicating to electronic health record systems using medical device integration middleware. Project management oversees the entire integration and members of various subgroups, from biomedical engineering to networking staff, participate at different stages across the enterprise implementation.

competing, interests, expertise, objectives, and motivations. A project manager who oversees the rollout must be cognizant of the talent, training, and skills each member brings. The project manager must work with team members to effect the rollout within what can oftentimes be a tight schedule carried out in parallel with other projects, and may even fall within the implementation scheduling timeline of the EHR.

Implementing the MDI solution involves

- Assembling the project team
- Facilitating an enterprise walk-through
- Planning, defining scope, and setting weekly contact meetings
- Deployment and system configuration
- Unit testing
- Integrated system testing
- Support and operational training
- Parallel charting and transition to live
- Post-live support

It is necessary for the healthcare enterprise to assemble a project team under a project manager or leader. The team includes the aforementioned staff members plus the EHR and MDI system vendors. Following team assembly, the project manager facilitates refinement of the configuration and deployment by scheduling an enterprise walk-through of the affected clinical spaces to determine specifics on configuration, facilities, networking, clinical workflow, and other environmental particulars. This serves to identify the target deployment environments and establish an understanding of the specific implementation, facilities modifications, and other impacts.

The walk-through, combined with an overall EHR deployment schedule and timeline leads to the creation of a detailed project plan together with an organized and regular set of standing meetings to measure progress. During the rollout, hardware and software will be deployed, both by the MDI vendor in concert with hospital personnel. Progress on deployment is reported at the regular stand-up meetings. Defining expectations for the team in terms of which hospitals and departments are to be deployed is a key goal of the project manager, as well as identifying specific tasks and dependencies for completion—with individuals identified by name.

Implementation of software includes medical device driver software. It is important for the project manager to work with the information technology, data center and networking teams to establish test environments in which to stage new software and upgrades prior to rolling into production settings. To this end, software component testing is followed by end-to-end integrated systems testing, from point-of-care data collection to EHR. This is the phase in which data mapping to the EHR needs to be validated and data posting to the chart is verified. This is an iterative process and can take some time. As such, it is essential that the project manager maintain tight reign over action item creation and closure, together with identification of individuals responsible for ensuring closure.

Training and support workflows are conducted by the MDI vendor with the project team and all stakeholders. The project manager must ensure that all stakeholders are scheduled for training and that the MDI vendor provides a comprehensive training plan prior to go-live, with all operational staff clearly identified as to specific expectations for them and clearly delineated success criteria. If training certification is offered, it is imperative that the project manager work with operational and affected technical staff to ensure requirements are met for certification, continuing education, and qualification on hardware and software before go-live.

Prior to go-live, a good practice is to conduct a "soft opening" or parallel charting, in which live charting occurs in parallel with a legacy system (e.g., other EHR or paper). The process can require as much time as is necessary depending on the complexity of the rollout, comfort level of clinicians, and findings requiring corrective action. During this stage, daily meetings may be necessary. Once all issues are resolved or a plan to resolve has been accepted by all and current issues do not represent a hindrance to live operations, transition to live operations takes place. The healthcare system, led by project management, should convene regular meetings with the EHR and MDI vendors to assess feedback on operations, report lessons learned, identify improvement needs, and facilitate a continuing and active relationship among all parties.

Section Summary

In this section a review of key team collaboration competencies was conducted. These included

■ Communication
■ Focus
■ Honesty
■ Integrity
■ Listening
■ Organization
■ Respect

All of these are key elements of successful team collaboration. The successful facilitator or team leader will seek to nurture all elements in team members and understand that a better outcome will be achieved by enabling participants to express themselves appropriately and creatively while focusing the efforts toward the objective or outcome.

Chapter 18

Understanding the Multi-Generational Workplace

By Dr. Laura Marks

CPHIMS, PharmD, RPh

Contents

Keywords:

Workforce Generations
Generationalism
Multi-Generational Workplace
Baby Boomers
Traditionalist
Baby Boomer
Gen X
Millenial
Gen Z
Leadership Style
Values

Introduction

Americans are facing a much longer work-life expectancy, which means we will now have 20-year-old employees in the workforce with those more than 50 years older. It has been common to identify the different workforce generations and to perhaps stereotype one another along age lines. As our workforce continues to evolve this may be less appropriate and we will need to put on a "post-generational" mindset. The premise of this chapter is that we cannot move beyond generationalism until we fully understand how the generations differ and, perhaps more importantly, how they are similar.

A "generation" is defined as a group of individuals born and living contemporaneously per Merriam-Webster dictionary. What this means if that over a span of 15–25 years there are significant forces at work that develop similarities within the group of people in their formative years during that time. That doesn't mean that everyone in a generation is exactly alike. Imagine a ruler and as you hold it in front of you can see that some people lean toward the left-hand side and are more introverted, sensing, or feeling, but other people lean toward the right-hand side and are more extroverted, intuitive, or thinking. With a generation that ruler can collectively be moved one direction or another to perhaps value Achievement over Power or Individualism over Universalism. We will discuss this more as we work our way through understanding the multi-generational workplace.

I became interested in the different generations when I was quite young because my family is made up of a Traditionalist Matriarch (Grandma, my mother); 11 children (8 Baby Boomers, 3 GenX); 18 grandchildren (9 GenX, 9 Millenials); and 9 great-grandchildren (Generation Z). I am the tenth child out of the 11 and so was an X'er being raised by a Traditionalist Mother and Baby Boomer elder siblings. Because of this I show a mixed set of traits that made me "different" than other children my age. As I've matured and become more comfortable in myself I show more of my native GenX traits, but will always carry certain values that were promoted by my mother (Self-Direction, Universalism, Benevolence, Tradition). My sisters Joyce and Barbara were born within the year of the Baby Boomer cutoff of 1964 making them "Cusp" children. Cusp children will show characteristics of both the generation before and after them. All this simply means that statements about a generation are merely generalizations and not everyone within the generation will conform to those generalities.

Leadership Style

To better understand how members of different generations are motivated we need to understand leadership and power. There are three types of leadership styles as defined by Kurt Lewin (1939).

- ■ Authoritarian: This leader makes all decisions without necessarily taking input from others. They may give directions only for one step of a process leaving members in the dark about future plans. This is more of the "do as I say" approach to leadership. This leader tends to be friendly and/or impersonal and uses very personal praise or criticism to motivate.
- ■ Democratic: This leader uses team input and facilitates group discussion for decision-making. This leader may give members a list of options and then encourage members to work with each other to determine the process needed to achieve the end result. This leader works freely with the group and uses objective praise or criticism to motivate.

- Laissez-Faire: This leader allows the group complete freedom to make decisions and achieve goals without participating unless requested. This leader does not offer praise or criticism unless directly asked.

Power Types

The leadership style is then combined with a base of power to achieve desired goals. French and Raven (1960) define five types of power.

- Legitimate or Positional Power: This power is bestowed on the manager through a title or role. The team members understand this role/title and believe that this position gives the manager the right to give direction. This is typically demonstrated through some type of organizational hierarchy (manager, director, vice president). This type of power uses directing, delegating, and expectations of compliance to achieve goals.
- Coercive Power: Using this power the manager enforces compliance with an order through the threat of punishment. Punishment may be official (written warning) or non-official (disappointing the leader, group pressure).
- Reward Power: Using this power the manager gives some form of reward to the member to reinforce desired behavior. This can take the form of money or incentives, gifts, or other tangible compensation. It may also be intangible such as recognition, prestige, or a word of praise.
- Referent or Personal Power: This power is based on the member's respect for the manager and a desire to emulate them. Personal Power leads by example or empowerment which leans heavily on trust between the individual and the manager. This leader uses motivation, persuasion, and cooperation to achieve goals.
- Expert Power: This power is based on a belief that the member has exceptional knowledge or skill which merits them authority perhaps beyond what their organizational hierarchy warrants. This leader uses education, expert guidance, and expertise to achieve goals.

As we discuss the generations we will discover which type of leadership style and power type works and what isn't as successful. We will also find that different generations carry different types of values, so let's review the types of values and their definitions.

Types of Values

- Power: Social status, control over people or resources; may include social power, authority, wealth, and public image
- Achievement: Success through demonstrating competence according to social standards
- Hedonism: Pleasure, sensuality, enjoyment of life
- Stimulation: Excitement, novelty, and challenge
- Self-direction: Independent thought and action
- Universalism: Tolerance, appreciation, protected welfare of all
- Benevolence: Preservation and enhancement of personal welfare

- Tradition: Respect and acceptance of long-standing customs and ideas
- Conformity: Restraint of actions and impulses likely to upset or harm others
- Security: Safety, harmony, stability of society or relationships and self

For this writing I will be using the AARP definition of the generations:

- *Traditionalist Generation (born 1945 or before)*: Also known as Silent, World War II, Builders, Matures, Industrialists, Depression Babies, GI Joes, Greatest Generation
- *Baby Boomer Generation (born 1946–1964)*: Also known as Boomers, Vietnam, or Me Generation
- *Generation X (born 1965–1980)*: Also known as GenX, Baby Busters, Thirteenth Generation (since the American Revolution), or Post-Boomer Generation
- *Millennial Generation (born 1980–2000)*: Also known as Generation Y, Echo Boomers, Boomlet, Generation Next, Nexters, or Internet/Nintendo/Sunshine/Digital Generation
- *Generation Z (born 2001 and after)*: Also known as iGeneration

Note: Some consider the end of Millennials 1995 and the beginning of GenZ 1996

As you can see in Figure 18.1 there are substantially more Baby Boomers, Millennials, and GenZ than there are GenX and Silent Generation. According to the U.S. Department of Labor Statistics Employment Outlook 2010–2020, there will be 164.4 million workers by the year 2020. This means if we used the proportions shown in Figure 18.2, there will be 54 million GenY, 51 million GenZ, 46 million GenX, and 13 million Baby Boomers in the workforce in 2020; or stated another way, 64% of the total workforce will be Millennial or Generation Y.

For each generation there are seminal events that help shape the basic fabric of that generation. In previous generations these events were country specific; a person born in 1955 in the United States might have had different shaping events than a person with the same birthdate from another country. Once we reach the Millennial Generation we find that country and nationality does not have the same impact on the development of the generation. Due to worldwide media and cultural events future generations will be referred to globally and the demarcations of a generation's start and stop dates will be less clear.

Seminal events that are scandal, tragedies or war-like events are marked in red; cultural, science and social advances are blue.

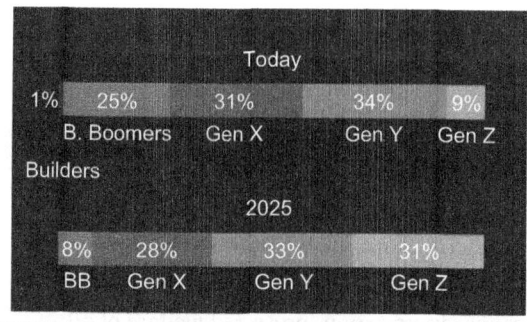

Figure 18.2 Workforce by generation. (From http://mccrindle.com.au/blog/2015/09/Future-Workforce-Generations.png.)

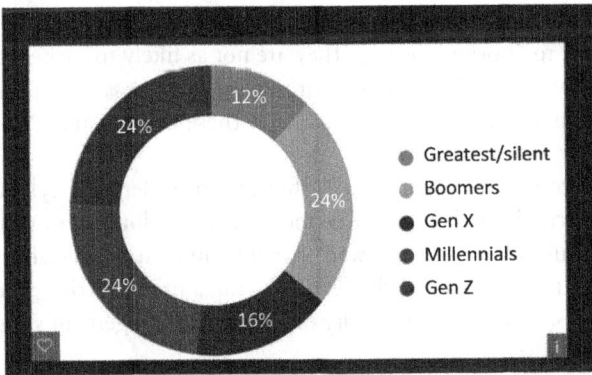

Figure 18.1 Population by generation. (From https://overtheshouldermedia.files.wordpress. com/2014/02/population-by-generation.jpg.)

Traditionalists (Born 1945 or Before)

- 1937: Hindenburg Tragedy; Disney's first animated feature (*Snow White*)
- 1941: Hitler invades Russia; Pearl Harbor; United States enters World War II
- 1945: World War II ends in Europe and Japan
- 1947: Jackie Robinson joins major league baseball; HUAC investigates film industry
- 1950: Korean war begins

This generation saw the beginning and end of World War II with all of its social, political, national, and personal tragedy. They endured rationing and other hardships while they sat around radios listening for an update on the war effort. They were much more likely to start and end their career for the same employer. They were given several compelling messages such as "Make do or do without"; "Stay in line"; "Sacrifice for the common good"; "Be heroic." The most influential technologies of this generation are the radio and the record player.

This generation's values include Benevolence, Tradition, Conformity, and Security.

Traditionalists are generalized as being a bit "Old School". This generation was taught how to do a thing and was then expected to do that thing *correctly* each time. This expectation comes with them into the workforce where they expect processes to "make sense" and assume that everyone will naturally do what is best for the good of everyone else around them.

Using my mother as an example, you don't dare trim celery and throw away the yellow, leafy innards because they can be used to make soup stock and you *never* throw away leftovers. My mother taught me how to pound a nail, stretch a fence, make a chocolate cake, and sew a dress. Each skill was taught with a minimum of fuss and covered all of the basics. Today when I cook with all of the herbs and spices used in my multi-ethnic dishes she sniffs and says she's not sure where I come from. . . a basic banana and peanut butter sandwich would do just as well.

Tradionalists now find themselves to be the minority in the workplace. This can become a negative if other generations feel Tradionalists are too focused on the "how" instead of the "what" (quality of the final goal). This can definitely be a positive if Tradionalists are given a platform to share their knowledge and experience and this is used to avoid "pitfalls" or inefficiencies.

This generation is very dedicated, focused, stable, and loyal. If they are made to feel a valuable part of the team they will use these attributes to help those around them to be more productive.

In working with this generation it is important to understand that they have been raised to not "brag" on themselves or to "bother" others. They are not as likely to express their feelings and are uncomfortable with conflict. If given a safe environment to express their thoughts they will share their concerns and opinions in a positive way. If not, these feelings may "come out sideways" in the form of criticisms or judgments.

Traditionalists are comfortable with an Authoritarian leadership style and prefer Positional Power. They prefer instructions that are clear and logical, set long-term goals, are fair and consistent, and are respectful. They can work well with a Democratic leadership style as long as they don't perceive it as too indecisive or touchy-feely. Having a manager that worries over making an unpopular decision or uses too much profanity or "trendy" management styles will not tend to be respected by a Traditionalist.

The best way to reward a Traditionalist is through tangible symbols of loyalty, respect, and commitment such as plaques and certificate. When communicating to Traditionalists it is best to use a slightly more formal language that avoids slang and profanity and to use memos, letters, and personal notes.

Remember that this generation will have adapted to technology at different rates depending on their personal abilities. Some may not even have a computer while others are on social media. If you are communicating with a group of this generation, regardless of their job or educational level, be ready to send the communication both electronically and via traditional mail. Radio ads and newsletters are effective tools for this generation.

Within the workplace this generation can contribute history, knowledge, and experience if given the proper platform. In return this generation needs to accept and accommodate the different modes of communication and leadership preferred by other generations.

Baby Boomers (Born 1946–1964)

- 1954: First transistor radio
- 1960: Birth control pill introduced
- 1962: John Glenn circles the earth
- 1963: Martin Luther King Jr leads march on Washington; President Kennedy assassinated
- 1965: United States sends troops to Vietnam
- 1966: Cultural Revolution in China begins
- 1967: World's first heart transplant
- 1969: U.S. moon landing; Woodstock
- 1970: Women's liberation demonstrations

This generation was witness to the medical, scientific, and social strides made in the post-war era. This generation was taught that you *can* make a difference and if you can then you should. It was still common to start and end your career working for one employer and American product loyalty was strong, although they have watched this erode in the following decades. Baby Boomers heard the compelling messages of "Be anything you want"; "Change the world"; "Work well with others"; "Duck and Cover." The most influential technology for this generation is the television.

This was the generation referred to in such movies as *It* and *Stand by Me* where children were given lunch sacks and a bicycle and told to come home by dark. They learned to negotiate within the group and work well with Democratic and Laissez-Faire leadership styles and they respond best to Personal and Reward power types. Boomers prefer to be led by consent and treated as equals whose opinions matter. When a leader sends the message to a Boomer that their input isn't needed or wanted, the Boomer's natural reaction is to withdraw support from that leader or project.

Baby Boomers' values include Hedonism, Stimulation, Universalism, and Benevolence.

Because Baby Boomers outnumbered the generations before and after them they have been accustomed to being able to use their collective strength to influence the workplace, communities, and the social world around them. It is only with the coming of age of the Millennials that there is a generation that equals the Baby Boomers' numbers and so we should see a shifting from a Boomer-modeled workplace to one more heavily influenced by the Millennials in the coming years.

Boomers are relationship oriented and require an interpersonal warm-up before conducting business, such as "I saw your child in the newspaper; very impressive win" or "How is your spouse doing, did they get that new job they were looking for?" They tend to be "big picture" oriented and value Universalism and Benevolence, which makes them ideal for service organizations.

Boomers prefer to use personal phone calls and meetings to make decisions or solve issues; "we just need to get the right people around the table." The tendency to see the "big picture" means that at times they don't value all of the detail pieces necessary to accomplish the tasks fully and so they rely on "group think" to fill in the details. Boomers tend to be sensitive to criticism and their preference for Democratic leadership styles means they tend to want universal agreement on group decisions and so work groups can at times suffer from "Analysis Paralysis" or "Death by Committee."

With all of that said, Boomers have a very valuable part to play in all organizations and work groups. By using the Democratic leadership style they are more likely to have "buy-in" on decisions and use the group's collective agreement to "lock-in" the process. This generation brings a personal touch, social awareness, and a teamwork orientation that would at times be overlooked by other generations. Boomers are invaluable for their ability to stay focused on the long-term goals and to stay the course once it is decided upon.

The best way to reward a Baby Boomer is through personal appreciation, promotion, or recognition. This generation values the handshake, the personal thank you, the mentioning of their contribution by name, and the ability to advance within the organization.

Remember that this generation doesn't always feel emails, text messages, or voice mail are the best methods of communication. Do not be surprised if after sending a detailed email to a Boomer that you receive a phone call in which they want to review it all in person. Personal communications by phone, one-on-one, or in group meetings will tend to be the Boomers' preferred methods.

Generation X (Born 1965–1980)

- 1972: Watergate Scandal
- 1973: Global energy crisis; Abortion legalized
- 1976: Tandy and Apple market the first Personal Computers
- 1978: Mass suicide in Jonestown
- 1979: Three-Mile-Island accident; Margaret Thatcher is first female British Prime Minister; Massive corporate layoffs.
- 1980: John Lennon killed
- 1981: AIDS identified
- 1986: Chernobyl disaster; Challenger disaster
- 1987: Stock market plummets
- 1989: Exxon Valdez oil spill; Berlin Wall falls; Tiananmen Square uprisings

When happily ever after fails and we've been poisoned by these fairy tales the lawyers dwell on small details, since daddy had to fly

Don Henley's *End of the Innocence*, 1989

With better methods of birth control and legal abortions, Boomer families were able to plan their children, which resulted in less children as their Traditionalist parents. With divorce rates doubling in the 1960s and 1970s, and the number of moms in the workplace doubling from 1969–1996, added to nuclear, religious, civil, and environmental disasters, this created a generation that clearly heard messages such as "Don't count on it"; "Heroes don't exist" or "Heroes are dead"; "Get Real"; and "Always ask why."

The most influential technology of this generation is the personal computer. While Boomers might see computers and technology as learning a foreign language, X'ers tend to be technology savvy, since they were there through the early years of computer development, AOL and The World Wide Web. This was the first generation to be more comfortable behind a keyboard or phone than in-person and so the preferred methods of communication for X'ers are voice mail and email.

X'ers, as a whole, are skeptical, cautious, independent, practical, and very adaptable. This generation tends to be "down to business," which can come across as blunt or proud. X'ers are more likely to be drawn to entrepreneurial or non-traditional work opportunities and feel it is better to "work to live, than live to work." What might appear to be a lack of interest is actually a tendency of the X'er to focus on their own task and assume that someone equally as competent is managing the other tasks. This generation prefers a Laissez-Faire leadership approach; give them a goal and let them do what is necessary to accomplish that goal. This generation can work with the Democratic leadership style as long as it doesn't stagnate or rely too much on bureaucratic "schmooze." Any type of leadership that is perceived as disingenuous (does not "walk the walk") or micro-manages and doesn't produce results will not be effective with this group. This generation respects Positional and Expert Power that they perceive as competent, straightforward, and genuine. FAST feedback (Frequent, Accurate, Specific, Timely) works well with this generation.

Generation X values are Achievement, Hedonism, Stimulation, and Self-Direction.

The best way to reward an X'er is to grant them flexible or free time, provide upgraded resources, or opportunities for growth and development. It is rare for this generation to work their entire career for the same employer and so this generation is more interested in certificates or degrees that make their career credentials portable.

Remember that this generation is about efficiency and "getting to the point," so when leaving a voice mail or sending an email to an X'er, keep the content brief and relevant. SBAR is a communication tool that summarizes information into Situation, Background, Assessment, and Recommendation. This type of bulleted communication style is very effective with Generation X.

Millennial Generation (Born 1980–2000)

- 1990: Nelson Mandela released; Hubble Telescope launched
- 1992: Collapse of Soviet Union; Bosnian Genocide begins; Rodney King riots
- 1993: Apartheid ends; Compound in Waco Texas
- 1994: Channel opens between Britain and France; Rwandan Genocide

- 1995: Bombing of Federal building Oklahoma City; Sarin Gas Tokyo Subway; eBay Founded
- 1997: Princess Diana dies
- 1998: Viagra marketed
- 1999: Y2K scare; Columbine school shooting
- 2001: World Trade Center attacks
- 2002: Enron, Worldcom and corporate scandal
- 2003: Iraq War begins
- 2004: Tsunami in Asian Ocean; Facebook founded
- 2005: Hurricane Katrina

Notice that the forming events for the Millennials are now global and include more natural disasters and terrorist threats. Belief that their fellow man is essentially good and means well is much lower than previous generations.

This is the first generation to be fully Techno-Natives, meaning, computers, smartphones, and social media have always existed for them and running multiple "gadgets" is a natural part of their daily lives. This means Millennials have the platform to act collectively, to be instantly famous, and to affect trends worldwide.

The parents of Millennials made sure these children were raised in child-centric families that focused on self-esteem and talent. In some instances the focus is perhaps on talent over success. If the X'ers had "free range" childhoods, the Millennials had the "helicopter parent" who was much more engaged and perhaps at times overprotective, focusing on providing the best education, extracurricular activities, and planned socialization while always keeping the child safe. This makes the Millennial more compatible with Authoritarian and Democratic leadership styles, whereas this generation really struggles with Laissez-Faire style if they haven't previously had the opportunity to learn to self-govern and self-motivate. This generation will not tolerate Coercive Power and might struggle with Positional Power unless it offers educational opportunities with a positive coaching and collaborating approach. Millennials respond very well to Reward Power, as demonstrated by the number of Apps that use coins and other small rewards for success. This generation will respect Personal and Expert Power as long as they don't perceive it as condescending, cynical, inconsistent, or resistant to input. A Multidimensional Power approach using a blend of the power types will be necessary for this multicultural, multiethnic, world-savvy generation. All of this combined to give Millennials messages like "You are Special"; "No one gets left behind"; "Connect 24/7"; "Achieve Now!"

The Millennial values are Power, Hedonism, Stimulation, and Security.

The most influential technology for this generation is the internet. This generation is always "plugged-in" and this can lead to some challenges in the workplace. Managers will be challenged to develop technology and connectivity policies not necessary for previous generations. They will have to answer questions like "When can members access their personal devices during the work day?" "Can we ask members to use personal devices for work purposes?" "What types of electronic security will we need to prevent hostile attacks and inadvertent viral contaminations"?

One word of caution for managers: If a Millennial is looking at their phone during a meeting they might be taking notes, so it is best to validate before chastising. Millennials are very sensitive to "isms" such as racism, sexism, ageism, etc. If inappropriate workplace behavior is not dealt with, leading the Millennial to feel unsafe or invalidated, they will tend to disengage or leave that work environment.

Millennials have perhaps spent more time using social media than engaging in interpersonal relationships. This can leave them unready for the messy challenges of work life. They may expect their manager to protect them from angry customers or rude co-workers. So, it is very important for the manager to set clear expectations with the newly hired Millennial for which situations they should handle and then to give them the tools to successfully do so. This generation is used to constant feedback in the form of likes, views, and followers; therefore, a management style of "If you don't hear from me you're doing okay" will not be successful with this generation. Managers will be challenged to find new mechanisms to stay in contact with these workers and learn to include IMs, blogs, text messages, email, and messengers.

64% of Millennials would rather earn $40,000 in a job they believe in than $100,000 in a job that bores them. It will be essential for employers to learn to relate to what the Millennials are passionate about, because the Millennials are climbing the employment ladder and they are bringing their passions with them. Organizations are already making changes to their marketing focuses to capture that $1 trillion in consumer spend by Millennials each year.

The best way to reward a Millennial is to give them tangible items of achievement such as awards, certifications, and other markers of credibility.

There is a growing phenomenon of the Millennial CEO with Facebook, Runescape, YouTube, Mozilla, and WordPress, just to name a few companies worth over $40 million that were founded and run by Millennials. These CEOs are facing the new business frontiers and applying their strengths of flexibility, creativity, social awareness, connectedness, and a willingness to use all available resources to work smarter instead of harder to garner business success.

Remember that Millennials feel you can never communicate too much. When communicating with this generation, be willing to use text messages, face time, or virtual connections to allow flexibility. Avoid sarcasm or telling them they are too young to contribute. If you pair a tech-savvy Millennial who lacks interpersonal inexperience with a mature Boomer who can accept assistance with technology while providing positive coaching on how to handle difficult interpersonal situations, you have a recipe for success.

For the purpose of this writing we will not go into depth on Generation Z, since they are only recently entering the workforce and are still in their formational stages. Some early predictions for this generation are that they may rebound from the more Authoritarian parenting style they are experiencing where parents freely check their personal and electronic space and track them via GPS. There is a downward trend in optimism, religion as the central tenant of life, and less concern with staying in style with fashion. This generation is very used to being able to digitally fact-check any piece of information and time will tell how this affects their relationships with authority such as teachers, police, and doctors, and social and religious leaders.

There is no question they will be the most cultural and ethnically diverse generation and their numbers added to the Millennials will give these two generations a platform to transform the entire business world, as we already see in progress.

Conclusion

What I hope to have conveyed in this writing is that we need to use a combination of leadership and power styles while being willing to be flexible in how we communicate and measure success. As we look to build this new workforce into one that is mobile and dynamic, I would propose the following suggestions:

- Foster collaboration and avoid silos
- Foster well-trained and highly accountable managers
- Reduce meetings to essentials and avoid inefficient use of time
- Allow flexibility in work and communications styles
- Give feedback in real time and communicate more than you think is enough

As we move into a post-generational mindset we will thoughtfully provide a work environment that has clearly identified mission, vision, and goals. This workplace will use a combination of communication styles to accommodate all needs and will allow a certain amount of flexibility in the workplace to include off-site, virtual, global, as well as in-person staffing models. This workplace model would respect all persons and accept the different cultural influences, providing needed training in multiple formats to create accountable managers.

There will be many stubbed toes and pitfalls as we move through the evolving workplace. But, if we keep an open ear and value each other's needs, we will see remarkable growth and success in the years to come.

Bibliography

1. AARP; Leading a Multigenerational Workforce; 2007.
2. Planning for Success in the Multigenerational Workforce; Mark Taylor; 2015; www.taylorprograms.com.
3. Tackling the Challenges of the Multigenerational Workforce; Nicole Fallon; *Business News Daily*; June 16, 2014.
4. Effectively Managing the Multigenerational Workforce; *Under30CEO*; August 25, 2011.
5. Leading a Multigenerational Nursing Workforce: Issues, Challenges and Strategies; Rose Sherman; *The Online Journal of Issues in Nursing*; 2006.
6. Why You Should Plan to Work Until Age 70; Emily Brandon; July 9, 2012.
7. Why can't Generation X get ahead at work? Ronald Alsop; July 11, 2013.
8. Old School Management Tweaks for a New Generation; Ryan Mead; August 12, 2015.
9. Facts about the Millennial Generation; Fred Dews; June 2, 2014; http://www.brookings.edu/blogs/brookings-now/posts/2014/06/11-facts-about-the-millennial-generation.
10. Leadership Styles and Bases of Power; David A. Victor, revised by Monica C. Turner; http://www.referenceforbusiness.com/management/Int-Loc/Leadership-Styles-and-Bases-of-Power.html.
11. Types and Values over Generations; Vera Routamaa, Katri Heinasou; Psychological Type and Culture—East & West: A Multicultural Research Conference, Honolulu, Hawaii, January 6–8, 2006; http://typeandculture.org/Pages/C_papers06/RoutamaaGenerations2.pdf.
12. Employee Outlook: 2010–2020—Occupational employment projections to 2020; C. Bret Lockard and Michael Wolf; *Monthly Labor Review*; 2012.

Chapter 19

Minding Your Manners in the Workplace and Beyond

By Michelle Cotton

CPA, CPHIMS, CIA, CFE, CCA

Contents

Abstract

Growing up, it is highly likely that you were told to say "please" and "thank you." While this is excellent advice, recognizing proper manners and etiquette in the workplace (and beyond) will serve your career in a very positive way.

Keywords:

Etiquette
Advice
Manners
Kindness
Constructive Criticism
Interruptions
Communication

Introduction

In this chapter, you will have the opportunity to recognize proper manners and etiquette in the workplace as we walk through five manners of the past and how to incorporate those prior learnings into your present and future. Please join us as we take a walk down memory lane and remember the importance of saying "please" and "thank you," being kind, paying attention, not interrupting, and holding the door for others.

Please and Thank You

Did you ever wonder why adults told you to say "please" when you were younger? Is it not quicker to just say what you need and drop the "please"? Beginning a request with "please" is a sign of respect. Without the "please," your request can come across as an order. Do you ever find yourself saying "Do this" or "I need that"? Statements beginning with those phrases can be perceived as orders and could immediately put others in a position where they are less willing or eager to do something for you. Regardless of whether the recipient of the request reports to you or is paid to perform the task, you should still treat him or her with respect. Would you not rather be politely asked to do something than told to do something?

And what about "thank you"? Most individuals enjoy gratitude in some form or fashion. Think about what a boost it was the last time someone thanked you for a job well done in front of your boss. Now pay it forward and do that for someone else when that someone else is deserving. If someone does you a favor, and you are gracious, that will likely warrant the receipt of favors from that individual in the future.

Be Kind

Remember hearing the phrase "kill them with kindness"? Interestingly enough, this also applies in the professional setting. Think about a time when you were conversing with someone regarding a problem that needed to be solved and brainstorming potential solutions where you had conflicting opinions. How did you respond when the individual proposed a solution that was in direct conflict with your opinion on how to solve the problem? Was your initial response "I don't think that's right," or "I disagree with you"? If so, you may want to consider rethinking your word choice. Responses of that nature often put the other individual in the conversation in a defensive position and could lead him/her to perceive that you are closed-minded and not open to a discussion. Now, try this: "OK, I think I'm following you. I'm seeing it a little differently, but maybe you can help me better understand your thinking." That opens the door for healthy dialogue while still getting your point across.

And what about those times when you have had to provide constructive criticism? It is of course important to have those tough conversations as it is a disservice to others to not, but you can always lead with kindness and respect. Let us think about two different approaches to these types of discussions and which we might prefer.

First, your boss sits you down and says, "I have significant concerns about your performance and fear you may not be able to do this job. You're going to have to make some changes." How would that make you feel? You might immediately engage from a defensive position into what one might consider a more hostile conversation. Now let us think about a second approach. In the same situation, your boss sits you down and says, "Thank you for the time and effort you put into this project. I'd like to chat about how we can improve the next time. We, myself included, always have opportunities to improve, and I'd like us to work through how we can make sure you have the necessary tools to do your job so we can be more successful in the future."

Safe to say, the majority of us would prefer this approach. While it may require a greater investment of time, the recipient of this message would likely be less defensive, and the boss would be able to get his or her point across while simultaneously preserving the relationship. So next time you have a tough conversation ahead of you, take a minute to think about how you can "kill them with kindness."

Pay Attention

Remember you parents telling you to pay attention and listen to others? The same goes for the professional environment. If you are at a presentation, meeting, or something of the like where someone has taken the time to prepare for the event, show them respect and pay attention. In these situations, it is important to give your undivided attention to the presenter or meeting leader. While you may believe you are quite talented when it comes to multitasking (and you probably are), if you are working on your computer, consistently checking your phone, or taking calls in the room, you are sending a message to those engaged in the discussion that you do not value their time nor do you value their contributions to the discussion.

If you are unable to give your undivided attention, it is best to bow out gracefully and conduct your work outside of the presentation or meeting setting. Now pay attention to this last thought: Everyone in the room notices your actions, and if you happen to be in a leadership position, what kind of example are you setting for others?

Don't Interrupt Others

It is important to remember to listen first and engage second. When you interrupt, you are likely losing out on valuable information you would have otherwise gained if you had just let the other individual complete his or her thought. You are also, albeit likely unintentionally, sending the message that what you have to say is more important than what others are attempting to contribute to the discussion. With that being said, we all know it happens from time to time. So when you do interrupt someone (again, hopefully unintentionally), simply apologize for the misstep (yes, another manner we learned as a child) and let the other individual complete his or her thought.

Now let us consider technology interruptions. In this fast-paced world we live in of everevolving technology and social media (constant emails, instant messages, texts, scheduling meetings over meetings), patience is quickly becoming a lost virtue. What we may forget is that some may perceive these "need it now" forms of communication as interruptions. Be mindful when communicating via technology and scheduling meetings. Think about what it is you need before selecting your method of communication. Is it a quick question like "Can you remind me how many people will be attending the design session tomorrow?" Or is it a question or need where a more detailed discussion is likely warranted, such as "Would you please share your ideas as to how we can best plan and prepare for the upcoming design session?" While the former might best be accomplished via instant messaging, the latter may require a phone call or in-person discussion. For the latter, a nice marriage of two communication methods might serve you best in that you could instant message the individual asking "Mind if I hop on your calendar for a quick discussion about the upcoming design session?" You can then follow up by scheduling a meeting when the individual is available. Incorporating other previously discussed manners of "please and thank you" and "be kind" will also serve you well in these situations.

Hold the Door

In its literal interpretation, we should of course still do this today (remember "be kind"), but how can we also apply this old-school learning in our professional environment? It is actually quite simple. Offer to help when help is needed. We often get bogged down in our own world and forget we have value to offer in other areas of the organization. By offering to help others, there are multiple benefits to be achieved. First, you are leading with kindness and that will be respected. Second, you are showing you are willing to do anything and that you do not have the "that's not my job" mindsight. Lastly, you will likely become a better employee as you will learn more about the individual you are helping as well as the organization as a whole; you will be more educated as a result.

A wise approach is to always raise your hand, literally and figuratively, when given the opportunity and rarely say no. While you may feel overworked from time to time (as we all do), the value in raising your hand when volunteers are requested and not turning down opportunities that come your way will greatly outweigh the cost of performing the work.

Conclusion

To sum it up, surprise surprise, something you learned as a child is actually relevant in your adult life. Falling back on the manners outlined in this chapter will serve you well as you continue on your health IT journey. So remember, say "please" and "thank you," be kind, pay attention, don't interrupt, and hold the door for others. And now, last but not least, thank you for your time!

Chapter 20

Encouraging Diversity in the Workplace

By John A. Mandujano
CPHIMS, PMP

Contents

Abstract

Diversity in the workplace can take many forms like work ethics, cultural sensitivity, inclusionary behavior, patient care, and beyond. Identify the many ways that the health IT professional can ensure a balanced approach to diversity in all things health IT.

Keywords:
Diversity
Linguistic Relativism
Sensitivity
Mindful
Opportunities
Cultural Competence
Respect
Empathy

Introduction

The cultural and demographic character of the patient population is changing rapidly. To accept and prepare for this rapid change, the health information technology community, which is experiencing its own changes, must embrace diversity to be successful in their initiative to delivering quality healthcare. In addition, as patients become more educated on medical procedures and risks, they also have more information regarding health grades among competing medical providers. If a provider organization intends to succeed in this competitive environment, it must leverage the best personnel with the best ideas, which may come from unfamiliar ethnic and cultural backgrounds.

Access the Healthcare: A Statistical Review

Prior to the enactment of the The Patient Protection and Affordable Care Act (PPACA) of 2010, ethnic and minority groups did not have as much access to healthcare. In 2009, 79% of African Americans, 68% of Hispanic Americans, and 88% of white Americans had health coverage. The resulting lack of health coverage is reflected in chronic health statistics. African Americans have higher rates of obesity, diabetes, hypertension, and heart disease than another group. Hispanic women contract cervical cancer at twice the rate of white women. Hispanics are 50% more likely to die of diabetes as non-Hispanic whites [1]. In the United States, although the population is expected to grow more slowly, the mix of cultures, races, and nationalities will give that population a decidedly different content. By 2030, one in five Americans will be 65 or older. By 2044, more than half of all Americans are projected to belong to a minority group. And by 2060, nearly one in five of the United States' total population is expected to be foreign born. The Hispanic population in the United States is projected to increase from 55 million in 2014 to 119 million in 2060, an increase of 115%. Twenty-nine percent of the United States is projected to be Hispanic—more than one-quarter of the total population [2].

Respecting Cultural Sensitivities

In most industries, customer service representatives have to evaluate customers to determine their level of sensitivity. Healthcare workers are in a unique situation in that they are already aware, or should be aware, that all patients are especially sensitive. Patient families are also very sensitive.

Healthcare workers are mindful that emotions are raw and care has to be taken to explain circumstances and protocols. We take into account that some patients may opt not to have a blood transfusion or an organ transplant for religious reasons. Being aware of a patient's culture is part of delivering quality care. To a certain extent, that same courtesy should extend to fellow healthcare workers.

Shortages of Healthcare Workers

The current shortage of healthcare workers, particularly among nurses, will increase the demand for alternatives like using more foreign-born healthcare workers. Healthcare workers with less than a bachelor's degree are racially and ethnically more diverse and overwhelming female. Men are the minority of all of these professions except for emergency medical technicians and paramedics [3].

The aforementioned shortage of healthcare workers will also increase pressure to utilize more technology to improve productivity and allow healthcare specialists to give more attention to patients. Some of these technologies might consist of telemedicine and advanced monitoring systems, including implants. The health information technology community, largely responsible for the implementation of these technologies, has also demographically changed dramatically in the past 20 years largely due to the influx of H-1B non-immigrant workers [4] and the increasingly diverse population.

This is the situation: The landscape of the healthcare workplace is experiencing demographic changes in patient population, healthcare workers and IT technicians. Healthcare organizations need to establish new structural policies and procedures, also known as cultural competence, to encourage and leverage diversity on all levels and to work effectively in this cross-cultural environment [5].

Equal Employment Opportunities for All

Employers are required to provide equal employment opportunities (EEO) based on qualifications and related experience and not on the basis of extraneous factors such as race, color, religion, national origin, disability, age, gender, gender identity, sexual orientation, veteran status, or marital status. Employers further this policy by issuing guidelines regarding conduct in the workplace and typically enforce zero tolerance toward discrimination or harassment. These policies are commendable, but one cannot judge a policy based on intentions. Large corporations satisfy many EEO goals by recruiting minorities at college job fairs, but similar opportunities for more experienced professionals are lacking. A better metric would track how minority employees advance within a corporation. If minority employees are not given high-profile assignments, their chances for advancement are impacted. One could argue the assignment of work may be discriminatory. Eventually, it is reflected in the lack of minority representation on corporate boards of directors [6].

Diversity Programs that Respect ime Away from Employment

Diversity programs do not have to be a drudgery or stilted in regulation. It can be as simple of being more aware of holidays, including holidays we might take for granted. A foreign worker may not be aware that July 1 is Canadian Independence Day and July 4 is American Independence

Day in the United States. Most cultures have a holiday that celebrates the annual harvest like Thanksgiving, the fourth Thursday in November in the United States, but Canadian Thanksgiving is celebrated on the second Monday in October. Hindis in North America celebrate Diwali in autumn and often include elements of Thanksgiving. Inventive organizations incorporate Diwali with Thanksgiving for a celebration of food from all nationalities.

Some holidays are not actual holidays but if the majority of employees do not come to work, it may seem like a holiday. For example, at some companies in upstate New York and Pennsylvania, so many people arrange personal time off on the first day of deer hunting season it may seem like a holiday. In addition, someone originally from outside of the United States might be confused how Americans have appropriated St Patrick's Day and Cinco de Mayo into an unofficial holiday. Keeping everyone informed of respective holidays can be instructive and entertaining.

We can allow religion to divide us or unite us. Respecting each other's beliefs should direct us to concentrate on what we all have in common, like a belief in a higher power. A Muslim hijab is not very different than a veil or a habit a nun might wear or attire preferred by the Amish. Hindis might have a tilak on their forehead, much like Roman Catholics might have ashes on their forehead on Ash Wednesday. I believe the Camp David accord was successful because Jimmy Carter, Menachem Begin and Anwar El Sadat respected each others' religious beliefs and recognized the divinity inherent in all of us [7].

Linguistic Relativism

Linguistic relativism hypothesizes that language affects cognition [8]. Imagine hearing a phrase where you know all the words but the words does not connect to your reality. To tell someone they are "out in left field" or "off base" or warned they already have "two strikes" is meaningless to someone unfamiliar with the sport of baseball. Or someone unfamiliar with American football may not realize a "Hail Mary" is a last-minute, desperate attempt at success. Even among Americans there can be misunderstanding. Someone recently told me they read me "five by five." Apparently, this is a military term meaning they understood me loud and clear. However, since I was never in the military, their message was unclear to me. In an environment where people accept each other's differences, there is no fear of asking for a definition of a colloquial phrase. A helpful phrase like "bindaas" can build bridges across cultures. "Bindaas" is Hindi slang for "cool."

Management Awareness and Sensitivity

Being aware of current events in other cultures is also important. Personally, I have visited a hospital where the nurses were predominantly Filipino. Likewise, I also consulted at a pharmaceutical distribution corporation that used many contract IT workers from the Philippines. In either case, it is helpful to be aware when a typhoon impacts the Philippines. Understanding their concern for their families would be completely justified.

As some advance to middle management, many are now evaluated on how they have mentored others. Such mentoring initiatives can reap benefits throughout an entire organization. Like The Butterfly Effect in Chaos Theory [9] that says a butterfly flapping its wings at the right time and place in Africa could spur the creation of a hurricane in the Atlantic Ocean, encouragement at all levels to all employees has a ripple effect, encouraging advancement and productivity. Mentoring does not have to be a formal program. But it should recognize the importance of an encouraging environment. Identify talent and encourage it. The other side of that transaction is that we should all be open to accept mentoring and be willing to adapt. The extent to which you will improve is dependent upon your willingness to accept constructive guidance. If you are not comfortable with coaching or mentoring at work, seek out mentoring outside of the workplace. Mentors can be anyone you feel comfortable with.

When a complaint is made, it is absolutely vital that an organization act quickly and decisively on complaints. Not acting quickly sends the message that the organization does not take complaints of discrimination or harassment seriously. We should know better. We should not have to cite respective codes of professional responsibility. Treating each other with respect should be the norm.

The Under-represented Workforce

For those of us that are under-represented in the workforce, an honest self-examination is in order. What makes you different? Is it your race, heritage, religion, language, physical size, gender, sexual orientation, age, physical disability, political orientation, socio-economic status, occupational status, or geographical origin? Your differences might be based on your experiences. For example, in an acute care setting, your opinion may be dismissed because you were never a healthcare worker like a doctor or a nurse. The truth is, if you are a member of a minority group, it is not enough to be competent. Everyone expects you to be competent. To advance, you have to obtain certifications, pursue advanced education, and work harder. To stand out from your peers, you have to take the initiative, like volunteering for leadership positions. If those opportunities are not forthcoming at work, volunteer outside of work, build your confidence, and bring that confidence back to your job.

Opportunities are not delivered to your doorstep. You have to pursue them and be prepared to act. When should you pursue opportunities? Recent studies have shown that male applicants typically do not possess 100% of the qualifications for a position, while female applicants will only apply for a position if they have all 100% of the qualifications [10]. Hiring organizations need to evaluate their judgment and recognize that males are being judged for their potential and females are being judged on their track record. They should be judged by the same criteria and be aware of gender bias. Part of the self-examination process should include identifying instances when you have held yourself back.

The Dalai Lama has said, "If every 8 year old in the world is taught meditation, we would eliminate violence from the world within one generation [11]." Consider how that same dynamic could be applied to educating under-represented children. Boosting diversity in the workplace and, thereby, improving the competitive placement of healthcare organizations begins with encouraging children to pursue their interests in the sciences and technology. A balanced education that includes science and the arts, to encourage creativity, would greatly improve all children. If a young girl or minority shows interest in science, we should all encourage that interest.

Initiatives like "Take Your Children to Work Day" are wonderful for showing children what adults do at work. Understandably, many that work at acute care facilities are unable to participate in such initiatives due to the nature of their work, liability insurance issues, and safety. In the absence of such participation, parents and guardians should teach their children about their careers and they should also be involved in their children's education. I am most impressed with parents that take the time to work with their children on their home assignments. This degree of involvement is most admirable. Granted, due to circumstances beyond their control, not every guardian can meet this demand. A guardian's interest, any interest, in the progress of their progenies has a lasting impact.

Respecting Others

In addition to learning subjects in school, a child's upbringing should also include lessons at home regarding teaching respect of other people. Respect for others is good parenting. Guardians need to communicate to their children the importance of courteous behavior or else children will consider other sources of information like the internet, video games, or television programming as models of acceptable behavior. Learning respect for others begins with active parenting [12].

Patients and co-workers come from varied cultural backgrounds and experiences. Allow your good work ethic to guide your behavior. Concentrate on providing quality healthcare and excellent customer service and know that everyone around can contribute to that success.

Too often, we rely on what is legislated to guide our behavior. Too many unethically sanctioned legal policies like slavery, the Holocaust and segregation are abhorrent in a civilized society. Even great thinkers like Aristotle and Thomas Aquinas relegated women to an inferior moral status. If we recognize everyone has equal moral status, it is more logical to accept an egalitarian society where differences are accepted. Indeed, we are different but like two sides of a dollar bill, we are different and we are the same. We come from different backgrounds and have had different environmental factors that formed us. But together, we deliver healthcare to patients. Like the seal of the United States declares, "E Pluribus Unum" which is Latin for "Out of many, one."

Many acute care facilities have interpreters on staff as well as post-operative care instructions in multiple languages. As a supplement to those efforts and to gain additional insight into the needs of a diverse and sometime unfamiliar patient population, I strongly suggest a tremendous resource on the web from the U.S. Department of Health and Human Services, National Library of Medicine, and National Institute of Health: https://sis.nlm.nih.gov/outreach/multicultural. html. This web portal is specifically for healthcare professionals. Topics include guidelines for cultural competency in a healthcare setting, standards for interpreters, and information on many healthcare topics designed for different cultures. More information can be found at https://sis.nlm. nih.gov/outreach/multicultural.html.

National Library of Medicine's Outreach and Special Populations Branch

In 2000, the National Library of Medicine (NLM) created the Office of Outreach and Special Populations (OOSP) in the Division of Specialized Information Services (SIS) as a way to focus efforts to reach its objectives of improving access to quality and accurate health information in underserved and special populations. In 2008, the Office was elevated to the Outreach and Special Populations Branch (OSPB).

Outreach programs are developed in an effort to eliminate disparities in accessing health information by providing community outreach support, training health professionals on NLM's health information databases, and designing special population websites that address specific concerns in various racial and ethnic groups. SIS outreach programs reach health professionals, public health workers, and the general public, especially about health issues that disproportionately impact minorities such as environmental exposures and HIV/AIDS. OSPB collaborates with other components of NLM involved in similar activities, particularly the National Network of Libraries of Medicine and the Office of Health Information Programs Development.

OSPB is committed to improving access to toxicology and environmental health information to underserved communities, improving access to health-related disaster information in Central America, improving access to HIV/AIDS information resources by community-based organizations, and improving access to health information for all minorities and underserved populations.

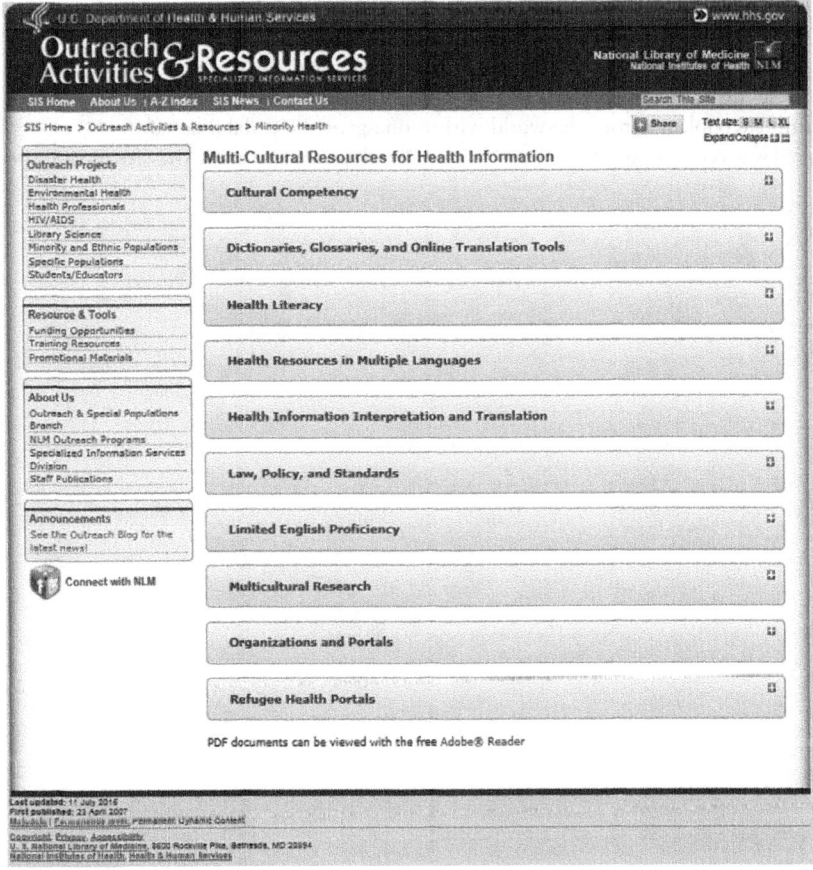

Summary

Patient, health care worker and health care vendor players are undergoing changes in their cultural, racial and gender makeup. In order to compete and accept the challenge of providing quality health care in this changing environment, all players need to embrace diversity. Recognizing similarities, accepting each other customs and realizing our customs may seem unusual to others helps to create an environment where we can all work together toward common goals.

References

1. https://www.americanprogress.org/issues/healthcare/news/2010/12/16/8762/fact-sheet-health-disparities-by-race-and-ethnicity/.
2. Colby, Sandra L. and Jennifer M. Ortman, Projections of the Size and Composition of the U.S. Population: 2014 to 2060, Current Population Reports, P25-1143, U.S. Census Bureau, Washington, DC, 2014.
3. http://www.rand.org/news/press/2013/11/04/index1.html.
4. http://www.judiciary.senate.gov/meetings/the-impact-of-high-skilled-immigration-on-us-workers.
5. http://www.nccccurricula.info/culturalcompetence.html.
6. http://www.nytimes.com/2014/06/01/business/not-walking-the-walk-on-board-diversity.html?_r=0.
7. http://www.npr.org/2014/09/16/348903279/-13-days-in-september-examines-1978-camp-david-conference.
8. http://www.linguisticsociety.org/resource/language-and-thought.
9. http://fractalfoundation.org/resources/what-is-chaos-theory/.
10. https://hbr.org/2014/08/why-women-dont-apply-for-jobs-unless-theyre-100-qualified.
11. https://responsiveuniverse.me/2012/11/20/if-every-8-year-old-in-the-world-is-taught-meditation-we-will-eliminate-violence-from-the-world-within-one-generation-dalai-lama/.
12. http://www.parents.com/toddlers-preschoolers/development/manners/the-return-of-respect/.

Chapter 21

The Aspiring Female Health IT Executive

Kristin Myers

MPH

Contents

Abstract

While the health IT workforce has traditionally been dominated by males, female health IT professionals are achieving recognition at faster rates than ever before. But there is more work to be done. Identify the challenges, barriers and opportunities facing the aspiring female health IT executive.

Keywords:

career ladder
Networking
Mentoring
Sponsorship
Career Development
Pay Differentials
Gender Parity

Salary Transparency
Negotiating Skills
Gender Stereotypes
Collaborative Environment
Advocating
Female leader

Introduction

As a female Vice President in the Information Technology Department at Mount Sinai Health System, a $7 billion not-for-profit organization, I have been fortunate to have had supervisors, senior executives, colleagues, and my team be supportive of my career aspirations and have received the training and education needed to progress. I have been entrusted with many complex transformative programs exceeding $100 million which make a difference to our patient lives every day.

For the majority of the last 20 years in health information technology, I have been very focused on my career development. My attitude has always been that I can achieve anything that I want to do or be, which was a common mantra from my parents since I was a child. My parents and brother always encouraged and supported me throughout my career and in all aspects of life.

However, in the last three years, after becoming a mother, I have had to change how I work, what I focus on and prioritize, and how I spend time with my son every single day. I have reflected on the many challenges, barriers, and opportunities that women face in the workplace and the many lessons learned in my career, which will be explored below. I recognize that not everyone has had a similar experience to me in their careers or the family support that I have had. I can only share what my experience has been to date in the workplace against the broader landscape of gender-related concerns.

Women in Healthcare

While 78% of the healthcare workforce is comprised of women, women continue to lag in the executive ranks [1]. According to a 2015 Rock Health study [1], only 34% of executives at Top 100 hospitals were women, 27% of board members at Top 100 hospitals were women, 21% of board members at Fortune 500 healthcare companies were women, and only 6% of CEOs of funded digital health companies were women.

In a research study by Health Data Management about women and healthcare IT careers conducted in April 2016 [2], women still are facing challenges as they progress in their career. Career obstacles cited were the old boys' network, lack of mentoring programs, perceived lack of management experience/skills, lack of a peer support group, lack of diversity/inclusion initiatives, lack of flex time, and lost career momentum due to family leave. 29% of women in the survey stated that gender was a reason that they were not offered a promotion at some point in their healthcare career. Women are financially penalized for having a family. There is a 20% "motherhood penalty" on salary as women who are unmarried without children make 20% more than married mothers [1].

Research by the Healthcare Information and Management Systems Society (HIMSS) in the 2015 HIMSS Salary Calculator and Compensation Survey [3] has shown that first-year female health information technology executives and senior managers receive 63% of the compensation of men in the same position. It takes a further 15 years to close the wage gap.

Gender pay differentials are unacceptable and must be acknowledged and addressed. Eliminating negotiations for pay and implementing salary transparency across organizations are two solutions that are frequently cited to end gender pay disparity. In the absence of these being implemented in the near future, women must add negotiating skills to their set of core competencies. This is an area that I have at times shied away from; however, after taking negotiation courses and at times, calling on a negotiation coach to work with, I recognize that it is an important skill to have.

Preparation is key to a successful negotiation by cataloguing your achievements and engaging in research about comparable salaries at other organizations similar to your own. This can be achieved informally by networking locally and at organizations that bring collective groups of health IT professionals together such as HIMSS. Practicing your negotiating skills with a mentor or a trusted advisor to refine your pitch is an important step in this process. According to Hannah Riley Bowles, a Harvard Law School course leader in negotiation, "use the pronoun 'we' instead of 'I' when making your pitch for a pay raise" [4]. Taking a communal approach to your salary negotiation as a woman "mitigates the negative reputational affects for women" [5]. Salary negotiations can be a difficult discussion to have with your supervisor; however, it is an important practice to develop and ultimately master for your economic well-being long term.

Unconscious Bias

There are some gender stereotypes that are deeply held in the workplace. An example is that women tend to be "nurturing and communal" and we expect men "to be ambitious and results-oriented." Studies have shown that in situations where identical help is given by both a man and a woman, "a man was significantly more likely to be recommended for promotions, important projects, raises and bonuses. A woman had to help just to get the same rating as a man who didn't help" [6].

The tendency is for women to assist others and mentor others more privately, which can be time-consuming. Women (and men) achieve "the highest performance and experience the lowest burnout when they prioritize their own needs along with the needs of others [7]." One example cited by Adam Grant that resonated with me was instead of meeting one-on-one with junior colleagues or team members, have group lunches. I have adopted this practice by having lunch sessions on a leadership development book with 10–12 colleagues at a time, which saves me time and also provides a forum for support and learning [7].

According to the 2015 Rock Health Study [1], 50% of women have adopted male behaviors in order to advance their career and 33% believe being female is disadvantageous to their career. It is hardly surprising that these views are held when many of the role models and mentors available to women have been men. Studies have shown that when "female executives spoke more than their peers, both men and women punished them with 14% lower ratings" [8].

Men and women at the workplace can counter the above narrative by creating a collaborative environment where ground rules are created and set by all members of the team at the beginning of the meeting, calling on women in meetings for their opinion and making sure that women sit at the table where the discussion is taking place. The more the workplace becomes accustomed to women speaking up, the more this bias. The longer-term solution is to increase the amount of women in leadership roles, which starts at the hiring process.

Networking

One of the most important lessons I have learned over the years in my career is that time must be invested in networking every week. This was not on area that I focused on for most of my career as I was too busy and immersed in my day-to-day work. No matter how content you are in your current job, it is essential to network, as increasingly leadership is about "your ability to connect to others" [9]. Many women do not feel they have time for networking as they balance their careers, families, and other personal interests; however, this is a missed opportunity. Networking internally at your own organization creates that "space where professional boundaries are softened by personality, often paving the way for women to be more effective in driving initiatives forward in the workplace" [9].

I typically block my Friday calendar to be able to catch up on the week and to spend at least 1–2 hours networking, whether it be lunch with colleagues, responding to LinkedIn requests, reaching out to other executives/mentors and coaches to discuss healthcare IT trends and giving/receiving advice. I also think it is important to join organizations/associations that align with your career aspirations, such as HIMSS, American College of Healthcare Executives (ACHE), American Medical Informatics Association (AMIA), College of Healthcare Information Management Executives (CHIME), and/or Project Management Institute (PMI). Joining your local chapter of these organizations can be a good first step.

Mentoring and Sponsorship

A critical component to career advancement is mentoring. Lack of access to mentors is still a barrier for women. Many women do not have a female mentor or do not have a mentor at all. In the Health Data Management Research Study: Most Powerful Women in Healthcare IT [2], lack of mentoring programs was cited as a top challenge. In my career, I have had different mentors for time periods in my career. Some of been formal, some have been more informal. The majority of the mentors that I have worked with have been men. More recently I have had the opportunity to meet other senior executive women outside of my workplace and have incorporated these women as part of my network to call upon when I need coaching and/or mentoring. It is important for women to take advantage of their network to identify mentors. I mentor both men and women; however, we have a special responsibility to coach, develop, and mentor other women.

One of my professors at Columbia University spoke about the concept of sponsorship in her career, which changed my viewpoint on mentoring in a fundamental way. While mentoring is important, securing sponsorship is more effective. Sponsoring is advocating for someone to receive a job or promotion, actively assisting that person advance. Sponsorship can make a real and significant difference in women helping other women advance in their careers:

"A sponsor can lean in on a woman's behalf, apprising others of her exceptional performance and keeping her on the fast track. With such a person—male or female—in her corner, our data shows, a woman is more likely to ask for a big opportunity, to seek a raise and to be satisfied with her rate of advancement" [10].

Moving Up the Career Ladder

In terms of career advancement, the only person who can make that happen is you. I have always been interested in understanding what it is like to work in different roles within information technology as well as hospital administration. Through my network, I have been fortunate enough to be able to reach out to contacts or referrals, people in positions of Chief Information Officer, Chief Operating Officer, or Chief of Staff to the Chief Executive Officer. In my discussions, I learn about their journey to the role, their education, why they were chosen, what key skills are important for the role, and what lessons learned would they advise someone considering the role. The knowledge imparted in these discussions has helped me refine my career goals. It also highlighted a gap in my education, as most of the people I spoke to had a master's degree, i.e., MBA or MPH. This led me to enroll and complete my Masters of Public Health at Columbia University.

It is also important once your career goals are refined to share them with your manager. At Mount Sinai Health System we have an opportunity to do this via an Individual Development Plan, which focuses on your career goals, what training and education you need, or exposure in the organization to reach the next level. If there is not a process in place, having a career discussion with your manager is important so he or she can either sponsor your career progression, provide feedback as to what competencies are required to progress, and also to be aware that you would like to take on greater responsibilities, so when these opportunities come up, you are on the short list to be chosen.

I also recommend at key career points having an external coach. This person can be a trusted friend or professional that is paid who is willing to speak the truth about your strengths, weaknesses, and areas of value and have challenged my perspective in a positive way.

What Are the Opportunities for Change?

In order for there to be gender parity in the workplace, we need men to be sponsors and advocates for the change. Frequently, organizations rely on women for gender and diversity initiatives. Men are untapped resources that need to be engaged and not alienated for the real and long-lasting organizational change. According to a study by the Catalyst group in 2009, "the higher men's awareness of gender bias, the more likely they were to feel that it was important to achieve gender equality" [11]. The study also demonstrated that "men who had been mentored by women were more aware of gender bias than men who had not had this experience" [11]. We need men to sponsor the organizational change around fairness, which starts with gender diversity in the hiring process and developing a culture that is based upon flexibility and is respectful of employee priorities. The organization environment needs to recognize the many ways that employees add value, such as informal mentoring and development of team members or volunteering. Each of us has had different life experiences that can be valuable to the team as a whole: "The overall goal in the workplace is to get to a point where you evaluate people by total contribution. But to get there, you have to be open to acknowledging biases. If men are willing to speak up for and advocate work that isn't being appreciated, it would improve equality for everyone" [12].

Conclusion

In conclusion, there are a number of opportunities for change in the workplace for women. As a female leader, I feel strongly that women supporting one another and sponsoring to create opportunities is a responsibility of leadership. It is critically important to career success to have a mentor and/or a sponsor. Seek out mentors and accept opportunities to mentor other women. View

202 ■ *The Handbook of Continuing Professional Development*

networking as a key to developing strong professional relationships rather than seeing it as political or insincere. There are many organizations and publications that focus on change and gender parity, such as HIMSS [13], TechWomen [14], and Healthcare IT News [15] to name a few. Getting involved in these networks can be a good first step. Finally, be intentional about your career and learn to negotiate.

References

1. Rock Health. 2015. The State of Women in Healthcare. https://rockhealth.com/reports/the-state-of-women-in-healthcare-2015/.
2. Health Data Management. 2016. Most Powerful Women in Healthcare IT: Research Study. http://www.healthdatamanagement.com/whitepaper/the-status-of-women-in-healthcare-it.
3. HIMSS. 2015. HIMSS Salary Calculator and Compensation Survey. http://www.himss.org/compensationSurvey.
4. Lutz, K. 2016. Salary Negotiation Skills Different for Men and Women. http://www.pon.harvard.edu/daily/salary-negotiations/salary-negotiation-skills-different-for-men-and-women/
5. Slavina, V. 2016. Why Women Must Ask (The Right Way). https://www.themuse.com/advice/why-women-must-ask-the-right-way-negotiation-advice-from-stanfords-margaret-a-neale.
6. Heilman, M.E. and Parks-Stamm, E.J. 2007. Gender stereotypes in the workplace: Obstacles to women's career progress. In S.J. Correll (Ed.), *Social Psychology of Gender. Advances in Group Processes* (Volume 24) 47–78. Elsevier, JAI Press.
7. Sandberg, S., and Grant, A. 2015. Madam CEO., Get Me a Coffee. http://www.nytimes.com/2015/02/08/opinion/sunday/sheryl-sandberg-and-adam-grant-on-women-doing-office-housework.html.
8. Sandberg, S., and Grant, A. 2015. Speaking While Female. http://www.nytimes.com/2015/01/11/opinion/sunday/speaking-while-female.html.
9. Bartz, C., and Lambert, L. 2014. Why Women Should Do Less and Network More. http://fortune.com/2014/11/12/why-women-should-do-less-and-network-more/.
10. Hewlett, S. 2013. Mentors are Good. Sponsors are Better. http://www.nytimes.com/2013/04/14/jobs/sponsors-seen-as-crucial-for-womens-career-advancement.html.
11. Catalyst. 2009. Engaging Men in Gender Initiatives. http://www.catalyst.org/system/files/Engaging_Men_In_Gender_Initiatives_What_Change_Agents_Need_To_Know.pdf.
12. Sandberg, S., and Grant, A. 2014. When talking about Bias Backfires. http://www.nytimes.com/2014/12/07/opinion/sunday/adam-grant-and-sheryl-sandberg-on-discrimination-at-work.html.
13. http://www.himss.org/get-involved/roundtables/women-health-it.
14. https://www.techwomen.org/.
15. http://www.healthcareitnews.com/womeninhit.

Chapter 22

Joining the C-Suite

By John P. Hoyt

FACHE, FHIMSS

Contents

Keywords:

Leadership
C-Suite
Competencies
Leading
Self-concept
Emotional Intelligence
Vision
Loyalty
Trust
Success
Mentoring

Active Listening
Team Building
Informal Power

Introduction

The CIO is a member of the C-Suite, but what does that really mean for a new CIO? What skills and competencies are expected of C-Suite members that are different from the skills needed for the day-to-day interactions that the former health information technology (health IT), now turned CIO, would have used with their staff in the last few years? In this chapter we will discuss the value of having the CIO as a member of the C-Suite and what competencies the CIO will need to exhibit to be successful as a member of the C-Suite.

Having the most senior person responsible for health IT becoming a member of the C-Suite was an idea championed by the College of Healthcare Information Management Executives (CHIME) in 1992 where the founding members defined the CIO as the "highest ranking IT executive of a provider organization and a member of the executive committee." That helped fuel the move of IT Directors into the C-Suite.

So quickly, what is the C-Suite? The C-Suite is generally also called the Executive Committee of the hospital or the health system. (This definition, of course, also applies to non-healthcare businesses as well). The C-Suite is the senior most committee for strategy development and execution directing in the organization. Typically, in a hospital or an Integrated Delivery Network (IDN) the C-Suite would include, but not be limited to the CEO, COO, CNO, CFO, CMO, and the CIO. Certainly there are variations in membership which will be a derivative of the size and complexity of the organization and its local market. No doubt, in highly competitive markets with a high managed care payer mix, we may likely see the senior most person for contract management and also the senior most person for marketing and public relations in the C-Suite. Large health systems with their own legal staff may also have the Chief Legal Counsel in the C-Suite.

So, why should the CIO be a member of the C-Suite? Today that question may seem superfluous, but in the 1990s that was an open question. This author clearly remembers conversations with a new CEO who wondered why the "IT guy" would need to be with executives. Doesn't the "IT guy" belong in the basement printing green bar paper? Well, clearly the world of healthcare delivery was changing as those thoughts were articulated.

As we know, health IT is so pervasively integral to the success of healthcare delivery that the CIO needs to be involved in the leadership of the health system. Other C-Suite members see it that way as well. The success of the CIO and the projects they lead and the investments they make need the support of the other C-Suite members. Conversely, the other C-Suite members need the CIO to be successful for their programs to be successful. It is a symbiotic relationship. This recognition of the integral nature of health IT to virtually all of the current healthcare initiatives, beginning with early EMRs in the early 1990s to the role of health IT for population health, marketing with websites and patient portals, plus finance and supply chain has led to the unquestionable need for the CIO to be in the Executive Committee.

The C-Suite has core members who are deeply involved in patient care: the CNO, CMO, VP of Professional Services, a VP over ambulatory practices. Other members are peripheral to patient care: the Chief Marketing Officer, CFO, and the CIO. However, the CIO can have a more of a positive or negative affect on patient care. It is imperative that the CIO understand the patient care processes throughout the continuum of care. The CIO should "walk the floors" with the fellow

C-Suite members, VP of Nursing or the Chief Medical Officer, to really be familiar with the processes that the health IT function needs to support.

So, What Skills and Competencies Are Needed for the C-Suite?

The C-Suite are the leaders of the organization; the managers of the organization report up to them. Is leading different than managing? Certainly so, say numerous academics since the 1970s such as Warren Bennis, who was one of the first to write extensively on leaders versus managers. Managing is maintaining the base, dealing with the status quo, making sure that there is no serious upheaval so that business as we know it can continue.

So, how is that different from leading? Leading is about creating new realities, about looking at the horizon more than looking at the bottom line. Leaders define a vision and, just as importantly, articulate and communicate the vision. Leaders inspire trust and ask what and why instead of how and when.

Are CIOs prepared to do this after a career as a health IT Director? Where a health IT director has been focusing inward to "run the business of health IT," the CIO will look outward and into the future to help define how IT will serve the enterprise in new future initiatives. To better understand how health IT investments can assist in patient care, the CIO will need a solid understanding of the patient care processes.

Key Competencies for Leadership

The book, *Exceptional Leadership*, by authors Carson F. Dye and Andrew N. Garman, published by Health Administration Press, provides excellent guidance on the competencies needed for leadership by the CEO and members of the C-Suite. This book is a guide to this next portion of this chapter. There are certain skills, or competencies as the authors put it, that define exceptional leadership, which is needed to make the health system successful in achieving its goals and successfully executing its strategy. The CIO, as an equal member of the C-Suite, needs to be equally skilled in these competencies to be successful as a contributing member of the leadership team. So what are these main competencies?

Positive Self-Concept

Why would this be the first competency to mention? Leaders with a positive self-concept are confident in their ability to achieve what they set out to do. Leaders need a transformational style to move the organization in a significantly different direction than it has been steadily heading in the recent past. Leaders need followers and followers are intrigued by charismatic leadership, which fundamentally takes a positive self-concept. Leaders with a positive self-concept can certainly have failures; however, "failures and setbacks may bother them, but they do not tear them apart [1]."

Leaders with a positive self-concept are very capable of successfully working with others. As stated, leaders need followers. Executives who are very poor at working with others will simply have fewer followers, and thus a significantly diminished success rate: "Leaders with a positive self-concept do not have to tear down others to bring themselves up" [1].

CIOs need a positive self-concept as much as any other executive in the C-Suite. Is this different than they needed as a health IT Director? Probably not, except their audience and "followership" is much broader now that the entire enterprise is involved, so the skill may need to be stronger and more pronounced in the CIO's persona.

A positive self-concept enables the leader to live by their personal convictions. These personal convictions suggest to them how the world should be, according to Dye and Garman. That enables clarification of their vision, which we will address later.

There are boundaries to this competency as well. Being overly moralistic, or ascribing to "my way or the highway" because there is over-conviction, so to speak, will work against the CIO if they are perceived as being too self-righteous in their personal convictions.

Possessing Emotional Intelligence

"Long-term effectiveness depends on the quality of the leader's working relationships, which are in turn a function of the leader's capacity to understand and work effectively with emotions—of others as well as themselves [2]." Emotional intelligence is a concept that emerged in business academic writings in the early 1990s. Emotional intelligence pertains to the concept of understanding other people's emotions while understanding and managing your own emotions and responses to others. Emotions play a major role in leadership. There are discussions and planning sessions where emotions can get very "heated." The CIO is in a position to take blame for every fault that IT brings to the users. Angry medical staff members who feel that patient care is jeopardized will test the emotional intelligence of any CIO. Successful CIOs, like any successful C-Suite member, will have a strong emotional intelligence to help them map their way through the tumultuous waters of health IT deployment.

Emotional intelligence enables leaders to confidently engage in dialogue and planning with others, both internally and externally. Truthfully and selfishly engaging with others to work on common goals and strategies engenders trust and trust enables followers to follow. Remember, a leader is not a leader without followers.

The lack of sufficient emotional intelligence can appear as not trusting others. One major symptom of this is not delegating to staff and which, in turn, does not enable staff to develop. This creates a long-term problem for the entire organization, especially since so many health IT projects require successful, cross-functional teams to work together for several years. CIOs need to be cognizant of their emotional intelligence and hone the skill to enable successful leadership and comradery with fellow C-Suite members.

The Vision

It's all about the vision right? This is clearly a significant competency for the CEO who wants to lead the organization in a different direction than it has been in its recent past. The same can be said about the CIO who needs to define a vision and future state with the use of health IT. The CIO will be in a position to articulate the vision to board members and fellow executive committee members, as well as rank and file workers as investments in healthcare IT ramp up. Being a visionary means that the CIO needs to have a broad awareness of industry trends and needs to articulate the value of those trends to the enterprise stakeholder groups.

There are several key skills within this very important category. The first is knowing which of the broader trends in the industry are appropriate for the enterprise at this point in time. Some CIOs have been rightly accused of seeking "technology for technology's sake." This can be an extremely strong "turn-off" for other members of the executive committee. Is the organization a cautious, conservative organization that takes change slowly? If that is the case, then some technologies, such as RFID employee badges for logging hand-washing time, may be totally inappropriate. The CIO must be able to appropriately judge the value of the technology, the current enterprise strategy, and the role that health IT is expected to play in that strategy, as well as the organization's current ability to absorb and utilize technology.

Second, the CIO needs to define which evolving technologies best align with the organization's strategic plan. If the organization is intent on building an integrated delivery system (IDS) and a clinically integrated network (CIN), then the CIO must have the skillset to lead the organization in adopting the technologies that are most likely to serve accomplishing the strategic intent of the organization. Furthermore, the CIO must be able to resist those who may push for "the latest coolest thing" if it does not clearly serve the strategic needs of the organization. In the IT department, and even in the medical staff, there will be those who push for the adoption of cutting-edge technologies because they are new and "cool." The CIO must convincingly resist this as a distraction if it clearly does not meet the strategic needs of the organization. Failure to do so if it is not appropriate for the organization will certainly be a negative impression for the CIO among the C-Suite.

Third, articulating the vision. What good is a vision if it cannot be explained? The vision of health IT must be clearly explained to several audiences with widely different perspectives. The idea of articulating a vision is to teach its value and to engender support. Few Americans who were born before the late 1960s can forget hearing President John F. Kennedy's articulating the vision of landing an astronaut on the moon before the end of the decade of the1960s. The articulation of the vision achieved two purposes: Explain the vision and engender support for it.

CIOs must be able to do the very same thing, explain the vision and engender support for it. But, do CIOs have any particular issues in this competency to address that other members of the C-Suite may not have? This author believes that yes, they do. For many CIOs who have "come up through the ranks," their strength is in understanding and using technology. For those people who have used IT in a development mode for years have spent much "one-on-one" time with a keyboard and a monitor. This author thinks it is fair to say that this could lead to less developed verbal and social interaction skills than other members of the C-Suite. The CIO can quickly lose support with "techy talk" and too many CIOs often fall into that trap. So, this author thinks it is fair to say that the skill of articulating the vision may be more important, and possibly more of a challenge, for the CIO than other members of the executive committee. And thus, it could be a notable failure point that shortens CIO's careers.

Overreliance on the vision compared to other competencies can lead followers to lose faith in the vision. Too often overreliance can lead to multiple "visioning exercises" and thus followers may "wait this one out until we re-vision next year." An overreliance on the vision can also lead to an inadequate focus on operations. Of course, operational failures in the IT department can have an extremely detrimental effect on clinical and financial operations.

The CIO will be called upon to conduct visioning exercises where ideas are percolated for potential health IT investments and operational improvements. These exercises will be performed in executive committee and board retreats as well as with Directors, mid-level managers, and day-to-day users of systems. To manage these exercises effectively, the CIO will need to have excellent social skills, group dynamics understanding, and the ability to hear negative news without a defensive reaction. The first attribute that we mentioned, a healthy self-concept, is a key ingredient to manage visioning exercises where negative information may be a frequent subject.

The vision and the articulating of the vision are often cited as the major skillset that separate leaders from managers. This obviously is a skill for which the CIO will need to have an excellent grasp to be a successful member of the C-Suite.

Earning Loyalty and Trust

It was previously stated that leaders are not leaders without followers. Loyalty and trust makes followers stay with the leader "through thick and thin." But trust takes years to develop. Clearly, a leader has to earn trust, not demand it.

Well, how do you earn trust? Trust can be earned through openness of conversation by encouraging dissenting opinions, being accessible, and being a role model inside the workplace as well as outside the workplace. Many organizations ask their leadership to conduct charitable activities outside the workplace not only to assist in the value of the charitable activity, but to also engender trust of the organization's leadership.

So, how do you turn trust into loyalty? With success over time and with serving the self-interest of the followers, trusted leaders develop a loyal following: "Exceptional leaders are capable of taking these individual interests and finding ways to bring them into alignment with the organization's goals [3]."

So how would a CIO who has gained trust and loyalty lose it? By not "walking the walk and talking the talk." Failing to lead by example, and not taking ownership of the problems is a fast way that CIOs can lose trust and loyalty. How often can the CIO say "it's the vendor's fault," or "the end user made mistakes," etc. While there certainly are times when that will be the case, a CIO who consistently fails to lead by acknowledging their leadership responsibility will quickly lose trust and loyalty, and that is the beginning of the end for many CIOs.

Mentoring Others, Developing Teams and Being an Active Listener

So many tasks that IT leaders need to direct, manage, and see to fruition involve team efforts. Implementing clinical systems require health IT leadership to work closely with clinicians to make certain that the software and workflow processes work together to serve clinicians and to improve patient care. The CIO is responsible for building a sense of "we," of building self-supporting teams.

Mentoring is also a leadership skill that eventually serves individual mentees as well as the teams of which they are a member. Mentoring is the activity of providing advice to and guiding an individual to help them meet their potential to achieve their career goals. The art of mentoring and developing individuals is to enable them to not need as much guidance. In other words, one could say that a successful mentoring manager "should work themselves out of a job."

A very key skill that enables successful mentoring is active listening. CIOs need to be active listeners. Active listening involves demonstrating that you are listening, and not just waiting for your turn to speak. An active listening technique such as repeating back to the speaker "what I heard you say is …". Active listening helps the CIO understand the person and their aspirations and goals, thus enabling the CIO to staff project teams with a deeper level of interpersonal trust. Active listeners take the time to focus on the individual and their opinions. Active listeners do not make the speaker feel rushed or make the speaker feel like they have to avoid a volatile reaction.

So why are mentoring, team building, and active listening so important for an executive committee member such as the CIO? The CIO's direct reports as well as the project team members must be convinced that their individual interests are served by listening to and following the CIO. The CIO needs to build strong relationships with all direct reports and team members, not just those who obviously need assistance. That strong relationship is built upon a solid understanding of the individual's personal goals and a perception of a clear opportunity to personally grow to achieve those goals. It is the exceptional leader who enables the alignment of personal goals with organizational goals and staffs the project teams accordingly.

The delicate balancing of the interdependence of team members, each with their own goals, must result in an alignment these goals to a common purpose. Exceptional leadership involves the skills of mentoring, team building through trust development, team member selection, active listening, developing a spirit of seeking a common goal, and helping teams work through inevitable internal conflicts that teams will have.

Generating Informal Power

And what exactly is "informal power"? Informal power is defined as the ability to influence others. It is the ability to influence, attain cooperation from and most probably gain access to resources, funds, and opportunities inside the organization. A CIO will need to use both formal and informal power to achieve the goals to meet the intent of the strategic plan.

But how do you use power that is not "formal" as displayed on an organization chart? Dye and Garman tell us that it requires the knowledge and sensitivities of people's relationships and the ability to use that knowledge creatively. Politicians speak of "political capital" that is expended as needed to influence others. The exceptional leader CIO will generate such influence and will use it sparingly and appropriately. And such expending of informal power will not necessarily be with the names that always appear at the top of the organization chart. The CIO will need to know who may wield the most power and influence within a division or department.

Let us not be blind to the fact that informal power can be used too frequently to the detriment of the leader. Playing power politics, getting back at people who did not support you, and focusing too much on your own agenda could turn informal power against the CIO. So, it is clear that informal can take time to gain and not much time to lose.

Building Consensus and Making Decisions

For sure, not all decisions that executives make are consensus-backed decisions. First, the CIO leader needs census building skills. This relates so tightly with competencies that we have mentioned before:

- Creating and articulating a vision
- Building trust and loyalty
- Building teamwork

These competencies lay the groundwork for potential consensus. But only the potential. It is great if a CIO can have consensus for decisions without "blind yes man loyalty" as in a dictatorship. But if the consensus is not there, then decision-making skills will be needed.

Dye and Garman tell us that decision-making skills are learned skills that can be refined. Exceptional leaders "decide how to decide" and use a defined, predictable decision-making process. The authors suggest that exceptional leaders keep a log of their decisions so that they can study the log carefully over the years to determine if patterns emerge. CIOs need to show evidence that there is a strong degree of transparency in their decision-making process and that they act with consistency and integrity.

Failure to have a known decision-making process can wreak havoc on the organization. We are all familiar with the concept of analysis paralysis, which is often an indication of a fear of making a wrong decision or being extremely risk adverse. Good decision makers have an excellent sense of timing. Analysis paralysis is the antithesis to timely decision-making.

Driving Results to a Higher Level

Exceptional leaders from the C-Suite drive the organization to achieve a higher level of goals. But that gap between the leader's expectations and the mid-level managers needs to be addressed flexibly with the skills that still engender support and loyalty. Defining goals is not the same thing as driving results. CIOs need to establish a series of performance behaviors or performance habits. CIOs need to ensure that goals are clarified, that progress is regularly tracked, and, importantly, that success is acknowledged. This latter point cannot be underestimated for CIOs because of the nature of system design, implementation, and go-live support. These are tremendously stressful times for health IT project teams and we must ensure they are supported with recognition for their hard work. And this certainly can be extended to vendor partners as well. The CIO's responsibility is to build a solid relationship with the vendor side of the health IT projects and investment. There is no reason that celebrations of success should routinely exclude the vendor personnel as well.

Conclusion

When a CIO makes the move from a health IT Director or an Associate CIO to a position in the C-Suite, significantly different competencies are needed to work successfully with other, more experienced, members of the executive committee. There are numerous competencies that others may think of, but these should be considered the key competencies that the CIO must embrace and exhibit in day-to-day life. Developing and honing these skills is a lifetime effort. We always can improve them, but clearly, a new member of the C-Suite needs to focus on these competencies defined here. A CIO can find a mentor in the C-Suite to help them begin this self-development process. And certainly, other CIOs who have been successful members of C-Suite can also serve as a mentor.

References

1. Carson F. Dye and Andrew N. Garman, *Exceptional Leadership: 16 Critical Competencies for Healthcare Executives* (Chicago: Health Administration Press, 2006), xxvii.
2. Carson F. Dye and Andrew N. Garman, *Exceptional Leadership: 16 Critical Competencies for Healthcare Executives* (Chicago: Health Administration Press, 2006), 17.
3. Carson F. Dye and Andrew N. Garman, *Exceptional Leadership: 16 Critical Competencies for Healthcare Executives* (Chicago: Health Administration Press, 2006), 57.

THE IMPORTANCE OF LIFELONG LEARNING

Chapter 23

Earning an Advanced Degree

By Tiffany Champagne-Langabeer

PhD, MBA, RD, LD

Contents

Abstract

The decision to earn an advanced degree is both exciting and intimidating: exciting because it can open up new opportunities, but intimidating if one has not been in an academic setting for some time. Review the advantages and disadvantages of earning an advanced degree.

Keywords:

Advanced Degree
Opportunities

Graduate Education
Degree Program
Lifelong Learner
Advancement
Career
Program Modalities
Online Learning
Traditional Courses
Accreditation
Prospective Student
Undergraduate Degree
Graduate Degree

Introduction

This book illustrates the many facets of lifelong learning and its positive impact on the health information professional. In this chapter, the focus will build upon several concepts already discussed earlier, such as identifying your professional potential, diversifying your skillset, and developing your career roadmap. We will concentrate specifically however on the process of considering and earning an advanced degree.

This chapter is organized in five sections (or steps) that systematically move lifelong learning from a casual thought process to a concrete set of activities that culminate in earning a graduate degree. The first of these (Step 1) takes readers through the process of considering all options, which helps to explore the decision process for ensuring that you really can and should pursue a degree now. Step 2 describes the admission process and identifying the right program and university. Step 3 describes the process of gaining admission for that program and the types of activities necessary to complete before a university can accept you. Step 4 describes briefly what happens when you have been admitted and now must work your way through the 30–60 hour academic program. Finally, Step 5 provides some guidance on what learners should do when they graduate. Figure 23.1 summarizes the major stages of earning an advanced degree.

Considering the Graduate Degree Option (Step 1)

The decision to earn an advanced degree is both exciting and intimidating: Exciting because it can open up new opportunities, but intimidating if one has not been in an academic setting for some time. Returning to school for advanced study will alter the quality of one's life, not only for

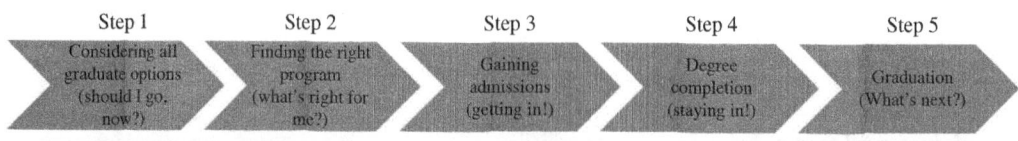

Step 1	Step 2	Step 3	Step 4	Step 5
Considering all graduate options (should I go, now?)	Finding the right program (what's right for me?)	Gaining admissions (getting in!)	Degree completion (staying in!)	Graduation (What's next?)

Figure 23.1 Stages of earning a graduate degree.

the short term but the long term as well. The choice to earn an advanced degree must be carefully considered. Seeking another degree will take a significant amount of time and resources and, depending on the degree, can impact up to 6 years of a person's life.

The rewards, however, are significant, including the potential for increased salary, advancement in one's career, and a substantial boost to personal confidence and efficacy. According to the career website Monster.com and the U.S. Bureau of Labor Statistics data, candidates with a bachelor's degree working as a health informatics specialist could expect to earn a median salary of $60,000, while one with a master's degree working in an information management position could earn as much as $90,000 (BLS, 2016; Monster.com, 2016). The field of health informatics has exploded as a result of the Health Information Technology for Economic and Clinical Health (HITECH) Act of 2009 and the resultant mandates for electronic medical records implementations and interoperability, not to mention the flourishing entrepreneurial mobile health (mHealth) field. There is a growing demand for those trained in health informatics. The opportunities are abundant for more and more highly skilled workers in the field.

In larger healthcare organizations, there are often hundreds and even thousands of information technology professionals. Some examples of potential positions which often require a graduate degree in the health information technology (HIT) field include the following: Director of Medical Informatics, Assistant Vice President of Information Management, Clinical Data Analyst, Lead Developer or Data Manager of EHR Applications, Compliance Officer (especially for those with a legal background), Chief Medical Information Officer (physician informaticist), Chief Nursing Information Officer (nurse informaticist), Research and Development, Systems Analyst, Clinical Informatician, and Senior Consultant. These are just a few examples among many possibilities depending on the professionals' background, area of interest, and desired career path. This does not take into account the myriad of fascinating options in the entrepreneurial field, where health IT professionals can develop new software, solutions, and companies. For many professionals, earning an advanced degree affords the chance to not only grow in their careers but to embark upon something new and exciting.

Before committing to a life-altering decision, there are several questions to consider:

- *What type of degree will I earn and in what type of organization?*
- *What modality works for my schedule, such as online or in person?*
- *If in person, are there evening classes?*
- *Should I consider a weekend only or executive program?*
- *What university is best for me to attend?*
- *How will I finance my education?*
- *What is the process for applying to graduate school?*
- *How will I balance work, family, and social life?*
- *Can I manage the additional stress of being a student…again?*
- *Where do I see myself after this degree?*

The next sections of this chapter will focus in detail on addressing these questions. This will later culminate in a decision matrix, which learners can adapt to their own needs to determine the best path forward. This practical tool can be used to assist professionals considering several programs to weigh the best options in an objective manner.

Finding the Right Program (Step 2)

Once a learner has determined they are ready to pursue a graduate degree, the second major step involves identifying the right degree program, campus, and university to apply for admission. This is more complicated than it seems. There are literally thousands of graduate programs and degree concentrations throughout the country. Some are online; some are accredited (or officially recognized by a governing body); some are low-cost; and some focus on healthcare primarily; while others offer only a few courses in health IT. In order to identify the right program for you, it is necessary to think through a number of areas, such as "which degree should I earn?"

Choosing a Degree Program

There are several types of graduate degrees a health IT professional can consider when seeking an advanced degree. After obtaining a bachelor's degree, the next obvious step is to seek either a graduate certificate or master's level degree. In this chapter, we will focus on a master's degree program. Most professionals currently working in health IT likely have a degree related to the field either in some type of technology or in a healthcare-related area. However, there are also many cases where successful professionals with liberal arts degrees are working in the field. In either case, the option to pursue an advanced degree for professional advancement should follow the desired and future career path. Someone with a Bachelor's of History or English should consider a master's level degree in the health IT field, given they would like to advance in health IT, as opposed to the in fields of history or English.

One of the first questions is to decide which specific degree to obtain. Although not an exhaustive list, Table 23.1 lists several of the degrees a student may encounter and consider for either a master's or doctorate level degree.

Although a few students may opt to directly seek a doctoral degree following their bachelor's programs, these students tend to be those that wish to pursue a scientist or academic profession, to become professors. For most working professionals, the master's level degree is the logical next step for those seeking an applied, professional path. For those who already have a master's degree and are considering a doctoral degree, this is a lengthy path and most often requires a full-time commitment to education. There are fewer program options for doctoral degrees in health information technology (health IT), and they tend to be more technically focused. These intense programs prepare students to become thought leaders, researchers, and university faculty. The finale of this path characteristically requires the student move locations for a faculty position, so additional consideration is required for making the doctoral leap. Some students who wish to attain a doctoral degree but not strictly for research may opt to focus on healthcare administration or another applied health field such as nursing (D.N.P.) or public health (Dr. P.H.) with a minor in health IT. Most programs with this level of specialization will be located in urban areas with major academic medical centers, such as in Houston, Boston, or Los Angeles.

The total number of credit hours required for a master's degree ranges from 36 to 60 hours; and similar to undergraduate courses, most classes are 3 hours per course. The time it takes to graduate will depend on a number of factors, including: full-time versus part-time attendance; how many courses are taken per semester; if summer coursework is available; and if a culminating thesis (or research project) is required. It is reasonable for a dedicated, full-time student to complete an advanced degree in 2 years; while a part-time student might take an additional year or two, depending on the course load. Seeking a doctoral degree from a master's degree will typically

Table 23.1 Listing of Degrees with Potential Health IT Concentration or Minor

M.S.	Master of Science in Bioinformatics, Project Management, Computer Science, Health Informatics, Clinical Informatics, Healthcare Information and Information Management	Primary degree focus and coursework in information sciences and management
M.S.M.I.	Master of Science in Medical Informatics	
M.S.I. or M.S.A.	Master of Science in Information; Master of Science in Analytics	
M.I.S.	Master of Information Systems	
M.S.I.M.	Master of Science in Information Management	
P.S.M.	Professional Science Masters also H.I. P.S.M. (Health Informatics)	
M.H.A	Master in Health Administration	Courses and concentrations available in information sciences and management
M.S.P.H.	Master of Science in Public Health	
M.P.H.	Master of Public Health	
M.B.A	Master of Business Administration	
Ph.D.	Doctor of Philosophy	
Dr. P.H.	Doctor of Public Health	
D.H.A	Doctor of Health Administration	

require an additional 48 hours of coursework plus research and an undetermined number of dissertation hours. Doctoral degrees vary largely in scope, breadth, and length and should be evaluated on a case-by-case basis. Universities establish reasonable limits on the estimated time they allow students to matriculate through their programs; this provides a good approximation of the time it takes doctoral students to graduate. Another excellent question all doctoral students should ask is, "How many students who begin, actually complete the doctoral degree?" It is estimated over half of all doctoral students never finish the complex dissertation stage of a doctoral program, so those considering a doctorate need to carefully evaluate their options before casually deciding on this path forward. Figure 23.2 shows the approximate number of hours it will take to earn an advanced degree, starting with the bachelor's degree for reference.

In 2015, the annual Healthcare Information and Management Systems Society (HIMSS) Annual Conference & Exhibition featured 29 universities and colleges. It is worthwhile to speak to these institutions while attending professional events. Universities typically have their senior student affairs staff and professors in the program at the convention. They are eager to speak to potential students and are competitively seeking the best candidates. The HIMSS Annual Conference & Exhibition offers a more relaxed format to get information from the top programs

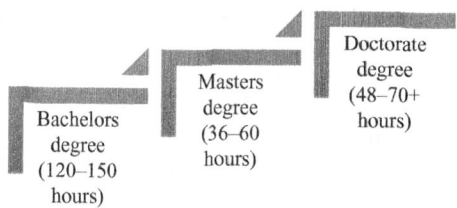

Figure 23.2 Approximate hours required for earning a degree.

in the health IT field; and potential students can ask honest questions about the program such as the number of hours, coursework, part-time options, and the modality (in person versus online) offered. Students should ask about the profile of other similar students in the program, their backgrounds, and the length of time the programs are taking to evaluate the "fit." It is also helpful to follow up with a contact at the university in case there are more specific questions after the event.

Graduate schools can be a much more personal experience than undergraduate programs, as the class sizes and cohort are typically smaller. It is worth the effort to get to know the university staff and administration. Several top programs in health IT admit only graduate students, so the student body, coursework, and research exist as the combined focus of the campus.

Choosing a Program Format/Modality

Students are not limited to their local university when seeking a degree in the health IT field, and there are many national options to evaluate and consider. Most advanced degrees in health IT will have some portion of their coursework delivered in an online medium. Many master's degrees are offered entirely online, meaning the student does not need to leave their home to take classes. Classes may be delivered through an online Learning Management System (LMS), which serves as an online classroom, convening students from various locations. As demand for health IT professionals increase, online programs are guaranteed to exist and even dominate the landscape of available degree plans. The most prestigious programs continue to evolve from traditional universities where courses are also available on a physical campus. A student may have the option to enroll in a hybrid program; whereby classes meet some of the time in person and the remainder of the coursework is completed remotely. The third option commonly offered is an executive-style program and is commonly offered for healthcare management degrees. Executive programs are condensed classes offered less frequently (for example, on Fridays and Saturdays) and may be offered similar to a working schedule of 8:00 a.m. to 6:00 p.m., instead of in 3-hour blocks. This format also offers less disruption and a more desirable schedule for students who do not live near the campus. The fourth option is the traditional program, where all courses are in person or face-to-face.

Each of these program modalities have benefits and disadvantages. For instance, traditional courses offer the ability to network and interact with professionals from other organizations, providing direct contact and exposure to potential contacts and job opportunities. Yet, traditional classes require students to adapt to a specific course schedule. Online learning offers complete flexibility as to scheduling and students can complete coursework on their own timetables, at midnight if they wish. But, online programs provide little exposure to a campus, professors, or fellow students for networking. Table 23.2 lists the four primary types of degree program options available.

Table 23.2   Classroom Formats for Graduate Degree Programs

Online	All coursework is completed via the internet, through an online Learning Management System
Hybrid	Online coursework is combined with face-to-face classes
Executive/Professional	Condensed classes offered all day for select days
Traditional	All courses are offered in-person

Choosing a University or College

When selecting the institution (university or college), there are a few things to keep in mind. First and foremost should be the quality of education you will receive, and this is typically reflected in the accrediting agencies that recognize the program and the overall integrity of the program. Accreditation is a means of ensuring adherence to standards of quality. The university should be "institutionally accredited" and the specific degree program should also be recognized as well.

Some of the best healthcare-focused programs are connected with external partners such as hospitals and academic medical centers, industry leaders in biotechnology or precision medicine, and entrepreneurs in health IT. The prospective student can find the links to these partners by searching the university's website. The website should be flawless in execution, engaging, and transparent. Those that are not might indicate problems with transparency of the program or quality of the education. Especially if you are considering an online degree program, the website needs to be even better. The student should be able to discover most of the desired information about the program, tuition, coursework, faculty, and other contacts a student would want to learn about the school. A description of each class is especially helpful for those seeking specialized interests such as entrepreneurship or advanced technical skills.

When exploring programs, identify the courses required in the degree plan. The degree plan is the assortment of courses necessary for successful completion of the degree. On school websites a sample degree plan should be available, but the university should also have courses in more esoteric subject matter areas such as natural language processing (NLP), cognitive science, leadership and entrepreneurship, healthcare delivery, strategic decision-making, or data mining. In addition to the required coursework, there should be alternate courses which are appealing to the student as electives and will serve as enhancements to one's career portfolio and skillset. Notice if the degree plan includes a capstone course, a thesis, or a culminating project. Depending on your skills and interests, one of these final options might make a difference. Table 23.3 provides a sample degree plan for a master's program in health informatics.

When researching the university website, a good graduate program will have a link on their website for "Current Students" and "Prospective Students." The first category should describe coursework, student events, and resources for students. There may be alumni statements, or some universities have videos of their current students stating why they chose the program. This is a great way to hear directly from real students who are actually engaged in coursework. The prospective student can gain an idea of the culture of the program and the expectations of the students, as well as any student activities or networking events. This is a perfect place to see if the university has recruiting events and any other resources a prospective student would need to consider in order to make a decision. Many reputable programs have alumni groups or events where graduates of the program can network or attend continuing education events throughout the year. These events

Table 23.3   Sample Master's Degree Plan (39 hours coursework + 3–6 hours thesis)

Introduction to Health Informatics	Legal and Ethical Aspects of Health IT
The U.S. Healthcare System	Security in Health IT
Introduction to Electronic Health Records	Quality and Outcome Improvement in Healthcare
Standards and Standards Development in Applied Health IT	System Analysis and Project Management
Technology Assessment and Evaluation	Clinical Decision Support System
Health Information Visualization and Visual Analytics	Health Information Exchange
Technical and Scientific Writing	Practicum or Thesis in Applied Health IT

and resources offer invaluable opportunities for the graduate to remain connected to the university and stay abreast of the latest developments in the field.

The reputation of a university is important, so the student should speak to influential colleagues in the health IT environment. Colleagues may be current employers or trusted peers who hold mid to senior level positions in health IT. Although this may weigh less in the final decision, it is a good decision point to gather information. For this reason, a student needs to consider the peers who will be joining them as classmates. Peer learning plays a larger role in a graduate degree when compared with an undergraduate degree. The student body may be more diverse and will have more experience in the work force. Students are encouraged to work in teams on large projects and writing assignments in graduate school, as this mirrors the working environment of a professional. While students are enrolled as classmates, outside hierarchy is left out of the classroom. Physicians will work equally with IT technicians; and nurses work seamlessly with software engineers and researchers. Classmates form important friendships and connections for networking in health IT after earning their degrees. Classmates get to know each other's competencies, weaknesses, and desired career paths. They make great references for future positions!

An excellent program has excellent professors. The people who teach the students are an essential and obvious component to the program; however, many students do not take advantage of the opportunity to engage with the faculty before applying to the program. All graduate programs should list their faculty along with the faculty's interests, degrees, and current research on the university website. Most questions can be answered through student affairs; however, students also have the option to contact the faculty directly.

Financing Graduate Education

Graduate school can be financially evaluated as a single purchase, in the same way one might buy a luxury vehicle or a home, depending on the institution. Since the total cost of earning a graduate degree can easily get into six figures, it is best to carefully examine how one will finance their degree. Some choices include student loans, scholarships, grants, or paying as you go.

Although in general, there are fewer subsidies such as grant opportunities offered to graduate students when compared with undergraduates, there are other factors which simplify the process. For example, graduate students receive the benefit of independence. No longer does one need to request tax documents from their parents to complete financial aid forms. The process is greatly simplified in this regard, as the Free Application for Federal Student Aid (FAFSA) only requires the student's tax return information. The calculation is made based upon the university's estimate of what it will cost students to attend and live reasonably while attending the program, then estimates the resources the student has to contribute to the cost of the enrolling. According to the U.S. Department of Education in 2016, current graduate students who meet the qualifications for aid and are entering their first semester of study can borrow up to $20,500 of unsubsidized federal loan money (Federal Student Aid Overview, 2016). Students should check with their program of interest to determine exact amounts, as schools establish their own cost of attendance. The interest on an unsubsidized loan accrues immediately, giving the student further incentive to finish on time.

Another option for financing graduate education is to seek company reimbursement or let someone else pay for it. Many large organizations offer generous tuition reimbursement programs for employees seeking to advance in their current position. The company considers this an investment in their human resources, and most will pay from 75% to 100% of the total tuition and fees for state universities and colleges.

As many of the programs are offered online, and this is undoubtedly a benefit, the downside is the student may face unexpected out-of-state tuition fees. Check the institution's in-state tuition policy versus out-of-state policy. Some state universities offer a waiver for out-of-state students or there may be a scholarship threshold, which qualifies the student for in-state tuition. For private institutions, the tuition is typically a set fee without negotiation. In this case, the best option is to seek financial aid or merit-based scholarship funds.

Based on available data from the Institute of Educational Sciences, the research and statistics section of the U.S. Department of Education, there are several excellent and affordable graduate programs across the country designed to meet the needs of working professionals. Table 23.4 lists a sample of a few of the more "affordable" programs, with the location, degree, and average annual cost.

Table 23.4   Affordable Graduate Programs with Master's Degrees in Health IT

University Program	Location	Degree	Cost of Attendance
The University of Texas Health Science Center in Houston School of Biomedical Informatics https://sbmi.uth.edu/prospective-students/index.htm	Houston, TX	M.S. Health Informatics	$6,075 per year
University of North Carolina at Charlotte http://hi.uncc.edu/admissions/tuition-and-fees	Charlotte, NC	H.I. P.S.M.	$8,662 per year
University of Utah http://fbs.admin.utah.edu/download/income/Graduate/BIFeeRes.pdf	Salt Lake City, UT	M.S. Biomedical Informatics	$9,195 per year

Source: University's individual websites.

Lifelong Learner Case Study: Examples

A student's individual backgrounds and experiences help determine which programs are better suited for their needs. To provide an example, below are 4 of the more common "types" of students.

Student A: Dual Degree Option, Early Career

A student is currently in a MPH program focusing on Health Promotion and Behavioral Sciences. She has a background in psychology and volunteer experience working at a clinic with EHRs. She would like to pursue a program, which utilizes her interests, bachelor's degree, and volunteer experience. Since she lives in a small town, she does not have a local program; so she pursues an online dual MPH/MSHI program. In order to finance her education, she applies to be a graduate research assistant. She also has the option to work in a clinic, complete a FAFSA and apply for an unsubsidized loan, or self-finance her education as she attends school part-time.

Student B: Entrepreneur with Broad Qualifications

A student with a liberal arts education and a medical degree has always been interested in technology. He is currently trying to build a start-up but does not have all the technical skills and industry connections necessary. He seeks a specialized program with an emphasis on mobile development and entrepreneurship. As part of his research, he checks the faculty profiles and industry connections of the university. He also researches the graduates of the program. He is results oriented, so he asks questions about the number of hours in the program and flexibility of the class schedule. He is employed by a hospital with a tuition reimbursement program and has also worked out a small stipend to work with a professor on a part-time basis.

Student C: Business Degree, Executive Experience, Career Change

A student with a business degree and executive management experience in the health insurance industry is considering an MBA. After further research and looking through the schedule of classes and meeting with professors, the student finds a program which utilizes her business background. She learns from former students this program will add new skills in integrated delivery systems, data management, and predictive analytics. She is fortunate to live near an academic medical center and negotiates time off from work to attend the executive MBA with a focus on health informatics. Her organization has an existing relationship with the university and receives a discount for the program. She also takes advantage of her company's tuition reimbursement program.

Student D: Registered Nurse, Looking for Advancement

A student has worked his way up in healthcare from a staff-level register nurse (RN) to supervisor over the past 15 years and for the past 5 years has worked in the IT department. He has substantial knowledge of patient workflow, EMR systems, and the healthcare system in general, but lacks certain technical skills to advance into management. Although the student is an excellent employee, advancing to the manager of the department will require more than experience. It will require a master's degree in an health IT-related field. The student considers online programs in MSIS, MIS, and MS in various fields to strengthen the specific areas of expertise needed. He learns there are many programs specific for nurses, including nursing informatics and program management degrees. He speaks with trusted colleagues and mentors, then considers programs which are taught at the local nursing school. Knowing informatics professionals with clinical backgrounds are in high demand, he works out a contract with his employer to commit 2 years of service for 2 years of tuition and returns to school full time.

Decision Matrix: Putting the Pieces Together

Once you have identified all of the information necessary to compare and evaluate the various degree program choices, one of the best ways to make a decision is through a structured decision matrix. A decision matrix helps to turn an otherwise qualitative decision into a quantitative one, where you place values and weights on the importance of key criteria to you. For example, if living in Denver were the most important factor in your decision, and a program was based in Denver, that criteria would receive higher scores and weighting. If online learning was your top priority, that should receive a higher weighting and any program that offers online degrees should receive higher scores. A sample decision matrix is shown in Table 23.5 below. Feel free to add or edit the criteria and weighting to fit your personal situation.

Gaining Admissions and Getting In (Step 3)

Once the learner has made the selection of the right degree program to pursue, the start of any new adventure requires planning to gain admission, which requires practical preparation. During the previous two steps for identifying and selecting the desired degree program and university, the admission criteria should have been closely examined. In this step, students should now begin preparing to meet those criteria.

Table 23.5   Program Selection Decision Matrix

Criteria	Weight (Importance)	Program 1	Program 2	Program 3
Course Format/Modality Aligned with Learner Preferences (e.g., Online, Traditional, Hybrid)	25%	9	5	
Institution Prestige, Rank, or Brand	20%	8	5	
Region/Location	5%	2	10	
Length of Program	5%	2	10	
Cost of Program/Financial Aid	20%	9	2	
Thesis versus No Thesis	5%	4	10	
Work/Life Balance	10%	7	2	
Probability of Success	10%	10	10	
Total Score	100%	7.75[a]	5.35	

[a] When interpreting the matrix, based on the weighted importance of each criterion and the score you gave the program, the total can be found in the bottom row. In this example, Program 1 would be a more attractive option (7.75 versus 5.35).

Typically, admissions criteria takes into consideration work experience and background, but there are also standard expectations for minimum grade point average (GPA) based on the student's undergraduate work, as well as scores on standardized graduate admissions exams. Those seriously considering graduate school should begin studying for the required admissions exam. Most graduate programs in the United States will require students to take the Graduate Record Examination (GRE). The GRE consists of three general sections: Verbal, quantitative, and writing skills. It may seem intimidating for someone who has not taken an exam in years; however, solid training and practice is the key to success for this exam. Many universities will make the average scores of their current students available, so applicants are aware of the range of scores expected. Some programs will focus more on quantitative reasoning, while other schools will want a high verbal score. The exam typical takes just under 4 hours and can be taken on a paper or computer-based format. More detailed information about the GRE is available at http://www.ets.org/gre/. There are many excellent study guides and courses you may take to help potential students prepare. These include:

- Kaplan Test Prep (https://www.kaptest.com/gre)
- Benchprep (https://benchprep.com/gre/gre-prep-course--2)
- The Princeton Review (http://www.princetonreview.com/grad/gre-test-prep)
- The Manhattan Review (http://www.manhattanreview.com/gre/)

The GRE was theoretically created to approximate the student's aptitude and ability to achieve in graduate school. GRE scores are valid and acceptable by most universities for 5 years; after 5 years, a student will need to retake the exam again.

In addition to excellent scores on the GRE, prospective students will be asked to submit former transcripts verifying a conferred undergraduate degree, as well as a resume of work accomplishments and a goal statement. The professors who will instruct the graduate students are the ones reading the goal statements; and these are taken as seriously as the scores on the GRE. Professors want to know students are serious about their educational goals, focused on their future, and have taken the time to research their specific degree program. Goal statements should be tailored for the university and degree program. The ideal statement should convey depth and passion while deferring from overly dramatic prose. Significant and relevant work or life experiences are worth noting, as are any major educational or health IT-related accomplishments, honors, or awards. It is always a good idea to have several trusted friends or colleagues proofread a goal statement. Ideally this statement should convey one's passion for advancement, interests in that university and degree programs, preferences for working with specific faculty, as well as being a writing sample in which the student feels a sense of pride.

Once an application is made to a program, it often takes weeks or even months to find out if a student is admitted or denied. It is worth mentioning, some universities may allow students to take graduate-level coursework prior to admission to a masters level program. The amount of coursework allowed will be limited, as will the conferred status as an admitted graduate student; however, this may be an efficient way to begin the journey. Otherwise, many schools work on admissions cycles, and these cycles dictate the communication timing. It is best to apply for multiple degree programs (based on your ranked preferences from the decision matrix), to ensure you get positive news from at least one.

Degree Completion: Staying In (Step 4)

When a prospective student receives their acceptance letter to graduate school, no matter the prior accomplishments, one should celebrate! Students should respond within the required deadlines and adhere to any guidelines established in the acceptance letter. This may include prerequisite coursework, forms, meetings, or mandatory orientation. Plan to spend at least 6–8 additional hours per week per course, especially in the first semester to get acclimated to graduate school. Depending on the timeline the student has established for completion, it is customary for students to take between one and two classes each semester, including summer terms. This creates a rhythm and inertia to coursework and the life of a graduate student. The suggested schedule, however, is highly dependent on the degree plan, workload, and individual capacity of the student.

Once you are admitted, there will be a registration process for the semester in which you are admitted. During registration, it is important that you follow the degree plan and select your first courses based on its timing of the degree plan (fundamental and introduction courses must be taken prior to advanced courses for instance). Take note of any courses that require prerequisites, as these must be taken first.

A key concern in the first (and subsequent) semesters should be around balancing work, family, and social life with the new educational endeavors. It is important to maintain a healthy position in all of these areas. Consider this when determining whether to enroll for one course (3 hours) or more. Obviously an individual that works full time should think carefully before enrolling for more than one to two courses per semester.

Lifelong learners will need to balance and manage the additional stress of being a student, again. Writing reports, developing presentations, analyzing data, developing computer scripts, and reading multiple chapters of textbooks require significant time and effort. The ability to manage time and coursework effectively in graduate school is as important as learning new concepts.

For students who work while attending school part-time, this is especially important. It is customary for professors to provide students with a schedule of assignments for the entire semester. This provides an opportunity for students to plan ahead and break larger assignments into smaller segments. Just as with projects at work, deadlines are serious, and missing an assignment carries serious consequences, including making a zero and possibly failing the course. Professors expect the same work product of all students, regardless of the outside demands. The assumption is even greater for full-time students: The majority of time is to be devoted to graduate work. While this may seem daunting, especially at first, many students find their creativity, effectiveness, and confidence soar as they get more immersed in graduate work. Recent studies have also shown that diligent scheduling actually produces a more productive life and can increase happiness overall (Hobson et al., 2001).

During your first semester, in addition to managing your course load, there are other considerations. Whether you are in an online or traditional format, it is important to connect and network with your colleagues and faculty. This provides significant opportunities for learning about new people, organizations, and positions. In many programs, there will likely be "team" projects, which require you and fellow classmates to get along and produce a collaborative report or project.

Work your way through the degree plan, semester by semester, with grades that are typically A or B level. Keep in mind that a 36-hour program is usually only 12 courses, so completion of the degree will be upon you before you know it!

Graduation and Next Steps: Where Am I Going? (Step 5)

Assuming the student was able to learn discipline and patience during the program, and continued to stay on top of all assignments, a few years later the graduate degree will be completed. This is a time to celebrate, as now new initials can be placed behind the name on email signatures and on resumes. These few letters can make all the difference for future earning power and job opportunities.

Now the question remains: What should you do next? This is the challenging part of earning a graduate degree. Obviously there were factors that stimulated your interest in pursuing the degree, and now might be the opportunity to make those happen. If you were unhappy being a staff nurse, then the new master's degree in informatics might allow you to apply for a new position as a Senior Clinical Informatician. Some others might be comfortable staying where they are, but earning more money; or, there is the option to relocate to a different region with a new position. Some even change to the healthcare industry from a different industry. Whatever your goals and desires, the graduate degree is now completed, and the lifelong learner must decide what to do next.

Whichever path is chosen, this author hopes you strive for excellence! Graduate degrees provide credentials, but the career strategy should now be the focus. Aiming high for a position that balances career goals, new educational platform, and personal interests will help ensure lifelong success. Subsequent chapters will describe this in even greater detail.

References

Bureau of Labor Statistics. (2016). Occupational Outlook Handbook. Available at www.bls.gov/ooh.

Federal Student Aid Overview. (2016). U.S. Department of Education. Available at https://studentaid.ed.gov.

Hobson, C., DeLunas, L., and Kesic, D. (2001). Compelling Evidence of the Need for Corporate Work/Life Balance Initiatives: Results from a National Survey of Stressful Life-Events. *Journal of Employment Counseling*, 38(1), 38–44.

Monster.com. (2016). 5 Healthcare Informatics Jobs and Salaries. Available at www.monster.com/healthcare/a/health-informatics-jobs.

Chapter 24

The Many Facets of Continuing Education

By Christine Hudak
Ph.D, RN-BC, CPHIMS, FHIMSS

Contents

Abstract

When participating in continuing professional development (CPD), an obvious choice may be to attend an in-person conference. But opportunities to engage in CPD abound both internally and externally to an organization. Define the many ways to develop competencies, expand one's professional practice, and achieve career goals.

Keywords:

Asynchronous Education
Certification
Competencies
Community of Practice
Continuing Professional Development (CPD)
eLearning
Evidence-Based Tweeting
Hybrid Program
Listservs
MOOC (Massive Online Open Courses)
Online Degree Program
Online Journal Club
Promotion
SPOC (Small Private Online Courses)
Synchronous Communication
Web 2.0 Tools
Webinars

Introduction

Continuing professional development has been defined in various ways. Wylie (2015) defines CPD as the "… means by which people maintain their knowledge and skills related to their professional lives …" The Chartered Institute of Personnel and Development (CIPD) defines CPD as "… the need for individuals to keep up to date with rapidly changing knowledge" (retrieved from http://www.cipd.co.uk/). The Institute of Hospitality defines CPD as: "a framework of learning and development activities which is seen as contributing to an individual's continued effectiveness as a professional" (retrieved from https://www.instituteofhospitality.org/Careers/cpd). In previous iterations, this term was known as Continuing Education, with each profession inserting their name between the two words; thus, we had Continuing Nursing Education, Continuing Medical Education, and the like. Regardless of what it is called, the activity shows a personal commitment to professionalism, personal responsibility for skill/knowledge enhancement, and a desire to challenge the expectations of a volatile, ever-changing business environment (Schambach and Blanton, 2002). The same applies to the healthcare sector.

Health IT professionals engage in continuing professional development (CPD) for a number of reasons. Whether it is to obtain or retain certification, obtain a promotion, maintain competence in their chosen area, learn and apply new knowledge, to improve job performance, or simply seeking out new learning for its own sake, (Mizell, 2010; Schambach and Blanton 2002), health IT professionals have multiple opportunities to engage in this activity. Whether it is a class for college credit, a webinar for CPHIMS/CAHIMS hours, a journal club for sharing and discussing new advancements, or even a vendor presentation to learn about new technology, the health IT professional has myriad ways to obtain the knowledge and skills to meet their individual goals.

Goal of the Chapter

In this chapter, we will define the many opportunities available to the health IT professional for professional development. We will define ways to meet the requirements for obtaining and retaining certification, methods to obtain new knowledge and expand professional practice, and paths to building and maintaining professional competence in health informatics. Through it we hope to assist the newly minted, mid-career, and seasoned professional to find the balance between personal and job-related responsibilities while finding time to accomplish professional goals.

Schambach and Blanton's Premise and How to Accomplish

Schambach and Blanton state that "IT professionals who want to maintain an appropriate degree of professional competence need effective professional development ... But because participation is generally voluntary, they have to be personally motivated ... before they are willing to participate" (2002, p. 84). The same can be said for health IT professionals: They may be motivated, but if the available opportunities do not allow for a work-life balance, they may be willing to forego the benefits that CPD can offer. So how do we offer CPD while maintaining the motivation of the employee? The next sections of this chapter will outline traditional and not so traditional methods and some new methods to reap the benefits of CPD. It will also classify these offerings as formal or informal.

Traditional Methods of CPD: Exemplar HIMSS Annual Conference

Many in health IT have probably attended a sponsored one-day or two-day workshop in their professional life. Indeed, if you have attended any HIMSS (Healthcare Information and Management Systems Society) Annual Conference & Exhibition, you have experienced at least three traditional and formal types of CPD.

Stand-Up, In-Person Presentations

Myriad in-person, stand-up, educational presentations abound at the Annual Conference. Multiple tracks reflecting current content in health informatics allow participants to attend those sessions that are of interest to them as well as sampling some not so familiar topics. Presentations are vetted by peer reviewers (the Annual Conference Education Committee or ACEC) for criteria such as originality, timeliness, relevance, data accuracy, and freedom from vendor bias. CAHIMS/CPHIMS holders can obtain credit for recertification. Nurses can receive Continuing Nursing Education (CNE) hours. Physicians can receive Category 1 Continuing Medical Education units. Pharmacists can receive Continuing Education Units, as can Board Certified Informaticists, Information Security Professionals, ACHE and AHIMA members and Certified CIOs (CHCIO). Project Managers can receive Professional Development Units (PDUs). This is a very traditional way of CPD in a compact, prevetted format that allows attendees to accumulate numerous hours in a short period of time.

Select stand-up presentations are recorded and made available in the HIMSS Learning Center so that additional hours can be earned by listening to the recordings of the sessions. Attendees can listen to extra sessions in the comfort of their home, office or car. The extension of the stand-up presentations to the mobile/home platform reflects the changing needs and the time constraints of the health IT professionals. Those who cannot attend the in-person event due to financial, time, organizational, or personal constraints still have the opportunity to benefit from the conference through the recordings.

Similar types of presentations can also be found at the individual HIMSS chapter level through smaller, more targeted conferences in a specific geographic area. Chapter programming as well as programming by other organizations rely primarily on these stand-up presentations to disseminate knowledge to the professional. Stand-up, formal presentations are also offered in individual healthcare organizations, though cost prohibitions see them decreasing over time.

Roundtables

Getting multiple experts in a single room to discuss a single topic in depth is a benefit of roundtable sessions at the Annual Conference as well as smaller HIMSS Chapter events. The opportunity to attend a session where CIOs or other hospital leaders discuss a singular topic provides a broader perspective to a problem and allows a deeper understanding of current issues in healthcare informatics. Panel discussion also falls into this category in their deep discussion, with varied viewpoints of a single topic.

Vendor Presentations/Demonstrations

Though not usually a way to obtain credits toward continuing education requirement, vendor presentations are another form of CPD. Software and hardware demonstrations are the standard way to tout features of a product or service to decision makers as well as staff persons. If the idea of keeping up to date with rapidly changing knowledge in hardware and software is integral to the job being done, then these vendor presentations are invaluable to this group. These same (or similar) presentations may also be seen in individual hospitals or other healthcare venues, where they are typically called in-service presentations or vendor demonstrations. They are frequently held when an organization is considering a new system, an updated system, or a replacement system. At the HIMSS Annual Conference, these demonstrations are readily accessible and cover the majority of hardware and software vendors for healthcare venues.

Interoperability Showcase

A not so traditional method of CPD held in a traditional in-person conference is the HIMSS Interoperability Showcase. Here the attendee can become the patient through a clinical use case scenario and will be able to see how their patient information can move from system to system. This method of using a clinical use case (a formal way of representing how a clinical system interacts with the environment) to demonstrate what can be accomplished if a system is interoperable is a powerful method to learn about this specific topic in the Annual Conference setting.

More Traditional and Formal CPD: Pursuing a First or Advanced Degree

Pursuit of a first degree, an advanced degree, or a different credential is a step that many health IT professionals decide is right for them. Demands of a current position, the pursuit of an advanced or different position, or simple enhancement of current knowledge and skills lead many health IT professionals back to school. However, "One problem for adults is the constant, competing tension between life obligations and educational obligations" (Pelletier, 2010, p. 3). What this means for the health informatics professional is that educational programs leading to a first, advanced, or new area of study must be congruent with the lifestyle and working situation of the potential student. Evening and weekend programs, accelerated programs, independent study programs, online degree programs with synchronous or asynchronous discussion (Internet only), distance-learning programs (real-time classes in remote locations), and hybrid programs (classroom and Internet) offer the first or advanced degree student multiple options for learning that fit into professional and personal life.

Academic transfer programs that allow completion of up to three years of work toward a baccalaureate degree at a community college with guaranteed transfer of credits assist those obtaining a first degree to meet their goal. The College Level Examination Program (https://clep.collegeboard.org/exam) allows the working professional to obtain college credit for those general education courses required of all baccalaureate degree programs (history and social sciences, composition and literature, science and mathematics, business and world languages).

More Traditional and Formal CPD: Non-Credit Courses (MOOCs and SPOCs)

Massive Online Open Courses (MOOC) as well as Small Private Online Courses (SPOC) have been touted as revolutionizing the academic and corporate education landscape (Kaplan and Haenlein 2016, p. 441). These MOOC and SPOC are offered by leading universities and provide the Health Informatics professional an alternative to traditional non-credit workshops and in-person courses. One or many courses can be taken at a single time and specializations can be obtained by completing sequences of recommended courses. With the completion of a capstone project, the student can receive a certificate of completion or a diploma.

MOOCs are accessible to anyone (massive enrollment) while SPOCs are designed for a small group targeting a specific subject. Participation in both of these methods of learning requires a high degree of "… intrinsic motivation and self-discipline. Successful graduates … tend to be older … (… 25–30 years) and already hold a first degree (80%), which they obtained through more traditional means. For most participants, a MOOC is … primarily a way to build new skills in order to strengthen an existing professional career" (Kaplan and Haenlein 2016, p. 444).

Both MOOCs and SPOCs can be synchronous or asynchronous, with the asynchronous mode dominating MOOCs and synchronous mode dominating SPOCs (Kaplan and Haenlein 2016). Testing of course material is conducted either online or in person at test centers. Multiple online providers offer these educational options through leading universities such as Duke, University of Michigan, Rice, Penn State, and Stanford. Costs are variable and discounts are applied if a student takes a series of courses leading to a specialization. Courses can be taken in such diverse areas as: Hospital and Health System Preparedness (Penn State Homeland Security Portfolio); Data Science (Johns Hopkins); a multi-course statistics specialization (Duke); and Bioinformatics Methods (University of Toronto).

Some Less Traditional and Informal Means of CPD: The Internet and Web 2.0

E-learning or E-CE is an all-encompassing term that can describe a number of informal options made possible by the Internet (Lam-Antoniades et al., 2009). Included in this designation are webinars, online journal clubs, mailing lists, blogs, evidence-based tweeting, LinkedIn™ discussion groups, podcasts, personal learning projects, and multiple Web 2.0 tools such as forums, bulletin boards, Wikis, tagging, and aggregators (Orok and Usoro 2015). Web 2.0 refers to services on the Internet that allow users to share data and interact with each other, (Constantinides and Fountain 2007). Though the tools were initially thought of as a new generation of Internet services (Dotsika and Patrick, 2007; Cosh et al., 2008), they have become ubiquitous in social communication and shown great promise in CPD and the acquisition of knowledge through virtual learning environments (Minocha, 2009; Chen et al., 2015). They have also shown great promise in the workplace for both in-place and mobile learning. The Web 2.0 technologies and the other entities included in E-learning or E-CE are appropriate additions to the more traditional methods of CPD.

The next section of this chapter will focus on these entities with brief descriptions of each.

Tools of the Internet

Webinars are one of the most prolific Internet tools for CPD by the working professional. Webinars are live meetings that take place over the Internet using tools such as Adobe Connect™, GoToMeeting™, WebEx™, or any other proprietary products that allow audio and video sharing of information (https://www.minitex.umn.edu/Training/Webinars.aspx). These meetings can be a discussion, a PowerPoint presentation for instruction, a demonstration of software or hardware, a panel presentation, or any other educational offering. They are generally 30–90 minutes in length and require nothing more than a web browser, and/or a telephone line. The webinars can accommodate large or small numbers of participants and can be found through professional organizations (http://www.himss.org/health-it-education/learning-center), the Federal government (https://www.healthit.gov/newsroom/2015-edition-webinars), universities and colleges (http://northernohio.himsschapter.org/event/ksu-nohimss-webinar-series) and vendors of health IT hardware and software, as examples. Organizations such as HIMSS offer access into Annual Conference presentations either during or after the conference through a webinar client. Continuing Education credits can be obtained through many of the webinars, making it an effective and efficient method of CPD for the Health Informatics professional.

Online Journal Clubs

Online journal clubs are a relatively new entry into the CPD arena. With a history dating back to the time of Sir William Osler, at McGill University in 1875, journal clubs provide a way for peers within and outside of individual institutions to meet and discuss knowledge and translate that knowledge into practice (Chan et al., 2015). The traditional journal club was usually found within a single medical specialty and was an in-person gathering either at a hospital, a clinician's home, or a remote location. A journal article or articles were distributed to the participants ahead of the meeting with explicit instructions to read and be ready to discuss. Despite the usefulness of this approach to knowledge sharing, traditional journal clubs have had low attendance and their value has been disputed among practitioners (Lizarondo et al., 2010).

Fast forward to the development of online journal clubs. These Internet-based entities offer distinct advantages over their face-to-face equivalent. First is the ability of the journal club to reach a wider audience of participants on a regular basis. It is possible to include colleagues outside of local borders, including international colleagues. Next is the convenience of the online version. With the use of webinar format, synchronous communication is possible. Since the journal club can be recorded, it is possible for those unable to attend in real time to listen to the discussion and contribute in an asynchronous fashion. Members can participate where and when they choose.

An asynchronous-only version of the online journal club is possible with the use of a facilitator or moderator who may use any number of tools at their disposal: Tutorials, research question development, discussion and appraisal of multiple literature sources and evaluation of the journal club itself (Lizarondo et al., 2010). The availability of full text services through the Internet, as well as the use of newsfeeds and improved search functions, extends the reach of the journal club to a larger number of practitioner views and opinions from a larger number of research and practice articles.

Originally designed as a way to promote better patient care and evidence-based practice, the online journal club allows this knowledge-sharing tool to be used by allied health professionals and health IT professionals. It allows them to keep pace with current literature, share use cases with each other, compare best practices in health information technology and solve problems of implementation and analytics using academic research.

To date, the online journal club format has been primarily used by Medical Informaticians, Nursing Informaticians and Bioinformatics practitioners. The use of this format by health Informaticians should be explored to a greater degree. Not only will it increase the CPD of the professional, but it will also bring to the forefront a more academic focus for the health informatics practitioner. The two articles noted in the reference list provide excellent tools for setting up an online journal club.

Listservs

Listservs are one of the earliest inventions on the Internet, but they are still relevant to the health informatics professional pursuing CPD. Though the Listserv was a program primarily created to manage email discussion lists (Manjoo, 2010), it has become much more in this age of burgeoning information. Further, if you want to have a real discussion about a topic, the Listserv is the most reliable tool available that will allow you to do this. While Facebook™, Tumblr, and Twitter™ allow an idea to be popularized, criticized, and widely disseminated, a Listserv allows you to really discuss an idea, in either a negative or positive way (Manjoo, 2010). In addition to the opportunity to really discuss an idea, a Listserv allows for longer and more meaningful messages.

Another advantage of the Listserv over Twitter™ or Facebook™ is that Listservs are closed. You must subscribe to be a part of them, and that allows for more honest discussion when an individual is sharing with a group invested in the topic of the Listserv.

So, how does one find a Listserv of interest? The best place to start is on Health Informatics websites. Many of the popular websites used by health IT professionals allow subscription on the first page. Type in your email address, perhaps send an email to the list with the command "Subscribe" and you will start receiving information about discussions of interest. For instance, if you want the latest information on Meaningful Use, the Office of the National Coordinator of Health Information technology allows subscriptions to various Listservs on the front page. Colleges and Universities frequently have Listservs for their students but may allow outsiders if they apply. Another way to find health Informatics Listservs is to go to http://www.lsoft.com/lists/list_q.html. This is a website that allows a user to search for Listservs related to their particular interest. You do not have to read all the discussion immediately; most Listservs archive the discussion activity, so you can return to it when you have the time.

While Listserv activity cannot be used to obtain recertification hours, it does provide an effective method of having a discussion of various sides of an issue with like-minded colleagues.

LinkedIn™ Discussion Groups (Communities of Practice)

Related to Listservs are the communities of practice built on a social media platform, such as LinkedIn. As defined by Trayner and Wenger-Trayner, "Communities of practice are groups of people who share a concern or a passion for something they do and learn how to do it better as they interact regularly" (2015, p. 1). The use of social media has been shown to be an effective tool in creating communities of practice as well as pursuing continuous professional development (Grajales et al., 2014; Moore, 1973). Communities of practice allow the participants to share and compare knowledge, but also to develop an identity as a member of that community. As an example, Dong et al. (2015), describe a LinkedIn group formed by hand surgeons called Hand Surgery International. This group develops, shares, and maintains specific knowledge about the practice of hand surgery, with a goal of members interacting with peers in the online Community of Practice to share knowledge about hand surgery and to develop their professional identity as hand surgeons.

Communities of Practice have not been frequently used in health informatics, though a cursory review of LinkedIn groups indicates multiple groups that relate to health informatics and could become communities of practice. Among these are: Healthcare IT and Electronic Medical Records, Health-IT/EHR/HIS, Health Information Technology, Healthcare Analytics and Informatics, HIEWatch, Healthcare Informatics Knowledge Network, Health Informatics Forum, CPHIMS, Clinical Informatics Leadership, HIMSS, American Nursing Informatics Association, American Medical Informatics Association and many, many more. While there is a plethora of groups relating to healthcare informatics, few of them have more than three or four messages posted and none of them act as a community of practice. In order for this to occur, moderators and members of these groups need to take an active role in the group and assign value to what is being written and discussed. Because the concept of communities of practice are not well known in healthcare informatics community, there are no shared domains of interest, few interactions or learning together, and many of the participants are not practitioners, merely persons whose interests lie in health informatics. Unless and until all elements (The Domain, The Community and The Practice) are combined and developed, these LinkedIn groups will not become communities of practice and will not contribute to CPD for health IT professionals (Trayner and Wenger-Trayner 2015).

It is important that the concept of communities of practice be developed among health IT professionals to take advantage of the sharing and learning opportunities that can be realized.

Evidence-Based Tweeting and Tweeting the Meeting

There are a growing number of healthcare professionals using Twitter™ for professional purposes. In 2010, it was estimated that there were 19,100 nurses on Twitter™ (Moorley and Chinn, 2014b). In 2014, there were 3,800 health communities, with 6.6 million healthcare Twitter profiles and 10,000 provider profiles (Moorley and Chinn, 2014b). There are multiple health IT-related hashtags (http://www.symplur.com/healthcare-hashtags/regular/page/1/I) that handle thousands of health IT-related tweets per day.

With the use of Twitter by health IT professionals in general and health IT professionals in particular, increasing, it is safe to infer that this social media platform can be a useful mechanism for CPD. Evidence-based tweeting and tweeting the meeting show the most promise.

Evidence-based tweeting uses URL links in the tweets to Pub Med articles about a particular topic (Djuricich, 2014). The information in the tweet allows those following the feed the opportunity to access evidence about the topic as well as peer-reviewed publications. Followers can join in on a live or asynchronous discussion using the URL provided by the tweet. Evidence has shown (Moorley and Chinn, 2014a) that either formal or informal use of Twitter through a formal community denoted by a hashtag contribute to CPD through the sharing of information, ideas, and opinions.

Tweeting the meeting, that is, setting up a hashtag prior to a local or national educational conference and using that hashtag as a filter, has seen increased use in the past five years (Djuricich, 2014; Chaudhry et al., 2012) Participants at the meeting are asked to tweet about the meeting itself or the content of the meeting such as research findings, treatment options, or to set up "tweet chats," prearranged synchronous online conversations with tweets posted to the same hashtag (Chaudhry et al., 2012).

Both evidence-based tweeting and tweeting the meeting can be useful tools for the health informatics professional to learn and disseminate information about important topics. Those in a meeting and outside of the meeting can potentially benefit from the live tweeting and the subsequent "conversations" that can take pace. The use of live tweeting, especially at a conference where groundbreaking findings are being released can outpace the normal rate of dissemination of either print or online information and can be used as a powerful tool for CPD.

Podcasts

Audio and video podcasts have been used in health professionals' education for multiple years. These podcasts consist of digital media made available on the Internet for download to a computer, a portable device, or a smartphone. Many podcasts are available by subscribing to a site and may be comprised of a series of presentations around a particular topic.

While audio podcasts are the predominant form of the tool, video podcasts have become increasingly popular. Video podcasts usually consist of a set of PowerPoint slides and an audio track that captures the narration. They can be used to augment or even replace a live lecture by removing geographic and time restrictions. Parts of the podcasts can be repeated at will.

The use of both audio and video podcasting could create relationships between professionals that allow them to engage in active discussions and seek out additional resources for learning. However, as useful and convenient as these tools are, many seeking out CPD view them as less stimulating than a live lecture and tend to use them only sporadically (Schreiber et al., 2010).

Blogs

The use of blogs in CPD can be a way to store opinions, thoughts, ideas, and reflections about a topic. As open access, personal web pages for a health informatics professional, a blog can be a way to share insights and encourage open and honest discussion through comments on the blog. While blogs are not peer reviewed, the discussion that occurs on them can be seen as a form of peer review as individuals react to postings (Moorley and Chinn, 2014b).

The reflective component of a blog can be used as a personal log of CPD and a method to review the thought processes that were at work in the individual postings. A user can put themselves in the shoes of any number of people to reflect on the various aspects of a situation and gather information that will enhance their own learning. Reflection on a topic and receiving feedback from like-minded individuals help the blogger to develop thinking in a structured manner and become more analytic (Moorley and Chinn, 2014b). While not used by many health IT professionals, this is a tool than can help an individual pursue CPD while recording their work experiences, their reflections, and their disappointments.

Wikis

While blogging is primarily a solitary exercise unless connected to other blogs, true collaboration for CPD can come from the use of wikis, long considered true social networking tools (Minocha, 2009). As a collaborative writing tool, the development of a wiki can aggregate the information from many professionals into a single document that reflects the totality of the users' knowledge.

Because of the collaborative nature of a wiki, it has occasionally been suggested that letting anyone edit allows for misinformation to be perpetuated (Kohs, 2015). Indeed, the recent experiment by Kohs (2015) indicates that even while trying to correct the misinformation, he was blocked from continuing and the old information was being restored. While that may be a potential problem in Wikipedia, the control exerted by a group of like-minded professionals collaborating on an article for publication, developing a knowledge base, and/or building community among themselves is a deterrent to deliberate misinformation in that wiki. The very nature of a collaborative effort supposes that there will be some mistakes made, perhaps some biased statements made. But collaboration is an activity that can assist in correcting these items and contributions made by the members of the wiki can be vetted by them. Wikipedia and a wiki for CPD by a group of like-minded professionals are two different entities and, as such, cannot be compared. It is a disservice to the concept of wiki to regard all wikis as clones of Wikipedia.

As a tool for collaboration and sharing among health IT professionals, a wiki can be a useful tool to build a knowledge base and share information.

Conclusion

CPD by health IT professionals can take a variety of forms and be pursued for various reasons. Whether it is a formal workshop to obtain certification renewal credits, the pursuit of a first or advanced degree, or an informal gathering of like-minded professionals sharing information through a blog, a wiki or a podcast, the pursuit of CPD is a necessity for obtaining and maintaining knowledge and skills.

Health IT professionals work in a complex and volatile environment as a result of changes in healthcare brought about by legislative, financial, and philosophical issues. Thus, CPD is no longer a solitary activity of an individual seeking further continuing education credits. It is, instead, a complex issue that resides at the organizational, departmental, and unit level. Changing the behavior of an individual is a reasonably difficult activity if the individual does not desire change. Changing that same behavior but in an organizational context, is more difficult due to the complexity of the situation and the number of individuals involved (Olson, 2012).

If we wish to change the practice of health informatics professionals, we must focus on the collaboration among professional teams and not on the individual professionals. Interprofessional education must become more commonplace and health IT professionals must emerge from their silos along with their physician and nurse counterparts and pursue CPD as a group.

There are multiple reasons to pursue CPD as an individual; there are more reasons to work in a collaborative and interprofessional way to achieve the goals of CPD.

References

Chan, T.M., Thoma, B., Radecki, R., Topf, J., Woo, H.H., Kao, L.S., Cochran, A., Hiremath, S., and Lin, M. (2015). Ten steps for setting up an online journal club. *Journal of Continuing Education in the Health Professions*, 35(2), 148–154.

Chaudhry, A., Glode, M., Gillman, M., and Miller, R.S. (2012). Trends in twitter use by physicians at the American society of clinical oncology annual meeting, 2010 and 2011. *Journal of Oncology Practice*, 8(3), 173–178.

Chen, Z.S.C., Yang, S.J.H., and Huang, J.J.S. (2015). Constructing an e-portfolio-based integrated learning environment supported by library resources. *The Electronic Library*, 33(2), 273–291.

Constantinides, E. and Fountain, S. (2007). Special issue papers. Web 2.0: Conceptual foundations and marketing Issues. *Journal of Direct, Data and Digital Marketing Practice*, 9(3), 231–244.

Cosh, K. J., Burns, R., and Daniel, T. (2008). Content clouds: Classifying content in Web 2.0. *Library Review*, 57(9), 722–729.

Djuricich, A. M. (2014). Social media, evidence-based tweeting, and JCEHP. *Journal of Continuing Education in the Health Professions*, 34(4), 202–204.

Dong, C., Cheema, M., Samarasekera, D., and Rajaratnam, V. (2015). Using LinkedIn for continuing community of practice among hand surgeons worldwide. *Journal of Continuing Education in the Health Professions*, 35(3), 185–191.

Dotsika, G. and Patrick, K. (2007). Knowledge sharing: Development from within. *The Learning Organization*, 14(5), 395–406.

Grajales, F.J., Sheps, S., Ho, K., Novak-Lauscher, H., and Eysenbach, G. (2014). Social media: A review and tutorial of applications in medicine and health care. *Journal of Medical Internet Research*, 16(2), e13.

Kaplan, A. M. and Haenlein, M. (2016). Higher education and the digital revolution: About MOOCs, SPOCS, social media and the cookie monster. *Business Horizons*, 59(4), 441–450.

Kohs, G. (2015). Experiment concludes: Most misinformation inserted into Wikipedia may persist. Retrieved from: http://wikipediocracy.com/2015/04/13/experiment-concludes-most-misinformation-inserted-into-wikipedia-may-persist/.

Lam-Antoniades, M., Ratnapalan, S., and Tait, G. (2009). Electronic continuing education in the health professions: An update on evidence from RCTs. *Journal of Continuing Education in the Health Professions*, 29(1), 44–51.

Lizarondo, L., Kumar, S., and Grimmer-Somers, K. (2010). Online journal clubs: An innovative approach to evidence-based practice. *Journal of Allied Health*, 39(1), E17–E22.

Manjoo, F. (2010). The joy of listservs. *Slate.* Retrieved from: http://www.slate.com/articles/technology/technology/2010/08/the_joy_of_listservs.html.

Minocha, S. (2009). Role of social software tools in education: A literature review. *Education and Training*, 51(5 & 6), 553–369.

Mizell, H. (2010). Why professional development matters. Retrieved from: https://learningforward.org/docs/pdf/why_pd_matters_web.pdf?sfvrsn=0.

Moore, M.G. (1973). Towards a theory of independent learning and teaching. *Journal of Higher Education*, 44(9), 661–679.

Moorley, C. and Chinn, T. (2014a). Nursing and Twitter: Creating an online community using hashtags. *Collegian*, 21(2), 103–109.

Moorley, C. and Chinn, T. (2014b). Using social media for continuous professional development. *Journal of Advanced Nursing*, 71(4), 713–717.

Olson, C.A. (2012). Twenty predictions for the future of CPD: Implications of the shift from the update model to improving clinical practice. *Journal of Continuing Education in the Health Professions*, 32(3), 151–152.

Orok, B. and Usoro, A. (2015). Factors affecting the effectiveness of web 2.0 as a mobile learning tool in the workplace: A conceptual view. *Computing & Information Systems*, 19(1), 6–14.

Pelletier, S. G. (2010). Success for adult students. *Public Purpose*, 1–6. Retrieved from: http://www.aascu.org/uploadedFiles/AASCU/Content/Root/MediaAndPublications/PublicPurposeMagazines/Issue/10fall_adultstudents.pdf.

Schambach, T.S. and Blanton, J.E. (2002). The professional development challenge for IT professionals. *Communications of the ACM*, 45(4), 83–87.

Schreiber, B.E., Fukuta, J., and Gordon, F. (2010). Live lecture versus video podcasts in undergraduate medical education: A randomized controlled trial. *BioMedCentral Medical Education*, 10(68), 1–6.

Trayner, E. and Wenger-Trayner, B. (2015). *Communities of Practice: A Brief Introduction.* Retrieved from: http://wenger-trayner.com/wp-content/uploads/2015/04/07-Brief-introduction-to-communities-of-practice.pdf.

Wenger, E. (1998). Communities of practice: Learning, meaning and identity. *Systems Thinker*, 9, 2–3.

Wylie, J. (2015). *10 Reason for Continuous Professional Development (CPD).* Retrieved from: https://www.linkedin.com/pulse/10-reasons-continuous-professional-development-cpd-jordan-ylie.

Bibliography

Al-Badi, A. M., Al Roobaea, R., and Mayhew, P. (2013). Improving usability of social networking systems: A case study of LinkedIn. *Journal of Internet, Society, Networks and Virtual Communities*, 1–23.

Harris, H. and Park, S. (2008). Educational uses of podcasting. *British Journal of Educational Technology*, 39(3), 548–551.

Chapter 25

Engaging Socially to Expand Professional Competency

By Colonel Kevin P. Seeley

Col, USAF, MSC, CPHIMS

Contents

Abstract

Engaging socially is no longer an option for those serious about developing one's competencies in health IT. Social sites like Twitter, LinkedIn, Facebook, and many others provide a level of unparalleled learning that supplements one's professional role. Review the challenges and opportunities with engaging socially.

Keywords:

Socialize
Competencies

Social Media Tools
Online Presence
Social Engagement
Learning
Career Advancement
Job Transition
Professional Reputation Branding
Collaboration
Contribution
Exposure
Growth
Thought Leadership
Beliefs
Digital Persona
Personal Learning Network
Learning
Sharing

socialize verb *so·cial·ize*\'sō-shə-ˌhz\

: to talk to and do things with other people in a friendly way
: to teach (someone) to behave in a way that is acceptable in society

intransitive verb
: to participate actively in a social group

Merriam-Webster.com

As health information technology (health IT) professionals working in a constantly changing healthcare system it has become imperative to network and engage socially with other health IT colleagues, peers, and thought leaders to ensure professional growth, development, and reciprocal mentorship. Regardless of whether you're a health IT executive (Chief Information Officer [CIO], Chief Medical Information Officer [CMIO], Chief Nursing Information Officer [CNIO], Chief Information Security Officer [CISO], Chief Technology Officer [CTO], Chief Digital/Data Officer [CDO]); physician, nurse, or pharmacist in a health IT-related position; informaticist; health data scientist, analyst or researcher; vendor salesperson; health systems architect, administrator, developer; front-line IT support technician; or IM/IT director; connecting with other health IT professionals will help you learn and gain outside expertise that you could not otherwise obtain on your own within your current organizational environment. As you commit to engaging socially, you not only improve and enrich other's careers, you also fill the roles of both teachers and students in a continuous learning cycle, advancing our health IT profession together as citizens of a community. Sharing information with other health IT professionals, both online and in person, helps create a personal learning environment that stimulates constructive dialogue and promotes the exchange of innovative ideas, insights, and experiences across the health IT and healthcare industry.

To develop and grow your health IT professional competencies, you should understand and embrace the role social engagement and social media play in supplementing your knowledge and expertise. As healthcare becomes increasingly connected, interoperable, and regulated, health IT professionals cannot limit themselves solely to local social networks. Career success now depends on using social media tools to establish a professional online presence and expand professional network connections. Without social media to maintain professional relationships and share the latest industry information, one risks being left behind (Arora 2014). So whether you're just starting out, or already have an extensive professional network and are fully connected online, this chapter will help guide your social engagement journey by (1) discovering "*why*" you need a personal vision and social engagement plan to get the most out of professional interactions, (2) exploring the different "*ways*" health IT professionals socialize online and in person, (3) discussing social media platforms as a primary "*means*" of discovering professional health IT learning and growth opportunities, and (4) distilling information on "*how*" to leverage LinkedIn, Facebook, Twitter, YouTube, GooglePlus, Pinterest, and other social media tools to boost the value of your engagement across the health IT community.

The Why

An important early step in your social engagement journey should be to establish a vision and goals for your future. Take a moment to inventory where you want to be in your health IT career in two, five, and ten years and consider how engaging socially, both online and in person, could help you get there, as well as what mutual benefits you can offer others across the profession. Ask yourself, "Why should I expend my time and energy to engage with other professionals, either online or in person, and what can I contribute back to the health IT community?" Examples of items to consider when answering could be your desires for: learning; career advancement; job transition(s); professional reputation branding and marketing; special interest problem-solving, collaboration and contribution; benefit(s) to patients, clinicians, customers and your organization; academic pursuits; human capital networking, exposure and growth; sharing specialized expertise; and local, regional or national thought leadership.

If you have trouble narrowing your career vision and goals, you can try the Warren Buffet method … that is, according to Angela Duckworth, author of *Grit: The Power of Passion and Perseverance*, there's a famous story about Warren Buffett telling his pilot to make a list of all the things he wanted to get done in life. As it turned out, like many of us, Buffet's pilot had a long list. Mr Buffet then tells him to circle his top five things and separate the rest of the items onto another list. He subsequently advises him to avoid at all costs anything that wasn't circled and to only focus on his five things. As it turns out, by identifying his top five things, Buffet helped his pilot discover his own personal theme, the "why" that motivated him to do the things that matter most, and ultimately the criteria upon which to base all his future decisions and priorities about where to expend time and energy. His lesson … you can't get everything done in life that you want to, so prioritize, then deprioritize the rest. (Duckworth 2016)

Another recommended method you may also want to try is to *Start With Why*, a book by author and speaker Simon Sinek which offers sage advice about identifying personal, professional, and organizational purpose. As the title states, Sinek encourages everyone to first start by answering a core question, "Why do you do the things you do?" rather than "What things do you do?" or "How you do things?" Sinek claims that too often most of us start with the "what" and "how" and do not spend enough time digging into the "why," which he emphasizes is the most powerful influence on our actions. The "why" reveals our core purpose, beliefs, and values that create our identity and drive our behaviors. The profound simplicity is that the "what" and "how" we do the things we do serve to outwardly support "why" we do them. He goes on to explain that since our brains are separated into feeling and logic functions it is easier for us to articulate our "what" and "how" logic, versus our "why" feelings, and only through conscious effort can we trace our "what" and "how" to our "why" (Sinek 2009). Regardless of how you get there, at the heart of every individual quest is a reason and purpose for expending valuable time and energy to act. Discovering why you identify with certain shared common values and beliefs should drive your personal health IT career vision and help you evaluate and establish goals upon which to plan your social engagements.

There are many different professional reasons why you should expend time and energy to engage socially; however, first understanding your personal reasons through self-reflection and introspective assessment will help shape and guide your personal plan for social engagement. To help you, an example outcome of performing the aforementioned self-assessment may read something like: *"As a current Electronic Health Record (EHR) Database Administrator I believe that technology will continue to transform and improve the future of healthcare delivery to benefit patients in my community and around the world. I feel I can contribute to that future throughout my career by optimizing health technology in my organization and helping others do the same. I see myself advancing from my current technical position to a Director of IT Operations in two to five years and then to a CIO position within ten years. To help me do this I will establish a strong professional digital presence on social media platforms where I will connect with colleagues directly, as well as join, subscribe and follow applicable online health IT groups and opinion leader forums. There I will share my work and expertise in partnering with clinicians and our CNIO to solve regional Health Information Exchange (HIE) data interface problems with our EHR, as well as my recent innovative solutions to our population health data hosting challenges. This will showcase my unique and relevant technical problem-solving skills and allow me to connect and learn from health IT peers, colleagues, and senior professionals about how they solved similar issues. I will also seek their mentoring and advice about obtaining an advanced degree in my field of interest. Furthermore, I will follow through with my social engagement by joining and participating in my local chapter and interest groups, and attending key events in-person that allow me to engage with Directors of health IT departments and healthcare CIOs face-to-face. My stretch goal would be to start a YouTube channel, Twitter feed, or LinkedIn forum to post and share how-to videos and advice to aid other health IT professionals."* Taking the time to write a similar paragraph in a statement tailored to your own circumstances and desires will give you a starting point of reference and personal social engagement strategic plan. This will help you focus and integrate your efforts with your health IT career goals and learning endeavors.

The Ways

Now that you've embraced your purpose for social engagement and developed a personal strategy, review the definition of "socialize" at the beginning of this chapter, and consider the different ways you can interact, teach, and participate in social groups across the health IT landscape. Social engagements can happen between you and others in *one-to-one, one-to-many, many-to-many,* or *many-to-one* relationships. When these quantitative relationships are cross-referenced with the three basic ways we professionally socialize and interact: (1) *Direct in person* (i.e., face-to-face), (2) *Direct virtual* (i.e., digital persona), (3) *Indirect third person* (i.e., word of mouth in-person or online), it renders practical examples of the different ways we engage and communicate socially. Table 25.1 provides examples of ways health IT professionals can interact and engage socially to expand their professional networks, remain visible, and learn, teach, and contribute across the health IT community.

Table 25.1 Ways to Socially Engage

	Direct In Person Examples	Direct Virtual Examples	Indirect Third Person Examples
One-to-One (you)	Face-to-face, formal and informal events, mixers mentor/protégé coffee, work lunches, outside work socials, post seminar Q&A discussion line	Online forums, social media, phone calls, media, blogs, vlogs, chat rooms, individual email, peer-to-peer gaming, file sharing, email, YouTube video tutorials, computer based training modules, instant message, avatar to avatar	Online or in-person word-of mouth; shared gossip; facial/name/ brand/reputation recognition; grapevine, re-tweets, my profile views, profiles I viewed, content/interest group recommendations/ sharing, forwarded email
One-to-Many (you)	Speaker to audience, keynote address, teacher to students, professional affiliation chapter board member, local special interest group leader	Host live-stream or recorded webinars, Twitter (other) feed host, blog host, online LinkedIn, Facebook (other) special interest group facilitator/ moderator, mobile SMS, author professional publication/articles	Interested listener, bystander, loiterer, watcher; monitor/share online activity with others, but do not subscribe, join, commit, para-social interaction, forwarded email to group, retweet, re-share, re-post to larger groups
Many-to-Many (you)	Round-table participant, working group member, conference attendee, think tanks, special interest groups, active local chapter participant, flash mob	Shared posts, chat-rooms, online collaboration tools, LinkedIn, Facebook special interest group discussion contributor, online gaming, avatar worlds, crowd-sourcing, Google Hangouts	Rumors, likes, dislikes, subscribers, voting, shared opinions, comment threads, retrospective analysis, shared group email with larger group, social media sharing/interest groups, re-post, re-pin, re-tweet
Many-to-One (you)	Audience to speaker, attendee at keynote address, conference plenary and break-out sessions conference Keynote	Twitter/RSS feed subscriber, blog/vlog subscriber, personal learning network, webinar attendee, e-Mentoring, live-stream webinar attendee, avatar attendance	Reference another's work, pass along referrals, gossip, rumors, reputation to friend/colleague, hearsay, likes, dislikes, para-social interaction, retweet, re-share, re-post, email blast recipient, Pinterest followers

Looking back to the earliest days of computing we can see a desire to leverage social digital engagement from the start. Long before Facebook or Twitter, or even MySpace, users would connect to bulletin board systems, or BBSs, where they exchanged some of the first instant messages and peer-to-peer files with other like-minded BBS users. BBSs were effectively the first widespread online digital chat rooms, and arguably the first digital "social media" tools prior to the introduction of the term. In the 1980s BBSs were primarily used by computer enthusiasts because it took special knowledge and tech savvy to navigate command lines and push and retrieve messages and files. Back then, in order to message different people on different BBSs, you had to hang-up your telephone modem and dial another BBS to connect with different social or interest groups, and if you received a busy signal you'd have to try back later. Avid BBS users had multiple phone lines installed so that they could be on multiple BBSs with multiple modems and computers at the same time.

Fast forward to today. In slightly less than one generation social media has become one of the most powerful tools and influences in our world. As shown in Table 25.1, the common thread in the "direct virtual" and "indirect third person" columns is the prevalent use of online interactive, virtual, and social media tools. Because social media is available 24 hours a day, 7 days a week, 365 days a year, individuals can now be digitally present anytime, anywhere and engage at their convenience without constraints of physical presence at specific times or places. Capitalizing on a no-cost or low-cost (depending on the social media services you choose) professional digital persona that's always on duty should entice you to set up and manage, or improve upon, your current social media profile(s). Doing so can amplify your reputation and name and face recognition across the health IT community at in-person organizational events, regional professional affiliation chapter gatherings, and national conferences. It also provides you with a way to invite, track, and maintain the connections you make in person with other professionals. Your social media profile is now the twenty-first-century equivalent to a business card ... health IT professionals should not be caught without one.

Table 25.1 again highlights the expanding role and growing number of ways to engage socially online. Virtual/digital social media engagement and networking can be initiated via blogs, fan pages, RSS (really simple syndication) feeds, interest groups, forums, podcasts, video/picture-sharing, vlogs, wall-postings, email, instant messaging, peer-to-peer content sharing, and unified communications tools. With the limitless reach of social media, individuals, businesses, academia, governments, and healthcare organizations can conduct more effective information sharing, promotion, and outreach to target audiences and like-minded people.

There are hundreds of social media applications, as well as an ever-growing number of social media management and aggregation tools to help holistically manage your digital presence. Depending on your personal goals and limited time, health IT professionals must carefully choose the ways to engage and which social media tools to leverage as a means of generating the best learning opportunities. Thoughtfully utilizing the right social media tools as a primary means to exchange information and make connections that focus on your goals will create the greatest value to you as a health IT professional.

The Means

Health IT professionals serious about social media engagement will immediately encounter an overwhelming number of social media platforms to choose from. To highlight just how many platforms exist, Table 25.2 lists 20 social media platform categories and over 250 social media tools, applications, and utilities. Many social media applications often cross multiple categories and

Table 25.2 Social Media Categories, Tools, Applications, and Services

Social Media Categories: (20)
Conversation Apps - Social networking - Micro-blogging - Publishing-Wikis - Photo Sharing - Aggregators - Audio - Video - Live Casting - RSS - Mobile - Crowd Sourcing - Virtual Worlds - Gaming - Search - Engagement - Marketing - Management - Analytics - Influencer

Social Media Tools, Applications, and Services: (250+) *alphabetical compilation*
100zakladok - Adfty - Adifni - Adobe/Omniture - ADV QR - Agorapulse - Amazon - Amen Me! - AngiesList - AOL Lifestream - AOL Mail - Appinions - APSense - Argyle Social - Arto - Attensity - AvatarsUnited - Awareness - Awasu - Baidu - Balatarin - Beat100 - Bebo - Bit.ly - BizSugar - Blab - Bland takkinn - Blogger - Blogkeen - Blogmarks - Bobrdobr - BonzoBox - Bookmarky.cz - Bookmerken - Box - Buddy Media - Buffer - Camyoo - Care2 - CSS Based - Cherry Share - CiteULike - CleanPrint - CleanSave - Cloob - Communicate - Copy Link - COSMiQ - CoTweet - Crimson Hexagon - Crowd Booster - Dashburst - Delicious - Diary.ru - Digg - Diggita - Diigo - Doc2Doc - Docphin - Douban - Doximity - Draugiem.lv - EdCast - EFactor - eHost - EngageSciences - EventBrite - Evernote - Exchangle - FabDesign - Fabulously40 - Facebook - Facebook Messenger - Facenama - Fai Informazione - Fancy - Fashiolista - FAVable - Fave - Favorites - Favoritus - Feedly - Financial Juice - Flickr - Flipboard - Folkd - FourSquare - FreeDictionary - FriendFeed - GG - G-mail - Go.vn - Google+ - Google Analytics - Google Bookmark - Google Classroom - Google Reader - Google Translate - GroupHigh - Hacker News - Hatena - Hearsay Social - Hedgehogs - historious - HootSuite - HTML Validator - Hyper - IFTTT - Indexor - Instagram - Instapaper - Involver - iOrbix - Jappy Ticker - Jugnoo - Kaixin Repaste - Kakao - Ketnooi - Kik - Kindle It - Kledy - Klout - Kred - LiDAR Online - LINE - LinkedIn - Linkuj.cz - Lithium - LiveJournal - Mail.ru - mar.gar.in - Markme - Medworm - meinVZ - Meltwater Buzz - Memonic - Memori.ru - Mendeley - Meneame - Mindomo - Mixi - Moemesto.ru - MouthShut - mRcNEtwORK - MS Lync - MS Outlook - MS Skype for Business - Myspace - myVidster - N4G - Nasza-klasa - Netvibes - Netvouz - NewsNetWire - NewsMeBack - Newsvine - Ning - Nujij - Nurses Lounge - Odnoklassniki - OKNOtizie - OpenTheDoor - Ovid - Oyyla - PageLever - pafnet. de - Path - PDFmyURL - Peach - Peek Analytics - People Browsr - Periscope - Pinboard - Pinterest - Plaxo - Plexus Engine - Plurk - Pocket - Posteezy - Postling - PrintFriendly - Pusha - QRSrc.com - Quantcast - QuantiaMD - Quora - Qzone - Radian6 - Reddit - Rediff MyPage - Renren - ResearchGate - Retellity - Safelinking - SAS - Scoop.it - Second Life - Sermo - Sharpreader - Shots - ShortStack - Shoutlet - Simply Measured - Sina Weibo - Skyrock Blog - Slack - Sloodle - SMI - SnapChat - Social - Bakers - Shots - SocialBro - SocialEngage - SocialFlow - SocialMention - SocialOomph - SodaHead - SpinSnap - Spredfast - Sprinklr - Sprout Social - Startaid - Startlap - studiVZ - Stuffpit - StumbleUpon - Stumpedia - SUP BRO - Surfinghird - Svejo - Swix - Symbaloo - Syncapse - Sysomos - Taringa! - TED - TEDMED - Telegram - Tencent QQ - Tencent Weibo - ThisNext - Tinder - TinyURL - Trackur - Trello - TrustedID Reppler - Tuenti - Tumblr - Tweepi - TweetDeck - Twitter - Typepad - Urlaubswerk - Viadeo - Viber - Vimeo - Vine - ViralHeat - Virb - Visible Technologies - Visitez Mon Site - Vitrue - Vkontakte - vKruguDruzei - Vocus - VoiceThread - VOXopolls - vybrall SME - Wanelo - Wayz - Wayback Machine - Web.com - WebMoney - WeChat - Weebly - WhatsApp - Whois Lookup - Wiggio - Wikipedia - Wildfire - WishMindr - Within3 - Wix - WordPress - Wykop - XING - Yahoo Mail - Yammer - Yelp - YikYak - Yo - Yookos - Yoolink - Yorumcuyum - YouMob - YouTube - Yummly - Yuuby - Zakladok.net - ZicZac - Zimbra - ZingMe - Zoho

Source: Compiled from web search results and Bard (2010), Baer (2015), and King (2011).

functions, making clear alignment of applications to categories difficult at best. The lists are not exhaustive and you'll notice the familiar mainstream social media applications are comingled with less recognizable applications. These lesser known applications sometimes offer niche capabilities and may come and go as fads with usage are often driven by hype or narrow use functionalilty. It's easy to get caught up in constant hype, suggestions, and referrals from friends and colleagues; however, the large mainstream applications provide stable, far-reaching platforms upon which to establish a solid digital persona and social media presence.

One of the first recommendations to maximize your limited social media engagement time and energy is to initially focus on the most popular market-share leaders like LinkedIn, Facebook, Twitter, Google Plus, YouTube, and Pinterest. These are the familiar mainstream applications that you consistently see on the primary "Share This" buttons located on nearly every corporate and social media webpage today. As you progress and advance your social media skills you can investigate and potentially leverage other tools, like those designed to be excusively for healthcare professionals (Ventola 2014). According to Debra Beck, author of "Social Media Vital to Professional Development," these mainstream tools offer the best immediate access to authors, educators, and opinion leaders and will most amplify your online presence and exposure to professional and career development resources. They present legitimate opportunities to not only share information and resources, but frequently enable individuals to initiate and invite direct engagement with industry leaders (Beck 2014).

LinkedIn is consistently recommended as a premier networking site for professionals and business people. Its primary focus is connecting professionals and sharing ideas and important information about work in a business-like atmosphere. Although Facebook was originally rooted in personal networking, it is now firmly established in the professional networking space too. An important factor to consider when using Facebook is the crossover potential between personal and professional profiles. It is important that a conscious effort is made to ensure your professional digital persona stays professional. Similarly, Twitter, Google Plus, YouTube, and Pinterest can be used as both personal and professional sharing platforms, yet all of these mainstream tools provide the means to establish your digital persona and connect with and learn from health IT professionals across town and around the globe.

One recurring theme for professionals that want to fully leverage the benefits of the mainstream social media giants is to adhere to a disciplined approach and commit to certain platforms for personal use and others as strictly professional. You may want to consider an "all professional content" approach with the mainstream social media applications and use the niche tools for sharing of personal life items. Whichever applications you choose to use, you must study and clearly understand how to use and maintain the often-changing privacy and security settings on each social media platform.

A good way to review your digital persona is to search for yourself, or watch a friend search for you, on the primary search engines such as Google, Yahoo, and Bing so you can see what other professionals see when they search for you. If you don't like what you find, you should clean up and update your profile(s) content, privacy, and security settings. Advanced users of multiple social media tools may want to consider aggregation and online image monitoring tools to manage all profiles.

The How

Although you may not recognize it, you already have what's described as an informal personal learning network (Arora 2014) made up of your relationships with the people you know and interact with frequently. These existing relationships are the foundation upon which to build and expand social media network connections and link to further professional development opportunities. To begin or advance your social engagement journey your next step should be to establish or improve online profile(s) on one or more mainstream social media tools.

A closer look at what LinkedIn, Facebook, Twitter, Google Plus, YouTube, Pinterest, and other tools can offer will help you choose which ones best fit your health IT professional learning needs. By summarizing the basics of mainstream social media platforms and how to establish a professional digital profile on each, you'll be able to quickly start leveraging their networking, content-sharing, and functional capabilities for your personal learning network. In every case you should reference and apply the repeatable generic social media "Do's and Don'ts Checklist" in Table 25.3. It summarizes important tips and reminders on configuring and maintaining social media profiles, privacy, and security settings.

As you step through setting up your social media profiles be sure to refer back to your "why" social engagement strategy to ensure your desired outcomes stay at the forefront. Specifically search each social media tool to find, bookmark, and connect with target health IT groups and individuals that match your career goals and personal objectives. Since LinkedIn has a professional focus and search results indicate 54,000+ individuals, groups, jobs, and posts related to health IT, and, more specifically, 1,784 groups related to health information practices, it is a great place to start connecting.

LinkedIn

LinkedIn claims to be the world's largest professional network with more than 300 million members in 200+ countries. Sixty-one percent of LinkedIn's members are located outside of the United States; members did nearly 4.2 billion professionally oriented searches on the platform in 2011. It offers a large database of other people's job titles, professions, career paths, companies, and career opportunities from which to mine, study and learn. Similar to other mainstream social media applications, LinkedIn has a powerful mobile app for Android and iOS, which allows you to remotely manage your profile and connections on the go (Prodromou, 2015).

Set up a LinkedIn account and complete your profile as thoroughly as possible using the automated interview. Be sure to include your current and two prior positions, skills, education, a professional photo, and professional career summary. Treat your profile as if it were your digital resume. The site provides you with a "profile completeness" metric from 0% to 100%. The higher your completeness, the more likely you are to appear higher up in LinkedIn's search results. Search health IT-related terms in your specific areas of interest to find and join one or more groups. Immediately connect with those already in your personal learning network sphere that also have a profile. To get your first "50 connections" in LinkedIn, make use of its many algorithms and data-mining features on the "People You May Know" page. Generously give and request endorsements and recommendations. To learn more about LinkedIn you can read *Ultimate Guide To: LinkedIn for Business*, by Ted Prodromou.

Facebook

Facebook has more than 1.28 billion active monthly users, which is roughly one-sixth of the entire world population. The social networking giant has introduced an extensive array of tools throughout its evolution that can be used effectively for professional growth. Whether it is Facebook groups, Business pages or Events, each of these functions is a great way of communicating with

Table 25.3   Checklist of Social Media Do's and Don'ts for Health IT Professionals

DO	DON'T

• Search for yourself to see what others see
• Remove unprofessional and personal content
• Develop a professional profile
  • Business-like email address only
  • Professional photos only
  • Consistent across platforms
  • Update every 2–3 months
  • Add professional sig block
• Make a great first digital impression
• Add health IT keywords/tags/current and future interest areas to profile so others can search and find you
• Join health IT interest groups/areas
• Only accept/seek professionals in your area(s) of interest that you want to learn from
• Contribute to your online forums … ratings are good value to your career
• Consider paying for premium services at strategic times in your career
• Create a professional signature on your email
• Consider aggregators to monitor multiple social sites in one place if advanced user
• Answer visitor messages
• Post, tweet, share, contribute twice a week
• Unfriend or disconnect with those acting unprofessionally
• Keep messages short and succinct
• Reduce/filter/delete irrelevant clutter/noise
	• Add unprofessional content (personal pix)
	• Post sexual, religious, political, cute content
	• Comingle personal and professional content
	• Completely replace in-person interaction
	• Accept invites to vague groups or evident solicitors; keep your network pure to you
	• Ignore your profile or set-it and forget it
	• Include phone numbers, just email or social media handle for contact
	• Where you live, the postal code of your place of employment is enough
	• Create different profiles for different social media platforms, all should be consistent
	• Ignore or relax privacy and security settings
	• Compromise your network by friending or allowing connections that tarnish your image
	• Make negative, insulting, or petty posts
	• Discuss controversial hot topics
	• Forget to add at least one attention getter picture to posts … still worth 1000 words
	• Forget that the information you put online benefits the company through aggregation and sale of information to other companies that use it to target audiences for products and services; refer to last item in "Do" list

Source: Adapted from Murray (2016) and Pollack (2012).

experts, spreading new ideas, building relationships and contacts, and trying new things (Arora 2014).

Create a professional Facebook page by adding the same information to your profile that you did on LinkedIn, then search for and take advantage of online communities to which you are already affiliated. This might include your organization's page, your university's wall, the Facebook fan page of a nonprofit you support, or an industry association listserv. Once you are a member, use the Facebook search tool to find and join health IT interest groups and friend-related companies. Connect with people and groups who share common interests. Comment on and participate in discussion threads. The Events feature will keep you informed about the latest learning opportunities happening in and around your city and update you on professional activities that you can attend for further networking. The search engine combines the job databases of US.jobs, Monster, Jobvite, BranchOut, and WORK4LABS, enabling discovery of exclusive job opportunities. Be sure to "Like" and "Share" professional interest pages, company and organizational pages, and content with others. Add descriptions titles and tags in the "About" section of your profile that reflect your health IT professional interests. Again, try to avoid personal likes and dislikes, hobbies, opinions, and descriptions. Use your "Status" to discuss your accomplishments and future goals. Become an active contributor to your connected group pages to build and enhance your professional network.

Twitter

According to the company's latest reports Twitter has over 250 million active users. Since Twitter accounts, tweets and pages are indexed by Google, Twitter can be a powerful online presence for users. Foremost it allows users to connect with like-minded learning professionals who follow shared interests, news stories, and industry trends. Twitter is also a powerful tool to research and connect with recruiters, industry experts, and colleagues. Even if you primarily "monitor" content more than you tweet, you'll value the information because it is customized to your professional interests.

After setting up a Twitter account you'll need to learn Twitter jargon. This social media tool has a small learning curve, but as you become familiar with terminology such as hashtags, tweets, promoted tweets, RT (retweet), RLRT (real-life retweet), IRL (in real life), MT (modified tweet), OH (overheard), Timestamp and Activities, you'll become a mature participant in no time. Actively sending and relaying informative/instructional tweets and participating in Twitter chats around a particular subject area can bolster career development by increasing your professional exposure and reputation. Additionally, companies are increasingly tweeting job postings so you can be the first to hear about and share career opportunities with others.

Twitter can set you apart in the health IT community not only by enabling you to stay current within the industry and your field of interest, but also by helping you prepare for interviews and keeping you engaged in real-time opportunities. Once on Twitter, consider following your university, health IT professional organizations, respected health IT professionals, companies of interest, and your current organization of employment. Use a short professional "handle" (username on Twitter) that people can refer to you by if your real name is long, and "hashtag" using words that are career related such as #HITjobs, #HITemployment, and #healthIT. Your tweets should include your career interests, goals, experience, and training. Use your profile to showcase your skills and capabilities to other professionals. Avid users may want to consider organizing followed Twitter pages into lists and grouping them by related topics. This will enable you to view grouped tweets separately so that you are not overwhelmed by other users' tweets.

Google Plus

Google+ is a well featured social network launched in 2011 with integrations across a number of Google products, including Buzz and Profiles. One key element of Google+ is a focus on targeted sharing within subsets of your social group, which are what Google calls Circles. Circles are simply small groups of people that you can share focused content with like EHR admins, certification holders, classmates, and co-workers. Google+ also offers a function specifically for viewing, managing, and editing multimedia. The photo tab takes a user to all of the photos he or she has shared, as well as the ones he or she is tagged in. It's not just photo tagging though: Google+ includes an image editor (with Instagram/Snapchat-like photo effects), privacy options, and sharing features.

Again, create a professional profile on Google+ containing the same elements previously discussed for LinkedIn and Facebook, then search for and add health IT connections. You can then join Google "Hangouts," which is a unique group chat feature. Instead of directly asking a peer to join a group chat, users click "start a Hangout" and they're instantly in a video chatroom alone. At the same time, a message goes out to social circles letting them know that a colleague is "hanging out." Connected users can then join the Hangout as long as they have been placed in a circle that was invited by the person who created the Hangout. This is great way to connect and grow your social network as well as share with and teach other professionals in real time.

YouTube

This ubiquitous video-sharing site has more than 1 billion unique monthly users. Created in 2007, the YouTube Partner program has 30,000+ partners from 27 countries around the world (Arora 2014). With estimates from 60 to multiple 100s of hours of video being uploaded every minute, users can find video resources on almost any topic imaginable. The large variety of instructional video available and the fact that its hosted content is linked to more sites across the web than any other makes YouTube one of the top interactive social media tools for professional development. Professionals can even start their own YouTube channel to produce and post educational and instructional videos and vlogs (video blogs) on topics of interest. It is a great means to demonstrate your individual personal strengths and professional public speaking and communication skills.

Pinterest

Pinterest can be used to create an online visual identity for networking purposes and build a profile that showcases you as a health IT professional. Professionals will "Pin" resumes, events, organizations, academic institutions, volunteer and charity work, former employers, inspirational quotes, and general things that they've created. The content that you showcase on Pinterest is important, so keep your content consistent. You can "Like," "Pin," and "Repin" images that reflect your interests, as well as cross-link your other social media profiles.

When using Pinterest be sure to choose images that represent you, your past accomplishments, future goals, and website links that are educational and meaningful to your health IT colleagues. Consider how the content you choose will showcase you. What you choose to share on your "Board" is the most important part of your profile. Everything that you "Pin" should lead to something that represents you as a health IT professional. Make your Pinterest Board interesting and visually pleasing with eye-catching pictures to attract and gain more followers.

Blogs

Blogging allows you to demonstrate your professional expertise or knowledge of a specific subject by writing about it. A few popular blogging sites are Wordpress, Tumblr, WorkBuzz, One Day, One Job and Blogger. Your blogs have the potential to be shared widely across the web and can lead to vast networking opportunities. Blog posts should be between 500 and 1000 words and include an enticing heading and a catchy summation title. This signals to potential readers that they can learn a lot for a small investment of time.

Professional bloggers keep blogs relevant and current and often include references to further materials, books, articles, and research. Like other social media posts, the success of your blog can also be easily increased by adding pictures, videos, and music. Check to see if a health IT professional that you like has a blog and "Follow" the blogs of those that share your interests. Be cautious of how you comment on other's blogs. Constructive and suggestive comments can be uplifting, while harsh comments reflect negativity and can be discouraging.

Aggregators

Social media aggregation tools such as Ning, Tumblr, TrustedID Reppler, TweetDeck, and Hootsuite are applications that automate the management of multiple social media platforms or profiles at once. These tools can help professionals manage information overload in an era where social media, email and 24-hour news cycles can inundate the savviest users. An increasing number of dashboards and platforms are available to bring accounts, services, and content together on a single central location for ease of use. Social media developers have consolidated applications such as RSS feeds, Facebook, LinkedIn, Wikipedia, and Twitter so they work together from within one account and user environment. For social media power users, aggregation allows for one-stop updating and information-monitoring in real time. It also enables busy professionals to monitor and view syndicated content from multiple sources simultaneously in one tool on the go using mobile devices and helps sift and filter real-time content across networks rather than searching the web or individual social media tools.

In addition, aggregation tools allow their users to add/remove content quickly, easily monitor streams, filter and create sub-streams, and respond, comment, and chat with people instantly. It powerfully schedules information retrieval using tracking tools and adapts content accordingly in one space. Some aggregators even aid in automated monitoring of your professional image, providing users with an "image score" using feedback algorithms that assess overall factors of having good social media pages such as language, phrases, activity, likes, dislikes, and types of individuals tied to your social media pages. This lets professionals know how their social media image comes across to others. Some can even alert you to privacy and security risks and provide you an activity summary of how information on your pages could negatively affect your online image.

HIMSS Resources

In addition to the mainstream social media tools, HIMSS.org is a tremendous professional learning and development resource tool with a "Members-In-Action Feed" and "Career Services" where you'll find hundreds of health IT professionals and thought leaders to connect with. The "HIMSS Learning Center" enables health IT career oriented professionals to join webinars and briefings, view online courses, and interact with speakers and user communities. The "HIMSS eMentor" initiative helps connect nurses, pharmacists, and executives via LinkedIn and Twitter. And yet another great way to learn as you determine your interests across the healthcare technology landscape is to consult with the Healthcare Information and Management Systems Society (HIMSS) and ask about how to get connected with one or more of its associated special interest or advocacy groups, professional communities, network forums, national committees, or local chapters. From informatics to medical devices, or from data interoperability standards to HIEs, there's bound to be something at HIMSS for you participate in. Once you're connected, take it a step further and volunteer some time to engage socially with your peers in person.

As a long-time HIMSS member, Certified Professional in Healthcare Information and Management System (CPHIMS), past chapter president, and most recently Chair of the HIMSS Federal Health Community, I've met other health IT professionals through online social media and in-person engagements who have influenced the course of my career and opened doors for me across our community. I've personally and professionally benefited by learning and sharing ideas with these colleagues and thought leaders. Specifically, my health IT connections helped me learn about the operational impacts of the Health Information Technology for Economic and Clinical Health (HITECH), Food and Drug Administration Safety and Innovation (FDASIA), and Federal Information Technology Acquisition Reform (FITARA) legislation on my healthcare organization; enabled me to participate in the first Meaningful Use request for information (RFI) analysis; inspired me to advocate for legislative grants in support health IT training and education; got me engaged me in Health Level Seven International Fast Healthcare Interoperability Resources (HL7/FHIR) working groups; and recently got me invited to moderate the HIMSS16 Annual Conference & Exhibition session with the White House Chief of Science and Technology. The knowledge gained and people I've met have helped advance my career and provide professional learning opportunities that I would not have experienced otherwise within my own organizational environment. For that I am sincerely grateful. And to all those engaged health IT professionals who helped me I owe you a measure of gratitude and say thank you.

Summary

In closing, how we decide to engage socially, participate professionally, or share of ourselves and how others decide to share with us, both online and in person, can change the healthcare industry one health IT professional at a time. With the growing number of ways to engage using social media, I encourage you to proactively start your social engagement journey today and stay open to learning from your health IT colleagues and the broader professional community. Don't wait for someone to invite you, but if you're the type of person who needs an invite to explore and engage socially, I extend that invitation to you now. Set up a profile on at least one of the aforementioned tools and turn the page to the next chapter in your career by putting your digital presence to work for you. And if the flow of information becomes overwhelming, return to your "why," narrow your focus, and remember that although information is available 24 hours a day, 7 days a week, 365 days a year, you decide when to access it and for how long. Leverage the valuable information in this book to keep learning continuously. Respect your inevitable learning curve and know that persistence will yield rich learning rewards (Beck 2014).

References

Arora, D. 2014. How to Use Social Media for Professional Development. SocialMediaToday.com. http://www.socialmediatoday.com/content/how-use-social-media-professional-development.

Baer, J. 2015. Clearing Clouds of Confusion: The 5 Categories of Social Media Software. Convinceand Convert.com. http://www.convinceandconvert.com/social-media-tools/clearing-clouds-of-confusion-the-5-categories-of-social-media-software/.

Bard, M. 2010. 15 Categories of Social Media. "The Social Web" graphic. http://www.mirnabard. com/2010/02/15-categories-of-social-media/.

Beck, D. 2014. *Social Media Vital to Professional Development*, University of Wyoming. http://evolllution. com/opinions/social-media-vital-professional-development/.

Duckworth, A. 2016. Warren Buffet's Famous Advice for Leading a Fulfilling Life is Simple. Business Insider Video. https:www.youtube.com/watch?v=Lf5ii3Q9AKs.

King, C. 2011. 22 Hot New Social Media Tools Worth Exploring. http://www.socialmediaexaminer. com/22-hot-new-social-media-tools-worth-exploring/.

Murray, J. 2016. Using Social Media for Professional Development. TeachHub.com. http://www.teachhub. com/using-social-media-professional-development.

Pollak, L. 2012. 10 Tips for Using Social Media in Your Job Search. Job Choices. https://www.roanestate. edu/webfolders/HARRISKB/placement/articles/students/10_Tips_for_Using_Social_Media_in_ Your_Job_Search.pdf.

Prodromou, T. 2015. *Ultimate Guide To: LinkedIn for Business*, 2nd Edition. Irvine, CA: Entrepreneur Press. https://books.google.com/books/about/Ultimate_Guide_to_LinkedIn_for_Business.html?id= Zlv_BgAAQBAJ&source=kp_cover&hl=en.

Sinek, S. 2009. *Start With Why: How Great Leaders Inspire Everyone to Take Action*. New York: Penguin Group (USA) Inc.

Ventola, C. L. 2014. Social Media and Health Care Professionals: Benefits, Risks, and Best Practices. MediMedia USA, Inc. http://www.ncbi.nlm.nih.gov/pmc/articles/PMC4103576/.Baer, J. 2015. Clearing Clouds of Confusion: The 5 Categories of Social Media Software. Convinceand Convert.com. http://www.convinceandconvert.com/social-media-tools/clearing-clouds-of-confusion-the-5-categories-of-social-media-software/.

Chapter 26

Viewing the Workplace for On-the-Job Training

By Dennis Winsten

Contents

Abstract

Health IT professionals who have an interest in expanding their knowledge of the many opportunities in the healthcare setting should look to on-the-job training as a source of continuing professional development (CPD).

Keywords:

Professional Learning
Growth
Professional Development
Advancement
Training
Skills Transfer
Skill Level

Preface

Health information technology (health IT) professionals who have an interest in expanding their knowledge of the many opportunities in the healthcare setting should look to on-the-job training (OJT) as a source of continuing professional development. OJT will equip the professional with additional skills, with greater depth of understanding of the role that he/she is in, and with increased potential for advancement in the field. The IT profession offers one of the most dynamic careers an individual can enjoy. OJT presents learning opportunities that offer the ability to stay abreast of the increasing demands and depth and breadth of skills that are required to succeed in this exciting field.

This chapter will:

- Provide alternative definitions of OJT consistent with today's health IT work environment.
- Recommend questions that the reader should ask herself/himself to help in making appropriate decisions about the types, scope and focus of OJT opportunities in which to engage as an avenue for professional growth and advancement.
- Describe some of the types of OJT programs being offered by healthcare institutions and healthcare systems vendors.
- Challenge the reader to think about OJT opportunities in a broader sense and to consider how to leverage/utilize OJT to meet current and future professional goals.

What is OJT?

Some common definitions of OJT are:

> On-the-Job Training (OJT) means training in the public or private sector that is given to a paid employee while he or she is engaged in productive work and that provides knowledge and skills essential to the full and adequate performance on the job.[*]
>
> On-the-job training is a form of training taking place in a normal working situation, sometimes called direct instruction, it is one of the earliest forms of training (observational learning is probably the earliest). It is a one-on-one training located at the job site, where someone who knows how to do a task shows another how to perform it.[†]
>
> On-the-job training focuses on the acquisition of skills within the work environment generally under normal working conditions. Through on-the-job training, workers acquire general skills that they can transfer from one job to another and specific skills that are unique to a particular job.[‡]

A definition that is broader, and reflecting today's expansion of OJT might be more relevant for the reader. In that context, an alternate definition could be:

---

[*] West Virginia Dept. of Health and Human Resources
[†] Wikipedia
[‡] *Encyclopedia of Business*, 2nd Edition

On-the Job Training (OJT) means training and/or education by employers in the public or private sector that is given to a paid employee, or self-financed by the employee, while he or she is engaged in productive work. OJT provides the knowledge and skills essential to the full and adequate performance of the employee's present job as well as opportunities for future job advancements and professional growth.

OJT programs are offered for different reasons. They benefit the employer by helping staff perform better on their job rather than learning new skills. To the employer, OJT is a way to develop a custom-trained workforce, and the investment that the employer makes in the employee reflects confidence in the employee's potential for growth and productivity, improves morale, and can generate the mutual loyalty of employee to employer and vice versa, of the employer to the employee. To the employee, OJT is a "free" opportunity for learning, growth, and job security, particularly in the fast-paced world of health IT. It uses the workplace and paid work hours to the benefit of both employee and employer, and is a learning opportunity that helps to prepare the employee for a fulfilling and productive future.

How can someone enhance her or his professional development using experiences gained while working in a health IT position? OJT doesn't necessarily have to be training offered by the employer. A broader view of OJT can include any education, learning experience or training that the employee undertakes while working at the job. This could include after work hours opportunities paid for by your employer such as community college or university courses, webinars by professional organizations, e.g. HIMSS, or by vendors. Some, but not all, of these options may provide continuing education units applicable towards the renewal of a credential. Regardless, the opportunity will add to your knowledge base. Some employers may offer tuition reimbursement and/or paid time off for studies.

Organization-sponsored or required OJT as a concept is not without issues. Often employees anticipate the training to be boring, disruptive to their project timetables, not beneficial to them personally and may trigger concern for their career future should they not perform well during the training.

However, the fields of information technology and healthcare have been and continue to evolve very rapidly. Keeping abreast of changes in computer technologies, networking, mobile applications, regulatory issues, medical advancements, etc. is a formidable task. On-the-job-training and education in the health IT domain is critical to maintain and/or obtain the necessary job skills to be successful in such a dynamic environment.

Types and Scope of OJT Offerings

What are the types and scope of on-the-job training offered today? It's useful to look at what a number of organizations are doing to get an idea of what you might look for in a current position or in seeing a future career opportunity. OJT offered by various healthcare institutions, health IT systems vendors, and professional organizations include:

Health Systems/Medical Centers/Hospitals

■ A large Michigan health system offers extensive professional development opportunities for both those in IT as well as departmental, e.g. laboratory, radiology, pharmacy informatics staff. Most of this is done though either "leadership academies" which are face-to-face courses or online education that uses the health system's online, self-paced learning management system (LMS) where access to thousands of hours of IT courses are available. Health IT staff are required to participate in at least one course per year. Many employees with a commitment to continuous learning take more courses. They know this is required for their best chance of success. In addition, annually, all staff attend an initial full two-day or one-day refresher Lean Six Sigma course. Group managers identify the most appropriate courses that will benefit an employee. Not all the course work is technical; other topics like project management, communications, and others are offered to employees for OJT.

■ A major university medical center in Maryland is engaged in a contract with Skillsoft for a broad range of online courses on IT and non-IT-related subjects available to its staff. To access this content, staff log onto the Skillsoft site with their institutional ID and password to access the training materials. A very broad range of IT and business-related content is available. Additionally, staff at the medical center receive tuition reimbursement for taking internal courses from the university's Computer Science department, its business school, its School of Public Health, all of which offer advanced degree graduate programs via evening and summer courses.

■ A major California cancer center provides support for its health IT staff allowing them to participate in various certification programs. Certification programs include the Project Management Institute's PMP (Project Management Professional) to help employees learn the competencies needed to lead and direct projects as well as the ITIL (Information Technology Infrastructure Library) practices and processes credential for ITT service management that aligns IT with the needs of the medical center. The PMP and ITIL programs are conducted externally by one of the certification organizations. Annually, on a quarterly basis, there are sessions for IT teams on high performance training. There is also an organizational leadership program offered to senior health IT staff at the director level and above. This "Leadership Academy" is an offsite one-week program administered by an external firm. All of these OJT programs are provided at no cost to the employee and are funded out of the IT budget.

IT Vendors

■ Microsoft Innovation Centers are offered by local government organizations, universities, industry organizations, software or hardware vendors who partner with Microsoft with whom they share a common goal to foster the growth of local software economies. These are state-of-the-art technology facilities that are open to students, developers, IT professionals, entrepreneurs, startups and academic researchers. The e-Learning library includes a broad array of classes, including basic computer skills, Microsoft Office software and advanced technical courses, ensuring that there is something for everyone regardless of current computer skill level.

■ One large EHR vendor reimburses its staff for additional ongoing training which includes classes, conferences, or webinars. In addition, staff members can access a "professional development fund" each year to purchase books related to their professions or work assignments, or, to learn more about a topic in healthcare.

■ A long-time Healthcare IT company in the Northeast provides a comprehensive training program for new hires. These training programs are conducted in classrooms as well as by webinars and through e-Learning modules that allow for self-paced learning. The training programs can last anywhere from two months to six to eight months depending on the participant's role. Employees also have the option to register for any number of continuing education offerings. Staff are permitted to attend classes on more specific or focused topics to further enhance their job training. The company provides all internal training, creates e-Learning modules and training materials, and offers access to educational websites free of charge to the staff member. The company also provides a tuition reimbursement program for staff who wish to pursue outside education opportunities provided it is with an accredited institution and is related to their specific role or to healthcare in general.

■ Another major Health IT/EHR vendor offers its staff a performance support tool with the sole purpose of OJT-related learning. The tool is intended to assist staff involved in sales, support or consulting to clients by providing pertinent information, guidance and training. Additionally, as part of an OJT experience, instructor-led training is provided to prepare staff members for client engagements.

Professional Organizations

■ HIMSS, the Healthcare Information and Management Systems Society offers many opportunities for professional learning and growth while working on-the-job. HIMSS Virtual Events provide insights into a number of industry important topics presented by health IT experts. HIMSS webinar events are offered on a complimentary basis. Many of the events provide credits for continuing education requirements for the Certified Professional in Healthcare Information and Management Systems (CPHIMS) or Certified Associate in Healthcare Information and Management Systems (CAHIMS). The HIMSS Annual Conference and Exhibition provides a forum to interact with other Health IT stakeholders, hear presentations on current health IT issues of importance, and see the latest in technological advancements at vendor exhibitions.

■ The American College of Healthcare Executives (ACHE), similarly, provides learning opportunities for its members. Face-to-face offerings include educational seminars for professional development with topics integral to healthcare management, customized, ACHE on-location programs held on-site at an organization, or specialized executive programs. Distance Education is provided via webinars and multi-week online seminars both of which provide ACHE Qualified Education credits.

The type and scope of OJT offered by healthcare institutions, health IT vendors and professional organizations varies but some form of OJT and educational support is almost always available to health IT staff who have an interest in furthering their professional development while attaining career goals.

Things to Think About

There are many questions that you need to ask yourself ... and answer as you consider job preparedness and advancement, career goals, and future opportunities in the health IT profession. Questions you may want to ask are: Is the cumulative experience gained in a single health IT position sufficient or is it better to gain knowledge from the perspectives of several, perhaps, radically different health IT jobs? Would experience gained in jobs outside of health IT be an advantage to broaden professional expertise and value to prospective employers? Can professional development be planned or simply based on opportunities that arise? Can you select OJT opportunities that will further your goals so that OJT could also mean "Objectives Job Training," where the training is intended to meet your personal professional objectives?

Any new job should require sufficient prior experience yet offer a considerable amount of new learning. The extent of new learning in a new job that one is willing to undertake depends on a person's tolerance for risk. "What if I can't do this? What if I fail?" Nelson Mandela once said: "I never lose. I win or I learn." Learning is not meant to be comfortable undertaking. Learning means change, and while change is inevitable, it can be very uncomfortable and incurs some level of risk. One advantage of OJT, as with any well-designed learning environment, is that the student is allowed to make mistakes – they are part of the learning process, in other words the risk is minimized.

Accepting a new position that requires basically the same skill levels and expertise that one already has is not a way to grow professionally. Employees need to add "layers" of new expertise and skills over the years. Consider how much of a "stretch" you are willing to make in a new job or new position in the same company.

Continuing professional development through OJT can help you make that stretch and can often be achieved from a plan based on your interests and aspirations. Do you wish to always be highly technical in your endeavors or would you prefer to move into progressive levels of management? The OJT steps that you take depend on your ultimate professional goal.

Suppose your long-term goal is to continue to be a technical "guru" and lead a technical project team or systems technical department. If so, your goal should be to obtain OJT that will further that objective. Steps that you could take are:

- Attend technical training courses offered by your employer, by universities or by vendors. HIMSS offers various webinars and special interest groups (SIGs) that can provide learning while on the job. Attending national and regional health IT-related conferences, e.g. HIMSS Annual Conference and Exhibition, can provide an excellent source of useful job-related information both from the presentations offered and the technologies displayed in the Exhibit Hall. Even if you can't attend in person, you can obtain session recordings via the HIMSS Learning Center.
- Study and consider the direction in which health IT will progress then "Google" and read all that you can on related subjects.
- Volunteer for projects that will utilize advanced technologies.
- Consider working in a different technical area, e.g. networking, mobile technologies, imaging... perhaps, even outside the healthcare domain.

Suppose you envision your long-term goal as that of a top-level manager in Health IT. If so, your goal should be to obtain OJT that will further your objectives. Steps that you could take are:

- Work to develop communications and "people" skills.
- Attend project management training courses offered by your employer, by universities, or by vendors.
- Consider earning a degree in a non-technical subject, e.g. business, human relations, psychology. You may be surprised at how much these non-technical disciplines will broaden your perspective and help you become a better manager.

Opportunities for OJT may not "knock on your door"; rather, you may need to seek them out. Be alert to opportunities in your workplace that may identify roles that you can play in addition to your current job responsibilities. Volunteering to take on some new functions and learn new skill sets, even on a limited basis can prepare you for a more advanced position in your organization. Case in point, a non-health IT individual who started out as a laboratory technician began helping the Health IT Department with some data entry and validation issues. Today, he is the director of the Health IT department in his hospital.

Summary

Most healthcare institutions and health IT vendors offer a varied range of OJT opportunities, many at no cost to the employee.

OJT opportunities can be either "passive" or "active." "Passive" OJT derives from employer-sponsored training programs whose emphasis is usually on benefits to the company, i.e. helping employees do a better job in their work capacity and lesser on the employees' professional career. "Active" OJT results from individual choices based on their career objectives, e.g. technical or management. These opportunities may be taken at the employee's expense or underwritten and supported by the employee's company.

For health IT professionals, there is a bright future in your industry. Technology has and will continue to expand in new and exciting ways. Rapid change is the "watchword" and professional advancement requires continuous learning and evolving practical experience. OJT, whether sponsored by employers or undertaken as an individual initiative will be a key factor in successfully meeting professional goals.

Chapter 27

Talent Management for the Health IT Professional

By Richard A. Biehl

PhD, CSQE, CSSBB

Contents

Abstract

While one typically thinks of talent management as a responsibility of the Human Resources Department, the astute health IT professional will become knowledgeable of the many components that will contribute to managing one's professional success.

Keywords:

Career Planning
Benchamrking
Trend Analysis
Value Analysis
Skills Inventory
Six Sigma
Job Description
Competency Model
Standards
Certifications
Mentoring
Coaching
360 degree feedback
Lifetime Employment
Talent Management
Workforce
Metrics
Time Management
Customer Surveys

Introduction

An organization conducts operations that consume skills and knowledge. It *demands* talent. As professionals, we use our skills and knowledge to work with, and for, operational organizations. We *supply* talent. That supply–demand relationship regarding talent is the centerpiece of our employment relationships as professionals. (Figure 27.1) The mechanisms by which that relationship is maintained have changed in our economy over a period of decades in ways that have altered how we actually perceive employment as a social institution.

Establishing an employment relationship (e.g., getting a job) requires demonstrating some minimum requirement for having the talent necessary to perform required duties. In some

Figure 27.1 Talent supply–demand perspectives.

organizations, that demonstration is in the form of a credential earned through education. Most relationships in healthcare that we would classify as professional positions use the basic four-year college degree as a minimum credential. Some professional positions require a much higher minimum.

Achieving that level of required credential has always been a self-managed process. While society as a whole might provide or even insist on everyone going through primary and secondary education, the notion of continuing education to achieve college-level credentials is left to individual choice. Until the minimum requirements have been met to achieve employment in a desired field, talent management is dominated by self-management of one's education.

Once employed, that situation undergoes a shift. A generation ago, a person entering a position in an organization expected her or his employer to take over responsibility for talent management. The employer saw the shift in the same way, usually putting significant human resource processes in place to make sure that everyone in the organization was being continuously trained to promote and enhance their talents for current and future positions and operations. The line between the talent you needed to demonstrate prior to gaining employment and the levels of talent you were expected to achieve throughout your career in employment was very clear. Your employer would take it from there.

Today, a person entering an organization holds few, if any, such expectations. The shift is largely the result of bigger and broader changes in the social relationship represented by employment generally. Few people think in terms of lifetime employment when they enter an organization anymore. Organizations are not enthusiastic to develop extensive new or additional talents in people who they now perceive as highly mobile in their employment. Indeed, people in organizations are less likely to be employees in a formal or legal sense anymore. Organizations are reluctant to make talent management investments in people with whom their relationship is only contingent. Under these circumstances, lifetime talent management has become self-managed.

The line between pre-employment talent management that was largely focused on going to college has shifted forward into one's career as a professional. For a few, talent management has become a permanent exercise in self-management. For most, talent management has become part of a portfolio that is shared with one's employer. If the ratio is dominated by the employer, less change is perceived or needed. If the ratio is dominated by self-development, either because of working for an employer that doesn't see talent management as a core responsibility anymore or because entrepreneurial interests might drive a career with many employment changes, the need to develop and manage one's own talents can become of paramount concern.

Many of the lines described here can be quite fuzzy. Employers might invest in certain types of talents, but not others. Developing talents for one's current or next position can be viewed differently from developing those involved in a career change. Talents that support licensure or accreditation might be managed very differently than others. Many talent categories aren't measured in clearly demarcated levels such as bachelor's, master's or doctoral degrees. Realistically, most talents needed to perform a professional function aren't covered directly by any such degrees. The pool of talents being managed for an individual can be diverse and evolving as career interests and opportunities change or emerge.

The bottom line out of all of this is that self-managing one's own talent development has become a critical skill for professionals throughout the economy, particularly in the fast-changing and dynamic healthcare and information technology sectors. The one talent this requires us all to have, therefore, is a talent for managing our own lifelong learning.

Adapting Standards into a Systemic Process

Since adopting and adapting industry standards is part of the set of recommendations for talent management offered later in this chapter, it's only fitting that this chapter use that approach. When we adopt existing standards, we accelerate the development of key talents called for in those standards, and we avoid the need to identify and characterize specific skills and knowledge. Letting a published standard do most of the work for us is a core competency if we're to effectively self-manage our personal talent pool.

To make effective use of a set of standards, whatever type and category of standards you ultimately choose as representing the domains against which you want to self-manage your talents, it helps to organize them into a framework that makes them easier to order and integrate in your planning. As process engineers, we are usually trying to build a system that converts inputs into outputs through an effective system design. As we build our talent management process, we want to identify standards that will define the outcomes we want to achieve through talent management (typically denoted as Ys). We also want to define input standards that can help identify the requirements that our talent management process must satisfy to be effective (typically denoted as Xs) (Figure 27.2).

Bridging our inputs to outputs is our talent management process or system. Its design and controls convert the input standard process guidelines into effective talent management outcomes (typically denoted by the transfer function $Y_1 = f(X_1, x_2, \ldots x_N)$) for any desired outcomes defined by our output standards. Since most published standards target organization or industry applications and scope, their use in this context typically requires refocusing both their scale and language to the individual personal management process that we're aiming for. That translation is made easier by the notion that we're developing a personal process for something that historically was the responsibility of the organization within which we worked. We're now trying to do the same thing for ourselves over the span of our careers, but the same effective functionality must be present for the process of managing talent to work at the individual level.

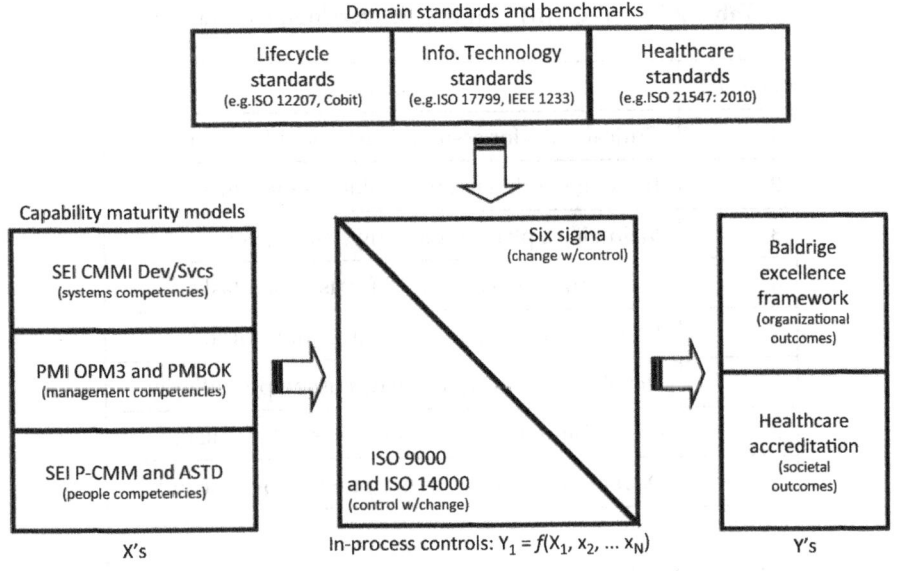

Figure 27.2   Standards integration framework.

Self-Guiding Talent Management

One output standard against which the quality of a talent management process can be measured is the *Baldrige Excellence Framework* of the Baldrige Performance Excellence Program in the United States. The fifth of the seven criteria categories evaluates *Workforce* outcomes. The core concern in this category is how the organization builds an effective and supportive workforce environment, and this is the area in which talent management processes would have an impact. Among the areas of concern are the capability and capacity of the workforce in terms of skills, competencies, and staffing levels. The criteria include maintaining a diversity of ideas and thinking, as well as ensuring that core competencies are capitalized upon in accomplishing work. The criteria also emphasize a continuing focus on customers and stakeholders working to exceed their performance expectations. As we implement a process to self-manage our talents throughout our lifelong careers, we must be accountable to ourselves to meet these requirements just as an organization for which we might work might be held accountable for meeting them with regard to their contributions to talent management in our career.

In order to define a process for talent self-management that will be capable of delivering the desired outcomes, we can turn, again, to an organizational standard that can be adapted for our own individual use. One such standard is the *People Capability Maturity Model* (P-CMM) from the Software Engineering Institute. The process area of interest in the P-CMM is *Training and Development*, and it covers those aspects of an organization's processes that must be in place to effectively ensure that individuals in the organization have the appropriate knowledge and skills to carry out their duties and that appropriate development opportunities are presented to each individual. Table 27.1 outlines the eight key practices that need to be present to satisfy the P-CMM Training & Development capability goals. These are precisely the focus of talent self-management, looking at ourselves as one-member organizations.

Table 27.1   P-CMM Training & Development Practices

Practice	Emphasis
1	Critical skills for assigned tasks are identified
2	Training needed in critical skills is identified
3	Maintains a plan for meeting training needs
4	Timely training is received for assigned tasks
5	Training progress is tracked and monitored
6	Development options are discussed periodically
7	Development opportunities are made available
8	Development activities are pursued by individuals

To the extent that the Baldrige framework provides the justification for focusing on talent management (the "why"), and the P-CMM provides a rationale for assessing whether a training management process is capable of meeting outcome expectations (the "what"), we still need is a procedure for ensuring that the practices modeled in the P-CMM actually get carried out (the "how"). Continuing the notion of adapting organizational standards to our individual efforts, we can turn to the quality management field for guidance on developing sound and systematic procedures; and one of the dominant models in quality management today is Six Sigma.

Personal Six Sigma Framework

As a quality movement, Six Sigma is about process capability. It emphasizes reducing the variation in a process, and increasing our control over a process, such that we can predict with considerable accuracy exactly how the process will behave. This level of capability can be used to implement improvements in the process where we set targets for future behaviors and achieve those targets within the levels of quality control that we choose to design into the improvements. This perspective on Six Sigma applies equally well in both individual and organizational settings, and yet the history of the Six Sigma movement is almost exclusively a history of organizational adoption and change. That history, as it applies to individuals, includes obtaining certification as a Green Belt or a Black Belt, always within the context of an organizational Six Sigma program.

A Six Sigma methodology can be adopted and adapted by individuals to personal self-management settings. In particular, it can be adapted to the development of job and career goals in order to create a regular periodic cycle of review, planning, and learning. Many large organizations have adopted Six Sigma practices as part of organizational quality initiatives. Working professionals in these organizations can sometimes find it difficult to adapt Six Sigma techniques to their own professional practice because the emphasis of the organizational initiative is on organization-wide and project-level implementation. Individuals working in organizations that are not adopting Six Sigma can feel completely overlooked by the Six Sigma movement. You can adopt the Six Sigma thought process to enhance or improve an operational process that you are involved with, regardless of whether or not the organization in which you work has adopted Six Sigma as an improvement model.

You can focus on learning and adapting Six Sigma techniques at a personal level, incorporating these techniques and tools into your professional practice even if you work in an organization that is not adopting Six Sigma. Readers involved in human development or leadership disciplines can consider expanding this approach to other individuals within their organizations.

Six Sigma DMAIC

Large organizational initiatives and projects tend to get the most attention in the Six Sigma literature. The intent of most organizations adopting Six Sigma is that the tools and thought processes of Six Sigma will eventually become so embedded throughout the organization that Six Sigma simply becomes the normal way of conducting business for everyone in the organization. Using this perspective, the idea of defining and conducting Six Sigma projects targeted at improving certain processes or products—the current dominant model in the Six Sigma world—can be viewed as an immature application of Six Sigma. As Six Sigma programs mature, the specific improvement project increasingly gives way to a continuous improvement of processes and products while they are being used (Figure 27.3).

Whether as a distinct project or an embedded activity, the Define-Measure-Analyze-Improve-Control (DMAIC) lifecycle of Six Sigma is applicable to a large variety of situations. Its application as an implicit embedded tool is not without precedent. For example, when a project manager or systems engineer tailors a standard organizational lifecycle into a project lifecycle, the tailoring act is an improvement activity preceded by a definition of the project, measurement of risks and opportunities, and an analysis of options for mitigating and managing scope and risk. The resulting tailored project lifecycle is then used to control the effort. The tailoring process is an implicit DMAIC cycle.

The DMAIC thought process can, and should, be used to improve and control virtually any process, whether or not the organization in which that process occurs is aware of its use. When added to existing practices; such as project tailoring, additional benefits and improvements will quickly materialize. The benefits are immediate and substantial when introduced into processes that do not already contain any implicit improvement capability. This is the basis for Personal Six Sigma.

Talent Self-Management

When personally adopting Six Sigma to a professional practice, an obvious starting point is in the application of Six Sigma thinking, and the DMAIC lifecycle model, to the management of your professional career. The DMAIC lifecycle can be used to understand the elements of a human resource management system that affect your personal career choices and opportunities (Figure 27.4).

The resulting model involves the process of improving personal competencies, where the key inputs are your current personal competencies, and the key outputs are your improved personal

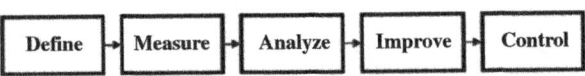

Figure 27.3   Six Sigma DMAIC Lifecycle.

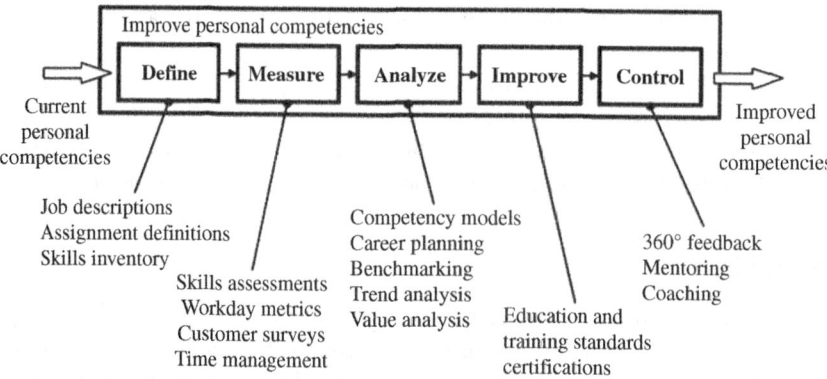

Figure 27.4 Personal Six Sigma Lifecycle.

Table 27.2 Personal Six Sigma Lifecycle

Phase	Emphasis
DEFINE	Understand positions, assignments, skills for current and future jobs
MEASURE	Assess actual skills use and how time is really spent
ANALYZE	Identify gaps and opportunities in skills and behaviors
IMPROVE	Enhance skills and develop adopted behaviors
CONTROL	Use feedback to monitor and initiate further improvements

competencies. Each of the Six Sigma phases offers opportunities to continuously recognize and improve talent needs through assessment, training, education, reviews, and continuous reflection. As a lifecycle, this process can be carried out as often as seems necessary. Initially, an arbitrary plan of conducting such an analysis annually might make sense. As the process matures, the aspects of the DMAIC Control Phase will determine how frequently you need to repeat the lifecycle (Table 27.2).

Define Phase

The Define Phase of Personal Six Sigma requires that your job competencies that are to be addressed be clearly and accurately defined so they can later be measured and improved. The inputs that drive this definition process are job descriptions, assignment descriptions, and a skills inventory. Define Phase activities are the most difficult to complete the first time Personal Six Sigma is put into practice. Subsequent passes through the lifecycle need only update materials created on previous iterations.

Job Descriptions

The first definitional activity requires establishing a detailed definition and model for your job and career path. This involves collecting or creating a job description for your current job, as well as detailing descriptions of any anticipated or desired jobs for the future. If you work in an organization that is good at creating and maintaining accurate and detailed job descriptions, this activity is much easier than if you work in an organization that only offers vague or superficial job descriptions.

It is critically important that a clear and detailed description of your current and future jobs be defined as the baseline model for the DMAIC improvement cycle. Future job descriptions can be especially challenging because there may be multiple career paths that you consider possibilities, including the potential for future jobs that do not yet exist in the current job market. Your definition need not be clairvoyant to be useful; a best estimate of the future is all that is needed since this DMAIC cycle will be repeated over and over throughout the course of the unfolding of those jobs. Your current view of the talent requirements that will materialize in the future need only be accurate enough to guide effective plans or decisions in the current cycle.

Assignment Descriptions

Job descriptions tend to provide a relatively static definition of your professional responsibilities. An additional layer of definition is provided by systematically defining your actual job assignments. The assignments you carry out in your job provide a more dynamic view of your professional practice. For many, assignments will be dominated by project work. However, even when project work constitutes the bulk of your assignments, there are typically still many aspects of your job that would be omitted if only project work was included. For some professionals, project work may even constitute only a small percentage of their responsibilities.

Where feasible, assignment descriptions should be projected into the future. Being able to forecast the assignments that you plan to undertake in the future can be a key element in career and competency planning. The level of difficulty of these descriptions will depend upon the level of detail and breadth of the job descriptions captured initially. Some job descriptions also describe assignments in a fair amount of detail; however, many do not. Even with detailed job descriptions it can be difficult to get an accurate picture of how a working professional will actually spend her or his days. A complete combination of job and assignment descriptions provides that picture and, to the extent that it projects into the future, will enable more effective measurement activities in the next phase.

Skills Inventory

The third definition activity in the Define Phase involves cataloging an inventory of all of the talents that are implied by the current and future jobs and assignments defined previously. Depending on how they were written, the job and assignment descriptions might already explicitly lay out the skills required. Even so, there are likely to be additional skills that should be included in the skills inventory beyond those explicitly identified. This inventory should be as complete as possible. It is important to capture all of the skills associated with your job, not just those that might be listed in an official job description or assignment.

Measure Phase

The Measure Phase of Personal Six Sigma requires that an accurate and quantified picture of actual job, assignment, and skills performance be collected so improvement opportunities that are well-grounded in the data can be identified. The inputs that drive this quantification process are skills assessments, workday metrics, customer surveys, and time management data.

Skills Assessment

A critical input to an understanding of professional talents is an honest and thorough skills assessment. A skills assessment involves reviewing each skill in the skills inventory created in the Define Phase and assessing whether or not you possess the required levels of skill. This measurement activity depends on establishing a scale for measuring competency levels and for determining the likelihood that you will need certain levels of skills in the future.

For example, you might use a five-point scale, where 0 indicates that you have no knowledge of the skill, 1 indicates a general familiarity with the skills but no current real capability, 2 indicates some knowledge or capability usually as the result of some training, 3 indicates sufficient competency to practice the skill, 4 indicates experienced competency to the point of being able to help others with the skill, and 5 indicates that you have mastered the skill to the point where you can teach, adapt, or extend the skill.

If an item in the skills inventory requires a 4 but your current capability is a 3, then action might be needed to improve the competency. However, if future job assignments might only require the skill at level 3, then the need for immediate capability enhancement might be mitigated. The use of current and future job and assignment descriptions, coupled with the ever-changing profile of job skills across the industry, makes a skills model rather complex. Here in the Measure Phase, the emphasis is on building accurate skill assessments, not making decisions about improvements. Improvement decisions need to be made based on an entire picture of your capabilities and plans, and will be the subject of the later Analysis Phase.

Workday Metrics

Each combination of job and assignment descriptions will have a unique profile of actual work activities that are conducted on a typical workday. Within this variation, however, it is important to be able to measure the actual activities performed. If you work in an organization that already collects time-reporting data, these metrics will be easier to identify and collect. However, since the objective here is competency development, it will be important to collect data beyond traditional time-recording mechanisms. In particular, while job and assignment activities and time should be tracked, so should actual utilization of your competencies in the skills inventory.

Depending upon the specifics of your professional practice, you will count different things. Typical metrics might include information about the timings and quality of the many different work products that you are responsible for in your position, including how and when you verified or validated those work products with peers or managers. Metrics should include the relative size of each artifact, time or effort expended, defect and issue data, rework time and scale, and skills actually used. In collecting workday metrics, try to think of yourself as a production line turning out products and services. The idea is to collect metrics regarding everything going on across your production line. Particular note should be made of any skills that you need to immediately improve in order to complete some activity.

Customer Surveys

A critical set of data needed for Personal Six Sigma is customer feedback. A challenge the first time through the cycle is to accurately identify all of the customers of your professional practice. We are often more accustomed to identifying our company's customers or even the customers of our projects; but the customers of our professional practice are sometimes less visible to us. The customers of interest are the individuals or work groups that directly receive our work products. The list will vary depending on job assignments. Think in terms of identifying the level of your customer's satisfaction with everything you produce, including the major work products that you are responsible for on a regular basis, as well as the many ad hoc or periodic work products or services that you provide as part of your job. Note that the customers of interest here are your direct and immediate customers.

Once your customers are identified, seek methods or occasions where direct customer feedback can be obtained. While this can be as formal as a feedback survey given to these individuals periodically, it need not be. Effective feedback can be obtained using less formal methods, including simple feedback discussions or a shared coffee break. Many such opportunities might already be available if an effective peer review program is in place in your organization.

Time Management

The fourth category of data to be collected during the Measure Phase is time data. How do you spend your time? Useful categorizations include value-added versus non-value-added time, as well as time on or off task. Time spent off task might include a variety of meeting types, training, or other administrative activities.

This type of data most closely aligns with data that might already be collected for time reporting in your organization. Depending upon the level of project management maturity in the organization, much of the data required might already be available. However, such data is less likely to be available for non-project work. If sufficiently detailed, this data will identify the aspects of your job assignments that are being completed on time and on budget, or late and over budget.

Do not limit your time data to on-the-job time. Pay particular attention to how you spend time outside of work hours. How much personal time are you spending for learning? How many professional journal articles are you reading per week? How much time are you devoting to professional society memberships? These time investments are strong enablers of career and talent growth that remain hidden if your measurement effort is limited to at-work activities.

Analyze Phase

The Analyze Phase of Personal Six Sigma requires that the metrics collected be reviewed objectively in order to identify trends and opportunities that can be addressed for improvement or growth. The inputs that drive this analysis process are competency models, career planning, benchmarking, trend analysis, and value analysis.

Competency Models

A comparison of your actual job description and assignments (from the Define Phase) to how often you actually use your competencies (from the Measure Phase) can serve as an indication of whether or not your talents are being developed and used in ways that are consistent with your career plans and goals. If not, then analyzing the gaps between your plan and actual competency use can help identify places where your talents might need to be realigned with real job opportunities, or job opportunities might need to be rethought in light of how your competency development is actually unfolding.

Career Planning

While your organization often has a career planning model available, it is typically limited to career options within the organization. Depending upon your personal goals, you might need to develop a career plan that extends beyond your current organization. If the workday metrics, customer data, and time management data point toward career change opportunities or needs, then potential career improvement might entail a rethinking of the job and assignment descriptions that currently form the basis of this DMAIC cycle. Be particularly alert to new career opportunities that might be emerging that were not available or considered during the Define Phase.

Benchmarking

Envisioning a change is always easier when the target change can be visualized or observed. You should continually look for opportunities to measure or observe other professionals as they progress through similar career paths. Professional publications and conferences are excellent sources of benchmark data: many trade publications provide periodic salary surveys, and many professional societies provide detailed body of knowledge materials to members. All of these sources provide a clear picture of what a might-be career target can include. This view can be used to help define a working path from your current asis model to some future to-be model.

Trend Analysis

Pay particular attention to trends in the data, even if they are small. Picturing your job five years ago can highlight how much can change over the course of time, and yet those changes rarely stand out during very short-term discussions or observations. The influence of technologies, organizational changes, and skill models are constantly changing the way your organization functions and the ways you experience being a part of your organization. By noting trends in the data you can spot areas that need improvement long before your supervisors or peers do. Such trends might include the frequency with which your skills are used or shifts in performance data related to certain types of artifacts meeting specifications. By planning for improvements in these areas, it is possible to prevent anyone else from ever observing slippages in your skills sets or performance.

Value Analysis

A particular form of analysis, perhaps viewable as a subset of trend analysis, is value analysis. What value are you providing to your customers over time? Ideally, there should be significant upward trends in the conducting of value-added activities that directly impact customers. On-time performance and skills utilization should continuously improve over time. As a Personal Six Sigma goal, these value measures should be improving notably faster than corresponding value measures for your entire organization. If not, you should work to identify reasons why not, and think about ways to improve such situations.

Improve Phase

The Improve Phase of Personal Six Sigma takes the information gleaned from analysis to directly implement improvements. The inputs that drive this improvement process are education and training, standards, and certification.

Education and Training

The most obvious improvement opportunities will involve forms of education and training. These might vary from focused training opportunities to improve specific skills, to full academic degree programs. Long-term planning will often involve both extremes. Professional conferences or professional society involvement can also provide for skills enablement or expansion. Simply reading publications from the many professional societies that cover aspects of your job can be an excellent improvement strategy.

Many other educational opportunities are likely to be available all around you in your current position. The many committees, task forces, or special assignments available in your workplace offer excellent opportunities to develop skills that might otherwise not be needed or practiced in the day-to-day activities of your job. The question shifts from whether or not you have the talents to participate, to whether or not participating will help you develop needed or desired talents. Very often these activities present opportunities to develop specific skills or relationships that would rarely be developed through your normal work assignments.

Standards

Standards are an important part of planning improvements. Standards have become an increasingly important aspect of most work or knowledge domains, so there are likely at least a few standards that provide guidance in the working of the tasks within your areas of responsibility. Identifying and adopting standards is the easiest way to improve the direction of your skills and career without needing to "reinvent the wheel." Adopting a standard can help even if the organization in which you work is not moving in the direction of that standard. (This chapter is an example of an adoption of Six Sigma if your organization isn't pursuing Six Sigma as an organizational strategy.) Many standards and guidelines are available through the Healthcare Information and Management Systems Society (HIMSS), the International Standards Organization (ISO), the Society for Human Resource Management (SHRM), the Project Management Institute (PMI), and many other related organizations. Don't overlook the myriad organizations that also promulgate technical standards that might be relevant to your position, now or in the future.

Certifications

As an extension of education and training, obtaining professional certification can be an important component of any competency improvement program. The body of knowledge for a certification program serves as a standard for the purposes of defining what needs to be learned. The examination process for the certification serves as an important benchmark for the level of competency that should be developed and how it should be measured. Because most certification programs also require some form of periodic recertification, they also serve as good initial components for the Control Phase.

Control Phase

The Control Phase of Personal Six Sigma works to institutionalize the improvements made, and assure that new cycles of DMAIC activity are driven by the data generated through the improved processes. The inputs that drive this improvement process are 360° feedback, mentoring, and coaching.

360° Feedback

Just as the Measure Phase includes soliciting customer input, the Control Phase also ties actual performance to stakeholder feedback. Data should be continuously collected from customers, suppliers, peers, and managers. Shifts in this feedback over time might represent signals that something has changed in the work environment, or your performance has shifted. In either event, such feedback can serve as an early warning that problems might be occurring that can be addressed through another iteration of this DMAIC lifecycle.

Mentoring

To obtain more future-oriented feedback, it is important to identify one or more mentors and to enter into mentoring relationships with those individuals. A mentor can often help you identify trends or opportunities that affect your future plans long before the details behind those trends become evident. In the most extreme case, such information might trigger a replanning of your job or career options that would necessitate a complete redefinition of future job, assignment, or skill opportunities.

Coaching

Try to identify individuals in your organization who can serve as coaches on a day-to-day basis. Coaching provides an additional control over whether things occurring in the environment are being properly interpreted and used to influence your plans over time. Again, the emphasis is on using the coaching relationship to identify data or thought shifts that would necessitate a recycling through this DMAIC lifecycle.

Personal Six Sigma offers a framework for you as an individual practitioner to adapt Six Sigma techniques and tools to your personal professional practice and talent management. Applications include using Six Sigma to model and improve your personal career path and opportunities, including an improvement cycle that can be repeated over time to help assure that your career is unfolding in the way you desire.

In addition to improving your personal career competencies, major opportunities exist for improving your technical performance in your job through understanding the mapping of Six Sigma processes and techniques against the processes and techniques of your work domain. Whether or not you ever actually create any of the common Six Sigma tools, you'll benefit from adapting Six Sigma thinking to the domain-specific tools you already use. As your knowledge of Six Sigma increases, you will increasingly use Six Sigma tools and techniques to supplement your domain-specific tools. The complementary nature of these tools will boost both your productivity and effectiveness. You will probably not spend as much time using Six Sigma tools as you typically spend using your domain-specific tools. That path is best reserved for individuals who choose the Six Sigma Black Belt career path. As a self-managing talent development practitioner, your roots will remain in your chosen disciplinary specialty while you develop additional Six Sigma skills to assist you in continuous improvement.

Conclusion

Managing one's own talent development, including assuring that current talents meet the needs of current positions while also developing new talents for desired positions in the future, is a critical competency for working professionals. To make that self-management more effective and efficient, systemically adapting industry and professional standards is a means to short-cut what would otherwise be a long and tedious process of identifying and defining individual needed talents and skills. Every individual might end up with a slightly different portfolio of standards around which talent management might develop.

Figure 27.2 presented one such framework that includes many of the standards that are relevant to managing talents in the Health IT field. Your personal framework might include these components, as well as a variety of others to suit your needs. In fact, the process development outlined in this chapter included three components of the Figure 27.2 framework: the Baldrige Excellence Framework defining outcomes (the "why"), the People CMM defining inputs (the "what"), and the adaptation of Six Sigma for personal use as the transformative process (the "how").

By adapting standards, we take advantage of a lot of other people doing much of the development work for us, and we ensure that the talents and skills we target for ourselves are both relevant and timely to our career needs. We want the process to be effective while consuming little of our resources, because the journey of lifelong learning is both continuous and never-ending.

References

1. Curtis, B., Hefley, B., and Miller, S. (2009). *People Capability Maturity Model* (P-CMM), Version 2.0, Second Edition. Software Engineering Institute, CMU/SEI-2009-TR-003.
2. National Institute of Standards and Technology. (2015). *Baldrige Excellence Framework: A Systems Approach to Improving Your Organization's Performance.* 2015–2016 Edition. Gaithersburg, MD: United States Department of Commerce.

Index